# DIRTY SOUTH

## OUTKAST, LIL WAYNE, SOULJA BOY, AND THE SOUTHERN RAPPERS WHO REINVENTED HIP-HOP

### BEN WESTHOFF

CHICAGO
REVIEW
PRESS

An A Cappella Book

Library of Congress Cataloging-in-Publication Data
Westhoff, Ben.
 Dirty South : Outkast, Lil Wayne, Soulja Boy, and the Southern rappers
who reinvented hip-hop / Ben Westhoff.
   p. cm.
 Includes bibliographical references and index.
 ISBN 978-1-56976-606-4 (pbk.)
 1. Rap (Music)—Southern States—History and criticism. 2. Rap
musicians—Southern States. I. Title.
 ML3531.W47 2011
 782.4216490975—dc22

                            2010053907

Cover and interior design: Jonathan Hahn
Cover photograph: Howard Huang/Contour by Getty Images

Portions of this book originally appeared in the *Village Voice*, the *Houston Press*, the *Dallas Observer*, *Miami New Times*, and *New Times Broward-Palm Beach*, which are all part of the Village Voice Media Holdings family of companies. They appear here with the kind permission of VVMH. Other portions originally appeared in Creative Loafing publications.

Published by Chicago Review Press, Incorporated
814 North Franklin Street
Chicago, Illinois 60610
ISBN 978-1-56976-606-4
Printed in the United States of America
5 4 3 2 1

*To Anna B and her curls*

# CONTENTS

# INTRODUCTION

MS. PEACHEZ favors bright clown wigs, press-on nails, and pastel blouses over her beefy, middle-aged frame. In the video for her 2006 song, "Fry That Chicken," she raps in a voice deeper than my uncle John's. The fact that she is a man is just one of many things that are odd about "Fry That Chicken."

Like many immediately catchy songs, it's so dumb it's genius. Something of a nursery rhyme crossed with a Mardi Gras march, its springy bass propels the beat along while high-register synth notes chime like Pavlov's bell. "I got a pan, and I got a plan/ I'ma fry this chicken in my hand!" she raps. "Everybody want a piece of my chicken/ Southern fried chicken/ Finger lickin'."

Its low-budget video takes place in the yard of a rural shack, surrounded by chicken coops. The scene is a good ol' country barbeque, with Ms. Peachez holding raw chickens and taunting a group of hungry grade-school children. Peachez's blue hair, and her T-shirt bearing an oversized peach, are nearly consumed by smoke from the grill, which heats a giant pan of bubbling, waiting grease. She passes thighs and legs through a bowl of flour, massaging them with her hands in time to the beat. After dropping the

1

segments into the pan, she shakes her hips and gets the hot sauce ready.

"Fry that chicken!" the kids demand, looking half-crazed as they pound on the picnic table and wave their arms. Peachez advises the kids to wash their hands, "'Cause you're gon' be lickin' 'em!" When the food is ready the kids tear into it, eating with their fingers and then, yes, licking them.

There's something innocent and funny about the video, and the song has a way of worming its way into your head. But there's also something creepy. It vaguely recalls a nineteenth-century blackface skit, although none of the participants are white, and the production appears to have been made in earnest, rather than as an ironic joke.

But a jive-talking, cartoonish drag queen hypnotizing a group of children with her southern-fried bird, seriously? Could the video's crafters possibly be unaware of its loaded stereotypes?

The oddness of the clip has been eclipsed only by its popularity. It's been seen 3.6 million times, and still gets thousands of views per day. But as "Fry That Chicken" went viral, it somehow became one of the most politicized hip-hop documents in years. To many, it epitomized the troubling turn rap music was taking. Despite the fact that bloggers and other Internet commentators knew nothing about Ms. Peachez—she didn't have a record deal and had never done an interview—they called her a degrading minstrel act that would set the civil rights movement back thirty years.

Even the *Washington Post* weighed in. Op-ed columnist Jabari Asim decried the antics of this "Aunt Jemima off her meds," whose video "engages—no, embraces—racial stereotypes." "Yes, it is the stuff of nightmares," he asserted. He added that it reminded him of a scene from D. W. Griffith's 1915 movie *The Birth of a Nation*, the granddaddy of American racial propaganda films, which warned of a Negro coup d'état and glorified the Ku Klux Klan.

"Maybe I've seen *Birth of a Nation* too many times, but it suddenly seemed mild when compared to 'Fry That Chicken,'" Asim wrote, adding, "How can anyone explain black performers willingly—and apparently joyfully—perpetuating such foolishness in the 21st century?"

Such criticism only seemed to spur Peachez's popularity, and she proceeded to release a series of follow-ups, each more outlandish than the last. Two and a half million more people watched her "In the Tub" video, a loose parody of 50 Cent's "In da Club." It finds her playing with rubber duckies and washing her bootie in an outdoor washbasin, her broad shoulders and flat chest exposed.

The most provocative in the series had to be "From da Country," which opens with a nearly toothless midget named Uncle Shorty, who wears a curly blond wig and chows down on some watermelon. There's a guy in a chicken suit, tractors, and Ms. Peachez showing off a plate of candied yams swarming with flies. Meanwhile, kids perform steps with names like "The Neck Bone," "The Corn Bread," and "The Collard Greens."

HIP-HOP started in the Bronx, was dominated by New Yorkers in the 1980s, and felt its center of gravity pulled toward the West Coast the next decade, through the success of gangsta rap acts like N.W.A.

As southern rap gained popularity in the 2000s, fans of "true" hip-hop said it appealed to our most base, childish instincts. Nursery rhyme jingles, they claimed, would be the downfall of an art form that has evolved from the good-time rhymes of the Sugarhill Gang three decades ago to the enlightened compositions of Nas. By the mid-aughts this chorus reached a fever pitch.

The problem wasn't just Ms. Peachez, who was presumed to be southern. There were plenty of other rappers to complain about, the ones responsible for the stripped-down, shucking-and-jiving ditties that were taking over the radio. These were "minstrel show" MCs, an epithet pegged to crunk artists like Lil Jon, who had a mouth full of platinum and carried around a pimp chalice.

But crunk was fading, and so the culprits became a new crop of young, blinged-out rappers whose songs often instructed listeners to do a new dance. These included Atlanta rapper Young Dro, whose hit "Shoulder Lean" told you to "bounce right to left and let your shoulder lean," and whose video features an older man dumping a bag of sugar directly into his pitcher of red Kool-Aid.

Then there was Atlanta group D4L ("Down for Life"), whose ubiquitous radio jam "Laffy Taffy" sounded mined from the presets of a child's mini Casio, only not so complex. The song uses the wax-paper-wrapped confection of the title as a metaphor for a bulbous rear end. "I'm lookin' fo' Mrs. Bubble Gum/ I'm Mr. Chick-O-Stick/ I wanna dun dun dunt/ 'Cause you so thick . . . Shake that laffy taffy."

Teenage Saint Louis rapper Jibbs earned his spot in this group for "Chain Hang Low," another massive hit that was an ode to his diamond pendant. The track borrows its singsong melody from the 1830s-era folk song "Zip Coon," which is also known as "Turkey in the Straw" and the ice cream truck jingle.

> Do your chain hang low?
> Do it wobble to the floor?
> Do it shine in the light?
> Is it platinum, is it gold?

Critics argued that these artists—and their complicit record labels—were indulging in the worst black stereotypes for the entertainment of white people. "Record labels are rushing out to sign the most coon-like negros they can find," declared popular hip-hop blogger Byron Crawford. Despite the fact that not all of the minstrel rappers were from the South, he insisted that the subgenre "obviously has its origins in shitty southern hip-hop."

Queens-bred rapper Nas, a charter member of New York's hip-hop elite, baited southern rappers with the title of his 2006 album *Hip Hop Is Dead*. Though he denied it was aimed specifically at them, it was easy to read between the lines, considering New York rap was declining and the southern style was ascendant. In 2009 he took a swipe at the alleged minstrel MCs, via an ostensible public service announcement known as "Eat That Watermelon."

The YouTube video begins with Nas narrating, in his most serious voice:

> There is a period of great distress in the rap universe. There was a time when hip-hop was a form of empowerment. Now the corporate world is quickly diluting our culture for nothing more than profit. With the ever mounting forces of ridiculous dances, ignorant behavior, and general buffoonery, it's only a matter of time before hip-hop's permanent annihilation. This is what the future holds if it don't stop.

The clip cuts to a pair of black-faced, blinged-out rappers called Shuck and Jive, who in their best Sambo voices set out to please "massah" with their dancin' and banjo-pickin'. Played by MTV sketch comedians Nick Cannon and Affion Crockett, the characters proceed to chow down on a giant rind of watermelon.

The clip is funny, preposterous, and slightly horrific. But it hit close to home. Only higher production values—and a wee bit of self-awareness—seemed to separate it from "Fry That Chicken."

WHEN MOST people think hip-hop beef they think of the 1990s-era feud between the East and West Coasts, culminating in the murders of hip-hop icons Notorious B.I.G. and Tupac Shakur.

But more recently rappers from both coasts have ganged up on southern MCs. Less blood feud than ideological battle and culture clash, it has nonetheless gotten nasty, particularly as southern artists began to dominate the charts.

New Yorkers have been voicing their strong displeasure with southern hip-hop since the 2 Live Crew. But the floodgates opened in 2007 when a teenage Atlanta rapper called Soulja Boy released a dance instructional called "Crank That," which became a phenomenon. None other than gangsta rap founding father Ice-T proceeded to rail against the seventeen-year-old, accusing him of having "single-handedly killed hip-hop."

Ice-T led a growing chorus of veteran coastal rappers who took umbrage with the South's new stars and their methods of success. Venerable Long Beach rapper Snoop Dogg also dissed Soulja Boy, along with the New Orleans rapper Lil Wayne, while New York kingpin Jay-Z released "D.O.A. (Death of Auto-Tune)," which took aim at the voice modulation software popularized by Tallahassee singer T-Pain.

Lyrical Staten Island clique Wu-Tang Clan was probably the loudest, with crew leader RZA insisting that southerners were less intelligent. "The South has evolved later than us," he told MTV News in 2010. He said southern students were likely to drop out of school early because of work obligations, poverty, or disinterest in the education system. "I got cousins out there that still live in the South," he went on. "They have not picked up on the wavelength of where their mind should be."

Other Wu-Tang members criticized "dance MCs." Ghostface Killah mocked D4L and Arlington, Texas, rappers GS Boyz (they of the song "Stanky Legg"). He called current radio hip-hop "bullshit," and contrasted it to the "real hip-hop" made by him and his New York brethren.

After Riverdale, Georgia, rapper Waka Flocka Flame claimed that lyricism wasn't particularly important to him—"The niggas who they say is lyrical, they ain't got no shows"—Wu-Tang's Method Man predicted his quick demise. Said Meth, "The shit that these niggas is doin' now ain't hip-hop. That's pop."

Meth's rhyming partner Raekwon allows that some southern MCs can spit, but says that popular rap these days (which just so happens to be dominated by southerners) is not for him. "When we were coming up, it was about skill and style," he tells me. "You had to be creative, and you had to come conceptually correct when you were writing your rhymes. But quality hip-hop is not important no more. It's all about image and marketing." He adds, "I think it's important for artists to really recognize that word, 'art.' If we stop making art, then how can we call ourselves artists?"

By the 2010s it had become something of a right of passage in northeastern MC circles to diss southern rappers. Rap audiences from the region did the same. During a 2009 show at New York's CMJ festival, the audience booed Atlanta rapper OJ da Juiceman off the stage. OJ happens to be Waka Flocka's crewmate; many in the crowd had come to see headliner Raekwon.

Even a New Jersey cab driver recently sought to explain to me how hip-hop had gone to hell in a handbasket. "When they came out with a song that was made up of nothing but whispering," he said, referring to Atlanta rappers Ying Yang Twins' "Wait (The Whisper Song)," "then it was all over."


THESE DISSES caused rumblings from southerners, including up-and-coming New Orleans MC Jay Electronica, who insisted rappers like Andre 3000 and Bun B were actually superior to their northern counterparts, and chastised RZA for his comments.

Before he died, Port Arthur, Texas, rapper Pimp C offered up an expletive-filled musical response to those who dissed his region, suggesting they put the coastal hip-hop on one side of the store and "country rap" on the other side, and see who sold out first.

"They sayin' hip-hop's dead," rapped Ludacris on fellow Atlanta rapper Shawty Lo's song, "Atlanta, GA." "I say we kept it alive." Others were content to let their success speak for itself. They knew that rap wasn't dead. It had just acquired a new home base.

In the early aughts hip-hop began to be dominated by southerners. OutKast's 2003 album *Speakerboxxx/The Love Below* became the greatest selling rap album of all time, and the genre's unofficial capital had relocated from New York to Atlanta. Many pioneering New York rappers, including Nas, followed. (Cheaper real estate and warmer weather helped.)

Suddenly, everyone on BET wore drooping, diamond-studded chains and drove candy-color cars with outlandishly sized rims. Rappers, singers, and producers from states like Florida, Texas, Virginia, and Georgia began dominating sales charts and radio. An August 2003 survey showed Virginia Beach producers the Neptunes alone accounted for more than 40 percent of songs played on US pop music radio stations that month. By one mid-decade count, southern artists were getting nearly twice as much radio play as their East Coast counterparts, and eight times more than west coasters.

Those trends continue. Music sales have been declining for years, but southern rappers like Young Jeezy, Rick Ross, T.I., Ludacris, and Lil Wayne—as well as hip-hop-focused southern singers like T-Pain, The-Dream, and Usher—continue to go gold and platinum. Of *Billboard*'s 2009 year-end top forty rap songs, 75 percent of them featured southerners. Down south artists dominate radio not just in the South, but in New York. Take the city's hip-hop and R&B station Hot 97, one of the most, if not *the* most, popular and influential in the country. During the first week of December 2009, all five of its most-played songs featured southern performers.

What characterizes southern hip-hop? It's often accused of being *simple*, and that's how a producer named Zaytoven, who has worked with Young Jeezy and Gucci Mane, describes it. Zaytoven was born in Germany and came of age in San Francisco, where he sold his beats to Bay Area rappers. He moved to Atlanta in 2000 and found he had to change his style for the local market. "I had to simplify things," he says. "The artists here weren't as complex as

Bay Area artists. In the Bay, they [like] their music more compli-cated. Here, it's almost like easy listening music. They want music they can sing along with."

Southern rap lyrics are full of hyper-regional slang. Formal structures and metaphor-heavy rhymes are often forsaken in favor of chants, grunts, and shouts, like when Lil Jon yells out, "OK!" Many MCs have distinctive, atonal voices. Lil Wayne sounds like a frog, and Lil Boosie's voice resembles a twelve-year-old girl's.

Sonically, the music features tinny percussion, danceable rhythms, and big bass, often courtesy of the Roland TR-808 drum machine, which you can recognize as that low, round, subwoofer sound. "You'll catch more people in the South with 15 woofers in the trunk cause they're mainly lookin' for bass," said No Limit pro-ducer KLC to *Murder Dog*. "It's all about the beat in South."

It's party music, full of hypnotic hooks and sing-along choruses that get the ladies on the dance floor. New York rap, on the other hand, tends to be more of a lyrically focused, cerebral boys' club.

But these are just generalizations, and flawed ones at that. Just because a song sounds like southern rap doesn't mean it *is* south-ern rap, after all. Many coastal rappers have appropriated southern styles, lock, stock, and barrel. If they want to stay on the radio, they don't have much choice.

THE MID-AUGHTS also saw a public debate about the role of racially coded language in popular culture. During a comedy show in West Hollywood in 2006, former *Seinfeld* star Michael Richards shouted *n*-bombs at black attendees, and the next year radio personality Don Imus was fired for calling members of the Rutgers women's basketball team "nappy-headed hos."

In July of 2007, thousands of folks, including the mayor of Detroit and the governor of Michigan, gathered in Motown at the NAACP's annual convention for a symbolic funeral for the *n*-word.

Def Jam Records cofounder Russell Simmons, meanwhile, called on the recording and broadcasting industries to censor the *n*-word, as well as "bitch" and "ho," while civil rights leaders Jesse Jackson and Al Sharpton called on rappers to regulate their own language.

"We're in an age where they are hanging nooses; they're locking our kids up in Jena and Florida," Sharpton told MTV News. "We do not need to be degrading ourselves. We get degraded enough. I think we need artists to lift us up, not lock us down." Sharpton's comments were in response to Nas's announcement that he would title his 2008 album *Nigger*. Nas claimed he was attempting to take back the slur from racists, but many suggested it was a publicity scheme. Eventually he caved to record label pressure and released the work as *Untitled*; it hit number one anyway.

On a 2006 show, New York public radio program *Soundcheck* addressed both the *n*-word controversies and minstrel rap, which similarly pitted the values of free expression against cultural and moral concerns. Duke University professor Mark Anthony Neal cited an "anxiety" among middle-class blacks about hip-hop from below the Mason-Dixon line. *The New Yorker* writer Kelefa Sanneh, meanwhile, noted the modern minstrel rap debate largely pitted urban, mainly northern blacks against rural, mainly southern blacks.

Naturally, Ms. Peachez worked her way into the discussion. Sanneh insisted that understanding context was important in this debate, but that in the case of "Fry That Chicken," that was impossible, since no one knew much of anything about her or her intentions. Nonetheless, Sanneh was willing to make an assumption: "I think 'Fry That Chicken,'" he said, "is very clearly a novelty and a parody."

BUT IS IT? I'm not so sure. "Fry That Chicken" doesn't feature any winks or nods, and its YouTube comment section is filled with racially charged name-calling. No, I have a strange feeling that Ms. Peachez isn't of the postmodern, tongue-in-cheek set.

But then again, what do I know? I figure the only way to get to the bottom of this is to hunt down Ms. Peachez herself. At the very least, someone at the center of a wide-ranging cultural debate—whose work was declared more offensive than *Birth of a Nation*—should have the chance to speak for herself. Himself.

And so I put on my Sherlock Holmes cap and attempt to track her down. From her MySpace profile I learn she's from Shreveport, Louisiana. Further inquiry shows she's allied with a rapper named Rico Da Body, who sells copies of her CD, *U Hear Me*, on his own site.

From his music videos, Rico seems to be Peachez's antithesis, a chiseled, self-serious, hypermasculine young MC who surrounds himself with groupies. An R-rated YouTube video for his song "Make Dat Ass Clap" features a pair of big-boned, barely clad girls in somebody's kitchen, rotating their rumps in physics-defying ways.

Rico's site lists his phone number, but in conversation he's not much help. "Ms. Peachez doesn't really do interviews," he says, though he promises to put in my request and get back to me. He never does that, but eventually I track down the phone number for a Shreveport record studio called Millennia Music Group, run by Rico's father, Dale Lynch. I begin leaving messages there, which also go unreturned. And so, to my chagrin, when it is time for me to fly to the South to begin research for this book, I have yet to make contact with Ms. Peachez.


WHY DO I want to get to the bottom of the Peachez phenomenon so badly? To me, she seems to epitomize what everyone, from the Wu-Tang Clan to some of my music critic buddies, hate about southern rap.

I personally find the genre worth defending, and suspect animosity toward it isn't based so much in music as in culture. The coastal/southern rap divide somewhat mirrors the red state/blue state political divide, which has plenty of poorly informed hysterics on both sides. This story needed to be told from the ground level, I decided, not from the perch inhabited by most critics, who tend to be based in the northeast and engage in little actual reporting.

I've been both critic and journalist in recent years, writing reviews and reporting on rappers for a variety of old- and new-media publications. But I was trained as a traditional news journalist, interning at the daily *St. Louis Post-Dispatch* while a student at Washington University, and starting with that city's weekly *Riverfront Times* in 2003.

My time in Saint Louis coincided with an explosion of interest in the city's hip-hop scene, with Nelly paving the way for artists like Murphy Lee, Chingy, J-Kwon, and Jibbs. Though Saint Louis is considered the Midwest, Missouri came into the union as a slave state, and has thick country accents and confederate-flag-bearing pickup trucks aplenty. Saint Louis rap has a distinctly southern flavor as well, with a focus on singsong melodies, slurred *rs*, and a booty-centric, iced-out image. It too has been ridiculed for breaking with formal, lyrical tradition.

After a year or so at the *Riverfront Times* I began focusing less on traditional news and cultural stories and more on rappers. I traveled to Beverly Hills with Chingy's producers the Track Starz, watched Jibbs perform before a roomful of screaming junior high students, and even started my own column, Yo! RFT Raps. I loved telling these artists' stories. Unlike rock bands, who often come from stable, middle-class (read: boring) backgrounds, rappers' biographies almost always have a compelling narrative arc, filled with struggle and triumph.

Yes, I'm a fan of Nelly, as well as Juvenile, Scarface, and Out-Kast, and just about everyone else in this book. (I also enjoy the work of this book's antagonists, coastal rappers like Ice-T, Nas, and Wu-Tang Clan, though they could all use more humility.) But just as much, I love uncovering details about these artists' lives, their breakthroughs, their dark moments. Even after moving to New York, and then New Jersey, I remained enamored with this endlessly fascinating, endlessly castigated genre.

MOST OF ALL, I want to know how a blue-wig-clad, cross-dressing rapper in a grainy YouTube video managed to piss off people all over the country. And so, having flown into New Orleans and spent a day prowling around the Hollygrove neighborhood where Lil Wayne grew up (folks there love being pried for details about his childhood, let me tell you), I pilot my tiny rented Hyundai Accent five hours northwest to Shreveport.

I still haven't lined up an interview with Peachez or anyone else, but I nonetheless book the cheapest room I can find on the Internet, which just so happens to be at a casino called Diamond Jacks. Seventy bucks gets me a mammoth suite with a Jacuzzi and three televisions, including one in the bathroom. Emerging from my soak I finally receive a callback from Dale, who says that, sadly, he can't introduce me to Ms. Peachez, as they've fallen out of touch and he doesn't have a current phone number. Still, if I want to talk to him and his son Rico, I can come by his studio tomorrow.

Millennia Music Group is surrounded by a moat of gravel in a pine-tree-studded, rural-feeling swath on the west side of town, next to a paint warehouse. Dale lets me inside the studios, which are larger and more professional than I'd expected, and boast a cozy lobby decorated with posters of Britney, Cristina, and Aaliyah. (Also, a fancy aquarium with no fish.) Bundled up in a thick work shirt for the unseasonably cold weather, Dale notes that he records everyone from gospel instrumentalists to the city's biggest rap star, Hurricane Chris.

Dale introduces me to Rico, who, unlike in most of his videos, is dressed, wearing a giant yellow jacket repping Grambling State, where he's a junior recreational therapy major on a track-and-field scholarship. A courteous twenty-year-old who speaks with a thick accent ("here" becomes "he-ah"), he's shy at first but eventually warms up, even explaining the genesis of his nickname, Rico Da Body. "Some females gave me the name in high school," he says. "I was one of the most muscular football players, and I always used to take my shirt off after practice."

For a couple of hours that afternoon he and Dale unravel the story of Ms. Peachez, whose real name is Nelson Boyd. Dale originally met him before he dressed in drag, he says, back when he was a little-known MC with the downright-unoriginal rap moniker of "Hip Hop."

Boyd came to Millennia to record one of his raps, and Dale eventually helped him craft a minor local hit called "Take Me to Get My Nails Did," which was featured in an independent film called *Dollar*. (This was in the pre–Ms. Peachez days, keep in mind, so the song's title comes from the perspective of a female love interest, not Boyd himself.)

At the time, Boyd was more of a hard-edged rapper in the vein of Tupac Shakur, which didn't seem to fit with his personality; in real life he's a hilarious, life-of-the-party type who sometimes performs as a stand-up comedian.

And so, after Boyd began spontaneously improvising a character he called Ms. Peachez one day in the studio, Dale enlisted her to provide comic relief for his free hip-hop DVD series called *Double X-Posure*. *Double X-Posure* featured interviews with rappers—Shreveport is known for a club-oriented subgenre called "ratchet"—and subsidized itself through ads for local businesses. After outfitting himself in a dress, wig, and press-on nails, Boyd-as-Ms.-Peachez performed in funny spots for Dale's advertisers. (You can see some of them on YouTube.)

Eventually the guys decided Ms. Peachez should be a rapper, and she began performing songs Rico created. Indeed, Rico was something like the man behind the curtain, doing everything from composing her music to arranging her songs. He even sang her hooks. When it came to the Ms. Peachez character, however, he was happy to step aside. "I wasn't going to dress up like a woman," Rico says. "I didn't feel like anyone would take me serious if I was in a Ms. Peachez video, so I just stay in the background."

"Fry That Chicken" was Peachez's first song, and Rico wrote it in 2006, when he was a junior in high school. "I wasn't hungry. I wasn't thinking about chicken or nothing," he remembers. "I knew I wanted to involve children, so I was just trying to think of a chant they could say that would be catchy, that no one had done before."

They filmed the video just down the street from the studio, on the property of a local guy Dale knew. They chose the spot because, well, the man had chickens. After we finish talking, they take me over. The owner isn't around, and neither are the chickens, but Dale and Rico lead a tour of the wooded, middle-of-nowhere plot of land surrounding the pastel green shack. The grounds are littered with abandoned cars, a rusty smoker, plastic swans, and other trinkets. There's even the patio furniture on which the group of kids—whom Rico says he assembled from his neighborhood— pounded their fists.

A true, backwoods country home, Rico says, one which was perfect for their goal of shooting a different kind of rap video. "We just wanted to show what normal people do in everyday life," he says. "We fry chicken. [The video] didn't have to have no rims, no cars, no lies. Just the truth. I wanted to do something positive. Nothing violent or sexual. Just something fun that everybody can enjoy."

"We live down south, and it's country," adds Dale, telling me he grew up in the small town of Winnfield, Louisiana, located a hundred miles to the southeast and the birthplace of slain Louisiana governor Huey Long. "We're used to horses, cows, chickens."

They had no idea the track would cause an uproar, and Rico says he was surprised when the nasty YouTube comments began pouring in. "There were a lot of racist comments, a lot of crazy stuff that's off track," he says. "It wasn't supposed to be that, it was supposed to be something fun for the kids, but people took it and made it what they wanted it to be."

Neither man gives much credence to the charge that the Peachez character perpetuates stereotypes. "I can see why they would say that, but that wasn't our point," says Dale. "The video was pure innocence. It had nothing to do with coonery, no negative vibe at all. The world made it controversial. We're used to seeing stuff like that in the South. We eat fried chicken! We eat watermelon!"

After visiting the "Fry That Chicken" set, Rico, Dale and I go downtown for lunch, to a restaurant and pub called the Blind Tiger. I order a shrimp po'boy, which contains nothing but bread and fried shrimp, and we talk more about Dale's work as a producer and Rico's track-and-field exploits. Turns out he throws discus and javelin, and in fact is the top javelin tosser in the Southwestern Athletic Conference, throwing one 197 feet recently, a personal best. Rico Da Body, indeed.

Both men are generous with their time, and I find them disarmingly friendly. From the moment we meet I sense that the Ms. Peachez creation wasn't meant to be offensive or subversive. Sure, she's a colorful personality designed to grab people's attention, but when Rico says "Fry That Chicken" was simply a song he hoped regular people could relate to, I believe him.

Nowadays, Dale has stopped doing the *Double X-Posure* magazine and is focusing on his gospel albums, while Rico is working on various solo projects. He's got a song called "Holiday Sex," which he's pretty excited about. He believes it will be even more popular than a similarly titled hit from an artist called Jeremih, called "Birthday Sex."

A FEW MONTHS later Dale finally tracks down Nelson Boyd's number, and I catch up with him over the phone. Like Dale, he disagrees that Ms. Peachez is politically incorrect. "I'm from the country, that's how we do," he says. "That's our lifestyle, that's a part of our heritage. Just 'cause I'm talking about it, that don't make it a bad thing."

He's still astonished by how popular Ms. Peachez became, and says he continues to be recognized regularly in Shreveport. "I was signing autographs in WalMart the other day," he says. "This chick working behind the photo counter followed me to the mouthwash section."

But it hasn't been all fun and games. Someone nearly tried to fight him, he says, after hearing a little kid singing the lyrics to "In the Tub." "Why you got those kids talking about thcy booties?" the man said. Though some have suggested that Boyd is gay, he notes his wife and kids. Besides, Martin Lawrence wore a dress, so why can't he?

He adds that he is too bowlegged to do traditional work, and survives off disability benefits. He and Dale had hoped to monetize Ms. Peachez's success, but couldn't agree about how to best market her as a rapper. By the time they finally secured a ringtone deal for "Fry That Chicken" and had finished her CD, interest had mostly died down.

Though he continues to perform the character at his stand-up shows, her hip-hop career has been effectively aborted. Still, he maintains a soft spot for her. "She's a real ghetto country backwoods [person]," he explains. "She's wannabe-city, wannabe-glamorous, wannabe-rich, and she's trying to be in the entertainment business no matter what. But you can't take the ghetto out of her."


MS. PEACHEZ obviously doesn't have the skill set of the other MCs and producers profiled in this book. But her story has taught me about the discrepancy between southern hip-hop's reality and its perception.

Despite what some have charged, down south rap is not rooted in a corporate conspiracy to dumb down America. In fact, quite the opposite, it's a largely grassroots movement that has succeeded in spite of, not because of, the big record labels.

Southern rappers had to work harder to succeed because they were being shut out by the coastal powers that be. And so, they developed populist sensibilities and sold their wares directly to the people.

Record label owners like Luke Campbell, J. Prince, and Tony Draper pioneered the independent hip-hop scene in the South. Their model thrived thanks to mom-and-pop distributors and shops, and it exploded with the arrival of Louisiana labels No Limit and Cash Money. That same do-it-yourself spirit was later championed by folks like Atlanta's DJ Drama, who went to jail for his street mixtapes, and even Soulja Boy, who used the Internet to build his fan base.

Though artists like OutKast, Geto Boys, and T.I. feature complex themes and brilliant innovation in their music, I'll admit that not all southern rappers are forward-thinking. But the genre has been tremendously adept at giving people what they want. It has reshaped the idea of what it means to be hip-hop artists and businessmen, and may just have saved the genre from obsolescence.

The criticisms by Ice-T, Method Man, and Ghostface Killah—rappers with declining commercial fortunes—smack of sour grapes. Surely they know that whoever can bring the hottest songs will command the most ears. If your beat is good and your rhymes are tight, it doesn't matter if you're rapping about Marcus Garvey or fried chicken.

Bronx-bred MC Fat Joe said it best when I talked to him a few years ago. Instead of complaining about southern rappers, he had begun collaborating with them, and wished others from his region would do the same. "Hip-hop is dead? No, it's not," he said. "Step your game up. Make some hits."

# 1

# LUKE CAMPBELL

■ ■ ■

## Bass and Booty

ONE SPRING evening at the Atlanta airport, I find myself stalking Luke Campbell. This is my first attempt to ambush someone, in a journalistic capacity or otherwise, and I don't think I'm cut out for it.

You probably know Luke's group the 2 Live Crew and their song "Me So Horny," off the 1989 *As Nasty As They Wanna Be* album, which local authorities deemed obscene. The subsequent free-speech battle went all the way to the Supreme Court.

Luke's a polarizing figure, and you may find him contemptible, what with his porn company, lewd stage shows, and songs like, "Head, Head, and More Head." Still, he's the undisputed godfather of southern rap music, and I've long been trying to talk to him. Tonight he's slated to perform at a Mexican restaurant in Athens— seventy miles east—and I plan to be there. On the trip over, I'm hoping we can knock out an interview.

The only problem is that I don't exactly have a scheduled appointment. A couple of months back he said he'd talk to me, but then stopped taking my phone calls. I've since gotten in touch with his booking agent, who said Luke should be able to meet up with me here in Georgia. But after informing me that Luke's Fort Lauderdale flight lands at 7:30, the booking agent dropped off the face as well.

Let me tell you: stalking isn't as easy as it sounds. For one thing, two Fort Lauderdale planes land at 7:30, one Delta and one AirTran, and each deposits into a different terminal. And so I decide to plant myself near the baggage claim, next to a set of escalators where most passengers arrive.

I send a text message to Luke to say I'm here, but, naturally, don't hear back. I pace. I sweat. I weigh my pros and cons.

On one hand, if I don't talk to this guy I don't really have a book. On the other hand, his bodyguard may tackle me.

I continue waiting. It's about 7:40 now. I've rented a car here in Atlanta, but in hopes he'll invite me to ride along with him, I've stashed it. For the same reason, my oversized travel bag is with me too.

Most likely, I will recognize him. In his solo videos from the 1990s, he usually wears a mischievous smile, flashing the gap in his front teeth while making filthy promises to his harem of bouncing dancers. In his 2008 VH1 reality show, *Luke's Parental Advisory*, he wears a more sober expression; balancing his line of work with family is not easy, you see. Lucky for him, his wife "understands that I'm like a gynecologist. If I don't see pussy every day, something's wrong," he notes.

At 7:45 he emerges, flanked by a sturdy-looking accomplice. Luke wears a small mustache and some scruff on his chin, and is clad in Adidas track pants and a University of Central Florida shirt. A middle-aged former football player, he looks and moves like an athlete, and quickly darts left toward the food court. Slinging my bag over my shoulder, I take off after him, dodging between folks approaching baggage carousels.

"Luke," I say softly, and then again, more loudly. "Luke!"

He turns. I introduce myself as the guy writing the book on southern rap he talked to a while back. "Sorry for stalking you," I say, with a half-giggle, noting that his booking agent green-lit this meeting, which is sort of true.

"He didn't tell me anything about that," Luke says, turning back around.

An inauspicious start, but I haven't explicitly been told to leave, and so I lurk a few steps behind as they approach a soul food stand called Paschal's. Everyone there seems to know him. The robust woman serving up his peach cobbler flirts with him, and he flirts right back. She wraps up his meal and proceeds to undercharge him.

As they head for the exits I realize time is probably running out, and summon the courage to mention the interview. "Maybe we could bang this out on the ride to Athens?" I suggest.

He laughs quietly, impressed by my audacity, and picks up his BlackBerry. "We'll see if there's room in the car," he says, dialing the show's promoter to arrange pickup. When a long SUV pulls up to the curb, Luke indicates I may climb aboard, and I scurry into the backseat.

He's not in a good mood, though, clearly annoyed with the transportation situation. He calls our vehicle a "1976 Excursion," thought it's at least two decades newer than that. Before we can start our interview, he insists I'm going to have to pay him for any valuable information. I suspect he's joking, but I'm not sure.

His mood improves when the promoter, who is driving the truck, hands him two stacks of cash. He counts it, stashes it, and leans back in his seat. Before I know it his tongue is loose. He begins reeling off some killer anecdotes, like the one about how he pissed off the Jacksonville police by showing them his ass, and the one about how he kicked butt at the Supreme Court.

Then there's the one about how he alone is responsible for southern hip-hop. "We inspired other cats from down here to be their own motherfuckers, to talk like where they were from," he says. "I started this shit, the whole fucking South."

IT'S TRUE. Long before Lil Wayne was performing tracks like "Pussy Monster," Luke battled censors to make rap safely profane. Before "Dirty South" was coined, he fought New Yorkers who didn't think the region made real hip-hop. Before independent labels like Rap-A-Lot, Cash Money, and No Limit began selling directly to their fans, Luke was plying his wares from his mother's washroom. Before "To the windows/ To the wall," before the "Laffy Taffy" or the "Crank That" dances, Luke was putting butts on dance floors.

"All that crunk stuff comes from Luke," says Three 6 Mafia's DJ Paul. Adds Mr. Collipark, the man responsible for Soulja Boy and Ying Yang Twins, "2 Live Crew is like the godfather of everything I do. As nasty as it was, it was so creative."

Indeed, perhaps Luke's greatest legacy is putting the *sex* in rap. All those fat-bootied, barely clad, gyrating women you see in videos? Luke started that. Back in the day, rap was just one of hip-hop culture's four "elements," alongside DJing, break dancing, and graffiti, all of which informed its imagery.

That was fine and good, but it wasn't Luke. "We didn't write on the walls in Miami, we booty-shaked," he says. "I looked at their shit, like, 'Motherfuckers flipping on their heads? How you gonna get some hos like that?'"

Starting directly out of high school in the mid-1970s, he plied his trade as a record-spinner and party promoter with a crew called Ghetto Style DJs. They bumped reggae, disco, rock, or anything with bass. Manipulating the knobs to maximize the low-end frequencies, they wanted the crowd to literally feel the music in their joints.

Miami bass is sometimes called the bastard stepchild of hip-hop, and indeed it takes some cues from the funk, electro, and 808 drum sounds of early New York rap. Owing to Miami's Caribbean immigrant population, bass music also has quick-paced, percussion-driven island sounds, sexually suggestive chants, and calls and response. It's not music for your mind, it's music to shake your rear. Think Tag Team's "Whoomp! (There It Is)."

Ghetto Style DJs didn't invent Miami bass. Collectives like Soul Survivor DJs and South Miami DJs had already kicked off the style, and Luke in particular looked up to a guy called Jeff Walker, whom he calls the "first mobile DJ."

But Luke and his crew made a name for themselves by hustling hard and performing anywhere—parks, car washes, beaches— until the police chased them away. "We'd set up in the big field in back of the school, take the lightbulb out, and pull the juice from the [socket]," he remembers. "Two to three thousand people out there on a Sunday, jamming like a motherfucker."

They used much of the same equipment as Jamaican DJs of the era, and the scene resembles early events in the Bronx, where originators like DJ Kool Herc and Grandmaster Flash set up impromptu, unauthorized soirees for neighborhood folks.

Luke says he wasn't familiar with them, however. One difference was that he didn't mine the "breaks," like Herc and company. What they did was isolate a song's break section—usually two-thirds of the way through the track, when all of the music stops except for the percussion—and play it over and over by going back and forth between two records. That's the technique that formed the basis for rap as we know it.

Instead, Luke and his contemporaries would speak over records, pulling the fader down to briefly silence a song, and adding their own ad-libs in place of the regular lyrics. Luke learned early on that creating a party atmosphere was important, and he knew just how to do it.

"[Girls] would be shakin' their ass, and I'd just make up the songs," he says, speaking of events at spots like Crandon Park and Miami's historically black Virginia Key beach. "I said, 'Take it off!

Take it off!' Then the crowd said, 'Take it off!' Before you know it, they're taking it off."

CONTRARY TO his wild image, Luke actually comes from a very stable family. Pops was an elementary school custodian from Jamaica, and Mom was a Nassau, Bahamas–bred beautician. They met in Cuba, and Luke was born in 1960, coming of age in Miami's Liberty City neighborhood, which he remembers for its brazen criminality. "It was the Nixon days, and everybody was robbing and selling drugs," he says. "It was like the wild, wild west."

Though his four brothers attended college, Luke didn't go that route. A pampered linebacker and defensive end who didn't learn to read until the eleventh grade, he lost interest once a coach explained his long odds of making the NFL.

Instead, he took a job as a cook and dishwasher at Mount Sinai Medical Center, playing records in his off hours. In those days being a successful DJ wasn't just about good technical skills or a large record collection. Rather, it was an arms race. Whoever had the most speakers won the day, so Luke set about building up his arsenal, acquiring all the fifteen-inch Electro-Voice brand subwoofers he could get his hands on. "You had to have stacks," he says, declining to say how he got the dough. "At first you needed sixteen [to be competitive], then it went to twenty-four, then forty-eight, then sixty-four."

Ghetto Style DJs were anxious to take him in, considering they only had a measly pair of speakers to call their own. Luke says he loved competing with his fellow turntablists. "I had to go deep in the crates and make some old shit sound good," he says. "I had to get some reggae, and then I had to talk some shit. I had to be more creative."

They inaugurated an event at the Sunshine skating rink called Pac Jam, with roller-skating in the early hours and a dance party later. Attempting to one-up his peers, Luke debuted his own songs, which he created by adding chants and catchphrases to other artists' music. For his first tune, "Ghetto Jump," he'd yell out, "Jump, Jump!" and the crowd would comply. Another track was called "Throw the D," which included a dance where guys pretended to thrust on women, often with their pants pulled down.

By the mid-eighties, Ghetto Style DJs were bringing nationally known acts to town, like Run-DMC. Luke maintained a full concert schedule. On Friday night he'd play a junior high cafeteria, Saturday he'd do a high school, and Sunday was Pac Jam, with scattered bar mitzvahs and weddings in between. All told he might perform before four thousand people over the course of a weekend.

It was around this time that a lightbulb went off in his head: he had a powerful platform to exploit. "I could break a song," he says. "If I played your [music], you were a hot group."


"COLLEGE TOWNS everywhere look the same," Luke says now, looking out the Excursion's window. "Same sports bar and wing places. Same Cracker Barrel, Waffle House. Same horny college girls."

It's nine o' clock, and we've arrived in Athens. There's a warm spring breeze, and said college girls are spilling out of dorm rooms (no idea if they're horny). We pass a random group of them waiting at a stoplight, led by a particularly comely blonde whom Luke has never seen before.

"I love you, Jenny!" he yells, sticking his head out the window. Everybody laughs.

The Excursion pulls up to the Hilton Garden Inn, a downtown spot decidedly more posh than the fleabag motel I've reserved on the outskirts of town. I follow the guys in. As the promoter pays for the rooms by way of another stack of cash, the clerk asks if I need a key card.

"No, I'm not staying here," I say, before Luke cuts in. It's either a gesture of goodwill or a way to get back at the promoter for the substandard SUV, but he insists I'm welcome to my own room, just so long as I'm on a different floor than he. "When my wife's not here, I have a good time," he says. He quickly corrects himself, "I mean, I have a good time when she's here, but . . ."

He turns his attention to the desk clerk, a recent University of Georgia graduate whose cheeks immediately flush. It's not that he's saying anything particularly salacious, it's just that he can't help himself from flirting. "I've got a gift," he imparts later.

Neither the clerk nor the bottle-blonde bartender who wanders over are very familiar with the 2 Live Crew, but it's clear they've got a celebrity on their hands, and so we're treated to a round of drinks at the bar.

These women aren't just talking to Luke, they're also talking to Luke's younger, bulkier accomplice, whose name I've learned is Chris. (Luke calls him his "road dawg," and also the "HHC," which I believe stands for "Honorary Hoe Coordinator.") But the weirdest thing is that the ladies are also talking to *me*. Luke mentions I'm writing a book about hip-hop, which they purport to find fascinating. It occurs to me that I've become part of Luke's entourage.

As we down lemon drop shots, the HHC breaks down the grittier requirements for membership in Luke's posse. A writer they met up with a few years back was required to—how to put this—insert a golf club into one of Luke's dancers. But as for me, I have a choice: I can either perform oral sex on stage or have oral sex performed on me. As a married, STD-free man, neither option bears much appeal, but all I can think to do is laugh noncommittally.

After briefly adjourning to our rooms, we meet back in the lobby at a quarter to one, about the time I usually return home from a night out. Luke now wears a black shirt and pants and a newsboy cap, and he and the HHC drink something from Styrofoam cups. We pile back into the Excursion and head a couple miles northeast, to an area which is off the Hilton's complimentary map.

The venue is a Mexican restaurant called El Paisano, which plays *cumbia* music and serves food in the front but transforms into a massive, barnlike club in the back, decked out with black lights and spinning laser beams.

A line of folks wait to pay twenty dollar cover charges, but we enter through the rear. Weed smoke fills the air, three or four hundred people groove on the dance floor, and I'm disoriented by massive, pounding bass. I set my hand atop a vibrating table, which begins to rattle off of its axis.

Luke takes the stage to little fanfare and, grabbing the mic, invites the room's hot chicks to join him. "Where my good-pussied bitches at?" he inquires.

BEFORE LUKE reimagined them as crotch-grabbing rabble-rousers, the 2 Live Crew was a vaguely conscious Southern California trio, formed around three airmen first class stationed at March Air Reserve Base in Riverside County. Aspiring rappers Chris Wong Won, who went by Fresh Kid Ice, and Yuri Vielot (Amazing V.), teamed up with producer David Hobbs, a.k.a. Mr. Mixx, the only guy in the barracks with turntables.

They held shows on and off base, and in 1984 released a single through an L.A. distribution company called Macola Records, who would later put out N.W.A's debut. The song was called "The Revelation," and it employs a dark tone. Amazing V. raps:

> Now your pocket is full, but can't you see
> That your soul will burn in hell for eternity?

"We didn't have an actual identity," Mr. Mixx says now. He never particularly cared for the whole damning-of-the-souls concept—that was V.'s idea—but the song nonetheless came together well. It takes its sonic cues from Bronx originator Afrika Bambaataa's track "Planet Rock"; after hearing it, Mixx was inspired to buy an 808 drum machine at a pawnshop for $300.

The flip side of the single was called "2 Live," and the record circulated all the way to Miami. Luke Campbell was so impressed that he invited them to come to South Florida and perform at the skating rink. "I was shocked that I got a phone call to go out there and do a show," recalls Mixx, adding that they were practically unknown in California and hadn't seen any money from their Macola situation. "I was like, 'You serious?'"

Luke promoted them by playing their music when he deejayed, and after coming down and playing some successful shows, they eventually moved to the area. Amazing V. dropped out, a new MC named Mark Ross (Brother Marquis) came on, and Luke became the group's manager.

The new lineup performed Luke's songs including "Ghetto Jump" and "Throw the D," the latter of which became a hit off their first album, 1986's *The 2 Live Crew Is What We Are*. "Throw the Dick," as it's now known, is an early Mr. Mixx classic, featuring New York elements like scratches and a singsongy cadence but also a more-danceable tempo, sped-up vocal effects, and unabashed raunch. "This ain't a dance from Mother Goose," Fresh Kid Ice warns. "Better freak your body and turn it loose."

Luke and Mr. Mixx shared comedic sensibilities, inspired by humorists like Clarence "Blowfly" Reid, Richard Pryor, and Rudy Ray Moore, a.k.a. Dolemite, who is sampled on "Throw the Dick." Luke remembers sneaking their naughty LPs out of his parents' stash while they were at work. "There weren't no dirty magazines, so we would listen to that," he says. "My [mother] would whoop your ass if she thought you were listening to that."

Another favorite was R&B singer Millie Jackson, who mixed in explicit routines with her music. "Millie was the first person I ever heard sing like that," Luke says. "So I said, 'Let's do some comedy shit like that.'

"Everything was done to be funny, it wasn't done to degrade nobody," he continues, adding that, considering his comic idols told dirty stories with relative impunity, he never thought he would be arrested for doing the same thing to music. Says Mr. Mixx, "We never thought we were raunchier than Richard Pryor or Dolemite or Andrew Dice Clay. We didn't realize that comedy is viewed differently."

BACK THEN Luke called himself Luke Skyywalker, and *The 2 Live Crew Is What We Are* came out on his fledgling record label, Luke Skyywalker Records, which he distributed out of his parents' house. He initiated the imprint because no one else would give his act the time of day.

"I didn't want to be in the record business, but I had to. In the days of hip-hop from New York, they weren't about to give no rappers from Miami a deal," he says, comparing such northern prejudice to "slavery." He adds that when they toured with artists like Salt-n-Peppa, Kid 'n Play, and Run-DMC, those New Yorkers would give 2 Live Crew crummy time slots and leave during their performances. He claims to have fought Public Enemy's road manager over one such dispute. Though *The 2 Live Crew Is What We Are* went gold, one imagines that the Miami act's barrage of puerile sing-alongs (see: "We Want Some Pussy") probably alienated their tour mates, whose material was more, shall we say, mature.

In the late eighties, the 2 Live Crew attended the New Music Seminar, a Gotham showcase where bands around the world performed before industry power players. Luke says his group was openly mocked, and that one mover and shaker stood up and claimed "southern music will never be nothing."

"And I stood up in the middle of the room and it was maybe 2000 people and I said, 'My man you will eat your words,'" Luke told writer Andrew Noz in an interview published on his blog, Cocaine Blunts. "I said, 'You don't understand the music business because if you knew how many records we were selling you'd have a different opinion.'"

"We were viewed as the outcasts of the industry," puts in Mr. Mixx.

Never a rapper, Luke didn't appear on stage with the 2 Live Crew in their early days. But after a month of lackluster shows, he decided to play a more significant role. "He felt Marquis and Fresh Kid were at a disadvantage, because they had the personalities of fucking turnips," says Mr. Mixx. As a DJ, Luke prided himself on grabbing a crowd's attention, so now as a hype man he did the same thing, shouting chants and revving up crowds with lewd catcalls.

He'd already taken a large role in shaping their music. While Mr. Mixx did the scratching and beat constructing, Luke plied him with concepts. He suggested sampling hot Miami songs like Herman Kelly and Life's "Dance to the Drummer's Beat," and twisting the Kinks' 1964 classic "All Day and All of the Night" into a sophomoric chant called "One and One." "One and one, we're having some fun/ In the bedroom, all day and all of the night," Luke sings on the track off 2 Live Crew's 1987 album *Move Somethin'*. It continues in this vein: "Four and four/ We fucked on the floor," et cetera.

After watching Stanley Kubrick's 1987 Vietnam film *Full Metal Jacket*, Luke got the idea to sample a prostitute character. "Me so horny," she pitched some American soldiers. "Me love you long time." The resulting song, "Me So Horny," off their 1989 album, *As Nasty as They Wanna Be*, became the group's most enduring hit. It also sparked controversy.

Luke says he tried to keep his R-rated music out of kids' hands, noting that he put warning labels on 2 Live Crew albums before

Tipper Gore and friends mandated them. Additionally, they recorded separate, less-offensive versions of their works, hence *As Clean as They Wanna Be*. Still, a slightly edited version of "Me So Horny" was all over my conservative Minnesota radio stations, and it was more risqué than anything my junior high classmates and I had heard. I didn't previously know the meaning of "horny," for one thing. Miami of the 1980s had a hedonistic, outlaw image, fostered by *Miami Vice* and *Scarface*, as well as reports of drug busts, shady millionaires, and massive Latin American immigration. The 2 Live Crew came to be the soundtrack for this out-of-control party; that they were selling tapes to white kids is probably why censors made an example out of them.

Authorities in Alabama and Florida had already sought to limit the sale of previous 2 Live Crew works, and *As Nasty as They Wanna Be* prompted a lawyer named Jack Thompson from the right-wing American Family Association to jump into the fray. It didn't help that Luke had recently campaigned against Thompson in his race for Dade County state attorney; instead, Luke supported the victor, Janet Reno, who would go on to be Bill Clinton's US attorney general.

Thompson convened with Florida governor Bob Martinez to take action, and before long Broward sheriff Mike Navarro moved to ban *Nasty* in that county, which borders Miami-Dade to the north.

The 2 Live Crew filed suit against Navarro, but a US district court judge decreed the album obscene, an unprecedented decision mandating that anyone selling *Nasty* or performing its songs face prosecution.

And thus, after an undercover officer purchased the work from a Fort Lauderdale store, its owner was arrested. A few days later authorities cracked down on an adults-only 2 Live Crew show at a club in nearby Hollywood. Luke remembers "horses and helicopters" surrounding the venue, and he and Fresh Kid Ice were cuffed shortly after the concert. (Brother Marquis had to turn himself in later, although Mr. Mixx didn't face charges since he hadn't performed any lyrics.) The arrests were national news, and the controversy helped spur *Nasty* sales well over a million.

Yet performing continued to be difficult. Insurers charged venue owners exorbitant rates to host the group's gigs, and dog-bearing cops surrounded 2 Live Crew in-store shows. When they did play, they continued to be arrested, though Luke says they were always quickly bailed out and were eventually acquitted of their charges.

At one point, Luke decided to have some fun with the cops. At a Jacksonville, Florida, solo concert, he saw the police lurking off-stage, ready to haul him in if he performed the taboo tracks. And so he asked the crowd to relay a message to the boys in blue for him. "Tell them to kiss my black ass!" he said, proceeding to drop his drawers and moon everyone.

The venue's engineer immediately triggered a massive light and sound display, blinding the police and giving Luke a chance to make his getaway. He removed his shirt, jumped into the crowd, and exited through the front door. There, he hopped into a waiting car and made his way out of town on south I-95. "The great escape," he remembers with a smirk. "Y'all got to wake up pretty early in the morning to catch me."

BACK IN Athens I stand at the rear of the stage, moving aside as women from the crowd climb up. Luke's not so much performing tonight as hosting, imploring the crowd to get loose as a rotund DJ spins CDs from Georgia artists like Young Jeezy, Gucci Mane, and Waka Flocka Flame. Out of deference to the godfather, there's an occasional Luke song, but almost everything else is trap rap, the southeastern subgenre focused on drug dealing and partying.

The kids know all the words. You can tell, because they shout them out when the DJ cuts the beat. But the odd thing is that barely any of these tracks get radio play. Most have never even seen proper release, coming instead off of mixtapes, the sometimes-unsanctioned, usually free compilations used to build buzz for artists. (Rappers like Jeezy, T.I., and Lil Wayne have used CD and MP3 mixtapes to propel themselves to platinum sales on their traditional releases.) "The mixtape DJs became kings," Luke says afterward, noting that he barely knew any of the songs in rotation. In any case, the beat is compulsive, and I find myself dancing unself-consciously, no mean feat for the only white person in the room.

More ladies take the stage. The party has a sleepwear theme, so many are clad in skimpy negligees; black, purple, and pink numbers that don't hide much. Following behind them are scores of dudes, some toting their own bottles of booze. "The guys must get down," rumble the half dozen security guards, although they're not particularly adamant about this request. By the time Luke announces that the "contest" will begin shortly, seemingly half of the crowd is up here.

I'm not sure what this contest will entail, but to lubricate the dozen participants Luke begins pouring tequila from a bottle of Patron directly into their throats. Some look very young, although I'm certain the girl with "Est 1987" tattooed across her chest plate is legal. The HHC, now feeling loose himself, tells me to help myself to the Bacardi and Coke, and before long I'm chatting up everyone in my vicinity. None of the girls know much of Luke's music, although some of them have seen his reality show.

Before long Luke announces the prize, $600, and with that the event begins. Forming a line, the women strut, pageantlike, across the stage, pausing to turn around and shake their butts very quickly, as if controlled by one of those vibrating weight-loss belts. They continue in this vein for a while, until Luke urges them to disrobe, implying that whoever gets the most naked will win the purse.

Tops quickly come off and then, to my astonishment, bottoms. Before long the exercise has devolved into a sweaty tongue-wrestling match, with a few naked and near-naked girls frolicking with each other.

"Kiss on the mouth, goddammit!" Luke yells, as the circle around them tightens. By now the bouncers have completely stopped keeping order, too busy trying to get a glimpse of the action. I can't see anything myself, which is why I'm not sure if the ladies comply with Luke's instructions to pleasure each other, although, judging from the crowd's reaction, I suspect they do.

It's at this point that the HHC suggests I jump in and join the festivities. I respectfully decline.

BY 1990 Luke Campbell was a household name. Chris Rock played him on a *Saturday Night Live* sketch, and Luke successfully exploited rising public sympathy with a new album featuring the 2 Live Crew called *Banned in the U.S.A.*, which became their highest-charting work.

The Bruce Springsteen–approved title track borrowed the melody from "Born in the U.S.A.," and it was hard not to feel sympathy with the message. Even if you disliked their songs, they certainly weren't any more offensive than an Eddie Murphy comedy album. Besides, the idea that *adults* shouldn't be able to buy the CDs they wanted didn't seem right.

That year, two decades before she was nominated by President Obama for the Supreme Court, Washington, DC, attorney Elena Kagan filed a brief with the 11th Circuit Court of Appeals. She argued that *As Nasty As They Wanna Be* "does not physically excite anyone who hears it, much less arouse a shameful and morbid sexual response," and had "undoubted artistic value," which helped get the obscenity ruling overturned. The Supreme Court concurred, and in 1992 declined to hear Broward County's appeal.

Luke dodged another bullet when the Supreme Court again sided with the group on their reworking of Roy Orbison's "Oh, Pretty Woman," off of *As Clean As They Wanna Be*. Their version, which mocked women with weaves and bald heads, ripped off the original's tune, causing Orbison publisher Acuff-Rose to sue Luke for copyright infringement. But in a landmark 1994 decision, the Court said the song qualified as parody and deserved fair use protections, noting it showed "how bland and banal the Orbison" song was.

Luke attributes his victory, in part, to what he calls a "meltdown" on behalf of Acuff-Rose's counsel. "He choked under pressure. My lawyer was cool, calm, and collected, like he was talking to some of his buddies. I have a big respect for the Supreme Court."

But other legal battles didn't go his way. *Star Wars* progenitor George Lucas sued in 1990 to stop him from using the "Skywalker" name; they came to terms out of court for a six-figure settlement. MC Shy-D, Atlanta's first successful rapper, who had recorded with Luke in the mid-eighties, won a judgment of $2.3 million against him for unpaid royalties.

Luke was forced into bankruptcy, and Shy-D's lawyer became Luke Records' trustee. Meanwhile, Luke's lawyer Joe Weinberger alleged that he owed him money as well, and was able to purchase 2 Live Crew's catalogue for $800,000. ("When you can buy something that's worth $10 to $15 million for about ten cents on the dollar," Weinberger told *Miami New Times*, "that's an excellent business opportunity.") Sony imprint Relativity proceeded to snap up Luke's platinum R&B act H-Town.

The 2 Live Crew had broken up by now. Its members also claimed Luke owed them cash, and Weinberger proceeded to sign the fragmented act to his Lil Joe Records. The group didn't have much success without Luke but are now on better terms with him, having performed together at VH1's 2010 Hip Hop Honors show.

Luke continues to harbor resentment toward Weinberger and Sony, as well as much of the national media, whom he contends hasn't given him his proper credit as southern rap's originator.

There's truth in this, and indeed one needn't be an aficionado to hear his bass beats, crude rhymes, and call-and-response chants in everything from crunk to snap to bounce. His independent distribution methods have been widely copied, and his bling-and-babes imagery has become rap's standard. But though southern hip-hop's heavy hitters pay him homage, mainstream approval—say, induction into the Rock and Roll Hall of Fame—appears unlikely.

But to say that all of this cramped his style would not be entirely accurate. Though his national celebrity has dimmed, he remains something of a Miami kingpin. This is true in the realm of music, as he helped usher in artists like Trick Daddy, Pitbull, and DJ Khaled. It is also true in football, where he became infamous for paying off University of Miami student athletes for successful plays and remains an influential youth coach.

But he's even better known for his urban pornography and pornlike stage shows, featuring the wild stylings of the Luke girls, dancers known to go well beyond the call of duty. For X-rated stories of sidekicks like Freaky Red and Gloria Velez, you can consult his 2006 CD/audio book, *My Life & Freaky Times*. Their lasciviousness is rivaled only by Luke's NBA, NFL, and college athlete acquaintances, who apparently have done some downright bizarre things to get these women's attentions.

AS THE GIRLS put their clothes back on, Luke declares a winner: She's a six-foot-tall lass with close-cropped hair, a small belly, and a tramp stamp tattoo that reads "Sexy." I'm not sure I would call her that, but being the first to disrobe probably won her bonus points.

If it sounds creepy for a nearly fifty-year-old man who nowadays calls himself "Uncle Luke" to be cavorting with these young ladies, it sort of is, although he's been doing it for so long it's tempting to give him a pass. It's not like he hasn't seen it all before. "I never understand why people go to parties and don't enjoy themselves," he says. "You should be *talking* about a party the next day."

When the 2 Live Crew yelled out, "Hey, we want some pussy!" it wasn't about offending anyone's sensibilities, he insists, but about saying what was on folks' minds. The women who take it off at his parties do so of their own volition and are simply expressing their inner freak, he adds.

But his attitude toward the fairer sex is often abrasive. He never fails to call women "hos," and refers to his children (except for he and his wife's young son) as "sperm donations." "To keep it real, that's what it is," he says. "When you don't have a relationship with somebody, it's a sperm donation. And the donation come in the form of a child support check."

Yet his kids' mothers sometimes grumble about said checks, and in 2009 he was briefly jailed, stemming from a legal dispute with one of them. He counters that his ex-flames are "gold diggers," and that others have attempted to entrap him over the years. "I spent a lot of time down at the University of Miami DNA clinic swabbing people," he told *Time Out New York*. "If anybody came to me and say, 'That's my kid,' I would take 'em down there and swab 'em."

Luke's legacy is a complicated one, somewhere between Chuck Berry and Joe Francis. It's sometimes hard to like him, but there's no denying he's been ahead of the curve when it comes to his music, his business, and his image. He opened the door for southern rappers, and for that reason it doesn't much matter to me if he was motivated by money, fame, art, or booty.

IT'S NEARING 2:30, and the club is emptying out. But the show's not over. In an attempt to hold onto the crowd, Luke takes his first stab at performing tonight, breaking into the first bars of "One and One."

> One and one, we're having some fun
> In the bedroom, all day and all of the night

Normally, the song goes all the way to ten (as in, "Ten and ten/ The bitch doin' it again") but this time he cuts himself off at four. It's clear that the kids don't know the lyrics and aren't interested. These rhymes may have sounded risqué back in 1987, but much of tonight's music was raunchier.

The party continues outside, however, in the parking lot of the adjacent Piggly Wiggly. Kids jump in their cars and cruise back and forth, sometimes slowly, sometimes squealing around corners. It's a chance to show off their wheels, their paint jobs, and their tires' rims—oversized, shiny pieces of chrome that sometimes spin in the opposite direction of the wheel. (Although, in my opinion, the coolest are the kind that look like they're not spinning at all.)

Once upon a time Luke might have stuck around to kick it with these folks, but tonight we all head straight back to the hotel. Turns out we didn't need an HHC after all.

# 2

# GETO BOYS

■■■

## Paranoia, Insanity, and Rap-A-Lot Records

SOUTHERN RAP'S gangsta roots can be traced to one group: Geto
Boys. There's nary a thug wannabe who didn't learn something
from these Houston trailblazers, who helped put hardcore hip-hop
on the map. They were every bit as tough as gangsta rap pioneers
N.W.A and Ice-T—the media's faces for late eighties gangland
menace—and even more twisted.

The group was masterminded by a luxury-used-car salesman
named J. Prince, a slight man who sometimes appears to be scowl-
ing and smiling simultaneously.

Over the years, Prince, who was born James Smith, has also
founded a condom company, managed champion boxer Floyd
Mayweather Jr., and donated millions to various local causes. But
rap will be his legacy, and he possesses impeccable taste when it
comes to the discipline, having fostered a who's who of Texas spitters, including Pimp C, Bun B, Trae, Z-Ro, Big Mello, Lil' Flip,
and Devin the Dude. Though he hasn't published many runaway

bestsellers, he's hasn't had many duds, either, and his Rap-A-Lot Records is hip-hop's longest-running independent imprint.

A native of Houston's downtrodden Fifth Ward, he's something of a southern cross between hip-hop moguls Sean "Diddy" Combs and Suge Knight. Like Diddy he's a flashy dresser who rolls in Bentleys, and like Knight he's been accused of manhandling his affiliates.

Everyone agrees that Prince partnered with a Seattle software engineer named Cliff Blodget to form Rap-A-Lot. Whether a now-imprisoned crack cocaine kingpin named Michael "Harry-O" Harris provided seed money for the label, as he claims, is disputed, however. Prince says it's untrue. (For what it's worth, Harris made the same claim about Knight's Death Row Records and won a judgment of more than $100 million. Harris's similar case against Prince never got any traction, however, and Prince has called him a "pathological lying snitch.")

As for Prince, some fear him, but many sing his eternal praises. Count former Rap-A-Lot artist Ganksta N-I-P among the latter, he a pioneer of the horrorcore rap subgenre that would influence the Geto Boys. One night in 1991 Prince saw him win a rap contest at a South Park spot called Club Infinity and after the performance asked him to come into the men's room for an audition. Joining them in the quieter, cramped space, N-I-P says, were some twenty men, "bodyguards and highly ranking Rap-A-Lot officials," he remembers.

N-I-P gave an impassioned performance, "breaking mirrors, hitting up against the wall," and Prince was impressed. They met the next morning in the club's parking lot, where Prince handed him a $20,000 check and signed him to a three-album deal. "I love him to this day," N-I-P says. "If I needed a car, he provided it. If I needed money, he provided it."


BUT IT WAS Geto Boys who proved to be Prince's greatest creation. As legend has it, in the mid-eighties he promised his younger brother Thelton and some of his buddies that he would release their rap record if they finished high school. Thus was born the original Ghetto Boys, whose members dressed like Run-DMC and were influenced by Miami and New York rap. Their song "Car Freak" got some local play. Featuring giant bass and goofy ad-libs, it's not gangsta but it is funny. "See, if you're walking down the street/ There's no conversation," it goes. "The girl wants a man with some damn transportation."

They didn't make much of a splash, but in the late eighties they changed the spelling of their name and shuffled their lineup; from the beginning Prince saw the group as a series of interchangeable parts. Staying on was DJ Ready Red, a New Jersey native who was a fan of pioneers Afrika Bambaataa and Grandmaster Flash. Though he would be the underappreciated architect of Geto Boys' raw, atmospheric compositions, he departed before they broke big, due to financial disputes with Prince.

Geto Boys' MCs included Bushwick Bill, a dwarf born in Jamaica who emigrated to America with his family when he was five and came up as break-dancer in Bushwick, Brooklyn. Though initially taken on as the group's dancer and hype man, after his rapping talents proved first-rate he was invited to become a full member. "[Prince] told me he didn't want me to be the hype man for the group," remembers Bill. "[He] was like, 'You think you can rap?'" Only two weeks later, Bill says, he was rhyming in the studio. In fact, he became the group's secret weapon, by way of mesmerizing chants and gory, over-the-top rhymes. "Motherfuckers be worried 'cause I'm sick," he raps on a Ganksta N-I-P ghostwritten song called "Chuckie." "Dead heads and frog legs/ Mmm... cake mix!" "My role was like Flava Flav," Bill goes on, "serious but with a comedic overtone that made the subject matter lighter."

Joining Red and Bill was a battle rapper named Willie D, a fierce Fifth Ward native and Golden Gloves boxer who once knocked out Furious Five member Melle Mel in a celebrity match. Possessing an angry bark and a coarse sense of humor, D wrote or cowrote many of the group's best-known tracks and also penned solo works like his anti-hairless-women anthem, "Bald-Headed Hoes," from his first solo album, *Controversy*. (The work's cover features four seemingly arbitrary expressions of the title: a woman in a bikini, a KKK member, a policeman, and a shirtless D himself.)

Rounding out the collective was a remarkable talent named Brad Jordan, an eighteen-year-old rapper and producer who called himself DJ Akshen. His obsession with Brian De Palma's 1983 film would later bring him a nickname that stuck: Scarface.

The new incarnation of the Geto Boys met for the first time when they arrived in the studio to record their 1989 album *Grip It! On That Other Level*. "That's why the album is so raw," Bill explained on *Yo! MTV Raps*.

Influenced by N.W.A and Ice-T, who found they didn't need to tone down their content to appeal to middle America, Geto Boys went even further. Rather than simply offering street-life rhymes and police-revenge fantasies, they made many of their songs as gruesome as possible. On "Mind of a Lunatic," Bill raps about spying on a woman, raping her, killing her, and having sex with her corpse. Adds Willie D, "I don't give a fuck if you're nine or ninety-nine/ Blind, crippled, and crazy, don't faze me/ Your funky ass will be pushin' up daisies."

"At that point, I was willing to say or do anything to make money and get people to pay attention," Willie D told Roni Sarig in his book *Third Coast*, though Scarface doesn't concur with this assessment. "I just wanted to speak what I knew," he says. "Bill may have done *anything*, but not Willie. Bill was a joker, but Willie was serious."

They found a champion in Def Jam cofounder Rick Rubin, famous for helping launch acts like Beastie Boys and Public Enemy. Rubin signed the group to his Def American label, who in 1990 released the Geto Boys' self-titled album featuring mostly *Grip It!* songs.

Distributor Geffen Records refused to circulate the work, however, citing its profane content. Though Warner Bros. Records eventually took it on, the controversy and Bob Dole's tut-tutting about the group brought it national attention.

Their 1991 follow-up *We Can't Be Stopped* still trades somewhat in the cartoonish shock-rap on which they'd built their name. But the songwriting shows an artistic evolution. Rather than just imagining psychopaths' behavior, the group began exploring their own increasingly twisted psyches. "Mind Playing Tricks on Me" features a melancholy Isaac Hayes soul sample and the stories of paranoiacs who think someone is out to get them.

Raps Scarface: "I can see him when I'm deep in the covers/ When I awake I don't see the motherfucker . . . Investigatin' the joint for traps/ Checkin' my telephone for taps." In a Hitchcockian twist, however, it comes to light that the man he fears so much is himself. "Mind Playing Tricks on Me" would become their most famous song; OutKast's Andre 3000 says it put southern rap on the map.

Like the 2 Live Crew, Geto Boys were humanized by their real-life adversaries, and on *We Can't Be Stopped*'s title track they shrewdly take on Geffen Records. "Can you believe those hypocrites/ Who distribute Guns N' Roses but not our shit?" asks Bill.

Many critics consider it an all-time top work, but not everyone found it so charming at the time. Similar to the 2 Live Crew's experience, Scarface says Geto Boys got a frigid reception at New York's New Music Seminar. (He can't remember if they attended in 1989 or 1990.)

"Everywhere in the country they loved the Geto Boys, but they booed the crap out of us there," he says, adding that much of the hate appeared to be coming from New York rappers. Still, he can understand why they felt the way they did. "'What's these dudes from Texas doing New York rap? You're not welcome to do that.' I understand that. [They] created this."

But the group was ahead of its time in its successful exploitation of real-life drama. In our age of micro-blogs and camera phones everyone does this, but Geto Boys' music often weaved fiction and nonfiction together so well that it wasn't always clear which was which. Bushwick Bill—who'd joined the group fresh out of Bible school—saw his fame lead to substance abuse, and his musical horror stories began coming to life. "I got introduced to having alcohol every day, and being influenced by drugs and alcohol," says Bill. "The way I dealt with things that hurt me or bothered me, I'd numb myself to the situation. . . . I saw the days by the bottles that I drank."

One night during the recording of *We Can't Be Stopped*, Bill, drunk and stoned, paid a visit to a girlfriend and asked her to shoot him in the face. She balked, he grabbed her baby and threatened it, and during the ensuing tussle the gun went off and a bullet pierced his right eyeball. The story is recounted on his solo track, "Ever So Clear."

Willie D and Scarface rushed to be with him in the hospital, and a picture of them wheeling Bill on a gurney—his bandage pulled down to reveal his bloody eye socket—serves as *We Can't Be Stopped*'s album cover.

The work sold more than a million copies, and the group's hyper-real image appealed not just to inner-city kids but suburban ones; affluent types could embrace the rebellion-by-proxy, imagining violent chauvinistic fantasies while singing along.

This archetype was hilariously portrayed by Austin, Texas–based filmmaker Mike Judge in his movie *Office Space*. Character Michael Bolton is a nerdy, undersexed tech worker who shares a name with the corny crooner; in the film he works out his angst by aggressively rapping along with a Scarface track while stuck in traffic. When a black man walks past the car selling flowers, however, Bolton cringes, quieting himself and locking the doors.

DESPITE BUSHWICK BILL and Willie D's contributions, Scarface quickly emerged as the group's dominant force. Near-universally regarded as the best southern rapper, he possess a rich, full baritone and is capable of taming complicated rhyme patterns. An absolute beast of a storyteller, his characters are criminals, convicts, and everyman sinners, some attempting to get things on track, some resigned to living in fear.

Though few can match his songs' nuance or moral complexity, his paternal attitude and exquisitely paced flow established the template for a hardcore rapper, and his influence can be heard in everyone from Tupac Shakur to Jay-Z. "Jay-Z [initially] was tongue twistin'," says Memphis rapper Eightball. "When he slowed that shit down, that was some southern shit, that was some Scarface shit he was doing."

'Face has always seemed older than his years. He's got a wide face, sturdy frame, bad posture, and tends to make jokes about subjects others might not necessarily find funny, like killing himself, as he did in an interview with video blog site VladTV. He came up in Houston's poor South Acres neighborhood, which he describes as close-knit. "Everybody was cool with each other," he says. "We really believed in our neighborhood. It ain't no different than the hood anywhere else."

Music ran in his family. He learned to play bass guitar from his uncle, and nowadays makes occasional surprise appearances at Houston rock shows as a guitar player. But his childhood was traumatic; he attempted suicide by slitting his wrists with a razor blade when he was twelve or thirteen. Before long he was shuttled off to the mental health ward at Houston International Hospital, where he was plied with lithium and antipsychotic drugs. "When you go crazy in the hospital, they get like five or six big ol' men to come in there and hold you down," he remembers. "They pop you with that Thorazine and you go *out*."

Even worse was when they locked him in a foreboding spot called the "quiet room," which contained little more than a small mattress with no covers. "I spent a lot of time in the quiet room, to the point where if anybody said anything about that quiet room I was like, 'OK! I'll be good! I'm not crazy anymore!'"

'Face says he had a schizophrenic uncle, who was "on drugs heavy, like he got high and never came down." Other than that, however, he can't point to any genetic or experiential reasons that may have sparked his mental health issues.

He remains unsatisfied with his treatment. During our phone conversation, he grows increasingly sarcastic and worked up as we discuss the subject, at one point Googling his doctor, who is now employed by the University of Texas Harris County Psychiatric Center. Scarface then proceeds to fire off an e-mail to him, which he reads aloud, pausing occasionally to laugh hysterically:

> I don't know if you remember me but my name is Brad Jordan. I was at Houston International Hospital in the early eighties. Thanks for your help in the past. I'm one of the greatest hip-hop artists of all time. You sucker!

There's something poetic about this note, with both its slightly vengeful and oddly warm notes. Indeed, Scarface's tribulations have repeatedly worked their way into his music. Unlike other rappers who'd have you *think* they're psychopaths, his honesty makes his voice resonate.

Obsessed with the thin line between sanity and craziness, between living and dying, he captures the desperation of men at their wits' end. "Everybody's got a different way of endin' it," he raps on, "I Seen a Man Die," "And when your number comes for souls then they send it in/ Now your time has arrived for your final test/ I see the fear in your eyes and in your final breath."

It wasn't necessarily his depression or treatment that informed his style, he says, but rather his therapy, which forced him to articulate what was going through his head. "We had one-on-one and also group meetings, where you had to talk," he says, adding with a laugh that thirteen-year-olds like himself were permitted to smoke cigarettes if they had their parents' permission. "It helped big time."

Not long after departing the hospital, Scarface left home and stayed with some friends through his middle-teen years. He dropped out of high school and later got his own place with long-time producer John Bido. His career as a rapper was kicking into gear; he'd come onto J. Prince's radar after an acquaintance passed along a tape of his song "Scarface."

But though the emerging mogul showed interest in signing him, Scarface was advised to stay away. "Everybody was like, 'Watch out for him,'" 'Face remembers. "Everybody."

I ask him why they said that.

"Everybody had their own little, whatever they wanted to say or do, but we never cared about that," he says, vaguely. "He ain't never did nothing but right by us. Rap-A-Lot and Scarface birthed each other. We were together when our careers started."

In fact, just as Geto Boys were gaining national renown, Scarface released his still-admired 1991 debut *Mr. Scarface Is Back*. The album went gold and kicked off his long-running solo career, and three years later he put out his high-watermark effort *The Diary*, which featured the remarkable "I Seen a Man Die" and saw his stories coming into sharper focus.

Near the turn of the decade he was recruited by Def Jam executive Lyor Cohen to be president of Def Jam South, a spin-off intended to give the New York company a toehold in the emerging Dixie market. For the imprint 'Face helped orchestrate the signing of Atlanta rapper Ludacris, who would become one of the bestselling MCs of all time.

Scarface released a career-defining album of his own for the label in 2002. *The Fix* had guest verses from Jay-Z and Nas, not to mention sparkling beats from Kanye West, the Neptunes, and collaborator Mike Dean. Dubbed overly commercial by J. Prince, 'Face calls it his "best work to date."

Though it debuted in *Billboard*'s top five, he wouldn't see that kind of success again. He attributes his relative commercial failings to his lack of dance songs, and it's something of a sore subject that his earnings haven't lived up to his stature. "Give me the money," he says. "I don't care if nobody knows me."

WHILE SCARFACE, Willie D, and Bushwick Bill were the public faces of Geto Boys, J. Prince controlled the group behind the scenes. "What people have to understand is that even though I'm a member of the Geto Boys, that's J.'s baby," Willie told *Murder Dog*. "J. owns the Geto Boys. . . . So regardless of what you hear happening with the Geto Boys, they always going to be J.'s group, period."

Their heyday coincided with a long-running Drug Enforcement Agency investigation centered around Prince. It commenced some time around 1988, when a car bearing dealer plates from a used-car lot he owned was stopped and found to be carrying a large quantity of cocaine. Prince's cousin sat in the passenger seat. The DEA undertook a partnership with Houston police in a vast, expensive operation intended to put Prince behind bars and shut down Rap-A-Lot.

Prince believed himself to be unfairly persecuted and feared for his life due to the involvement of an upper-echelon agent named Jack Schumacher, who had reportedly killed a number of his previous targets. Prince sought the help of California congresswoman Maxine Waters, whose husband Sidney Williams, a former NFL linebacker, grew up in Houston's Fifth Ward. In 1999 she complained to Attorney General Janet Reno, and the DEA's investigation ended shortly thereafter, with Schumacher simultaneously demoted.

In another bizarre twist, all of this occurred shortly after Al Gore visited the church to which Prince had reportedly donated more than a million dollars. Schumacher contended that Prince had made illegal contributions to the Gore campaign, and a leaked e-mail from another DEA agent asserted that political pressure had halted the investigation.

At one point Scarface himself became a target. The DEA nearly indicted the rapper on a federal drug conspiracy charge, the idea being, apparently, to get him to flip and testify against Prince.

If Scarface needed a reason to be paranoid this was it, a real-life, "Mind Playin Tricks on Me." Fittingly, then, he responded to the charges in rhyme on his 2000 album *The Last of a Dying Breed*.

> I can't get no peace cause Schumacher's been chasin'
>     me
> But I don't sell no dope . . . Fuck the DEA . . .
> I admit I use to sell rocks, but that was back in school
> Now I just do music, and smoke a little weed, but not
>     enough to run a dope house

The DEA's investigation resulted in numerous convictions against Prince associates, including a Houston police officer who was found to have aided a Rap-A-Lot employee as he robbed a drug dealer. But the case against Scarface was dropped, and Prince also walked away free. 'Face continues to vehemently deny the accusations. "We was young, and we was black, and we was getting money," he says. "That's an inviting [reason for persecution]. Young, black, and *not* dealing drugs? Shit, you gotta be doing something."

He contends that all of Prince's money was made legitimately. "Legal money and never forgetting what you came from, that's the long and the short of [our success]," he says. "We're tied in deeply to the people we grew up around. I'm a ghetto boy in real life."

The feds may have left Houston, but Prince popped up in the news again in 2007 when a record studio owner accused him of having him beaten after he refused to sell Prince part of his interest in the studio. "There's a conspiracy to destroy all black entrepreneurs in hip-hop by rat niggas and law enforcement," Prince responded to the allegation on the first track on Scarface's 2008 album, *Emeritus*. The charge, like all the rest, remains unsubstantiated.

Bun B, a Rap-A-Lot artist who credits Prince for nurturing him throughout his career, agrees that his boss is an unfair target. "If all this is happening, why hasn't there been any proof of anything?" Bun asks. "The company has been there for twenty-five years. People are going to say what they want to say about the man because they can't take him down."

MICHAEL BARNETT is a former Geto Boy known as Big Mike. He replaced Willie D in the group for one album, 1993's *Till Death Do Us Part*. In 2004 Mike was paroled and released from prison, where he had served three and a half years for torching a studio affiliated with Rap-A-Lot Records.

The offense was the culmination of simmering tensions between Big Mike and the label, which had released many of his albums. The trouble started when Rap-A-Lot wanted to lock him down under a long-term contract. According to Mike, J. Prince tried to make him an offer he couldn't refuse.

Mike came from New Orleans to Houston as a teenager and saw early success with a Rap-A-Lot duo called Convicts. He says he was soon contacted by Lydia Harris, wife of Michael "Harry-O" Harris, the convicted drug dealer who would later claim ownership stakes in both Rap-A-Lot and Death Row.

Lydia invited him and Houston rapper Mr. 3-2—Mike's Convicts partner—to come out to California to record. Before long Mike found himself working with Dr. Dre and sharing a room with an up-and-coming rapper named Snoop Doggy Dogg. According to Mike, they traded slang and he even taught Snoop Dogg down south phrases like, "I don't love dem hos."

But as Death Row cofounder Suge Knight dragged his feet on their project, Mike began to consider his options. A Rap-A-Lot representative told him that Willie D was leaving Geto Boys and invited him to fill the spot.

And so Mike returned to Houston and joined the group for their 1993 work *Till Death Do Us Part*. Though it was a strong album that would eventually go gold, at the time it was seen as something of a failure coming on the heels of the platinum *We Can't Be Stopped*.

Mike was booted from the act shortly after he and Scarface had a physical altercation of some sort; Mike suggests 'Face was jealous over Mike's increasing fame. But Mike now had a platform to launch his solo career from, and his first two Rap-A-Lot albums, *Somethin' Serious* and *Still Serious* cracked *Billboard*'s top forty. The latter, released in 1997, peaked at #16 and demonstrated his commercial viability.

It was around this time, Mike says, that he attempted to collect some money he was owed from the label. He called up Prince, who said that, sure, he could have his money, but he also wanted him to sign a new record contract. This was news to Mike. His old contract hadn't expired, and besides, other labels were expressing interest in his services. Unsure what to do, he balked.

Apparently this didn't go over too well with Prince. Mike remembers their call being put on speakerphone, with someone lurking on Prince's end of the line making threats. "Do you know who you're talking to?" Mike recalls the man saying. "Something could happen to you!"

Mike tried to put the conversation out of his mind. That night he went to sleep as normal at his house. But in the middle of the night, as he lay next to his pregnant girlfriend, something awoke him. "Did you just tell me to get up?" he asked his lady. She said she hadn't, so he lay back down, but sleep wouldn't return. Something felt eerie.

He walked into the living room and sat down. After pausing for a moment he lit a cigarette and began a conversation with his maker. "Lord, I feel like somebody's plotting against me," he prayed. "Please watch over me. Don't let nothing happen to me."

He made the sign of the cross and leaned over to ash his cigarette. At that very moment shots rang out and he heard glass smashing. A bullet penetrated the wall behind him, right where his head had been a moment earlier. He hustled out of the room, avoiding the bullets and injury. His girlfriend was OK too, thankfully, as were his children—who, against routine, happened to be with their mother that weekend. It was divine intervention, Mike thought.

Prince didn't respond to interview requests, and Mike doesn't come out and directly accuse him or anyone at Rap-A-Lot of orchestrating the shooting. "Draw your own conclusions," he says.

Still, he felt what he felt, and in the coming days he did a lot of thinking. He didn't go to the police, he says, because it violated his street code of ethics. Though initially intending to turn the other cheek, an encounter at a local club with a Rap-A-Lot security guard made him change his mind. Unprovoked, the man threw a drink at him, Mike says, and so Mike threw a couple of his own right back. "These people don't understand nothing else but guerrilla tactics," he remembers thinking, growing angry.

Shortly thereafter he made the decision that would alter the course of his life. He attempted to burn down a studio used by Rap-A-Lot, as well as the imprint's headquarters. He won't go into details about the evening, but he was quickly pinched for the studio fire. He served time in various spots around West Texas and was released a little more than halfway through his six-year sentence.

"It's hard to think about it now, because I lost so much off that one event," he says. "Time off my life, time with my children. My career suffered a blow from it."

These days he's attempting to reconnect with a fan base that once loved him and is working on a new album. Insisting he's not bitter, he maintains that his faith in God has helped him accept—and even feel grateful for—the hand he was dealt. "To the average person, it may feel like they won, that they were able to stomp on my name and throw dirt on it," he says. "But I know that it don't stop there. I'll always have another opportunity."

WILLIE D rejoined Geto Boys, but they've been relatively silent since their modestly received 2005 comeback album *The Foundation*. As this book went to press Scarface was in jail, reportedly for missing child support payments, while others associated with the group have fallen out of the spotlight. DJ Ready Red battled a crack cocaine addiction and is now back home in Trenton, New Jersey, where he has said he plans to start a chapter of Afrika Bambaataa's Zulu Nation.

Bushwick Bill has soldiered on with one eye, traveling around the country in a camper for a time, performing his hits. "See, driving is like stabbing somebody; it's very personal," he explained. "Whereas flying is like shooting somebody; it's more distant." In the late aughts he got sober and began recording gospel hip-hop as a born-again Christian. But in 2010 things went awry. After the shooting death of Houston DJ Lonnie Mack—the man who had helped launch Bill's career by introducing him to J. Prince—Bill fell off the wagon, and he was pulled over on a traffic stop outside of Atlanta and found to be in possession of cocaine and marijuana. Upon his arrest his immigrant status came to light: he had a green card, but because he'd never gotten around to filing the necessary paperwork he was not a US citizen. He was turned over to immigration officials who sought to deport him. His case was not helped by his prior convictions for battery and attempted arson, but in the end the judge granted him a reprieve, and he was allowed to stay in the country. "Everyone falls short of the glory of God," he tells me.

Willie D was not so lucky. In early 2009 he was arrested at Houston's George Bush Intercontinental Airport, accused of helping run an international scam in which he took money for iPhones and failed to deliver them. He pled guilty to wire fraud and in 2010 was sentenced to a year and a day in federal prison.

Despite his crime, it's tempting to sympathize with Willie D. Now in his mid-forties, he must face middle age as an underappreciated, underpaid rap trailblazer. "Even with all of the things I did, I have very little to show for it," he told *Murder Dog* in 2003. "Nobody makes that effort to make sure that history is preserved and the proper credit is passed out."

More accolades have come to J. Prince, who was honored, along with Luke Campbell, Jermaine Dupri, Timbaland, Master P, the 2 Live Crew, and Organized Noize at VH1's 2010 Hip Hop Honors show.

"Rap-A-Lot was very instrumental in awakening the sleeping giant," he said during the program. "I actually believe the South is a hungrier place, and always describe the East Coast as a piece of bread, and the West Coast as a piece of bread, and the South, the meat. Everybody's roots is from the South, so at the end of the day, we the meat."

'Face may have been up for the honor himself, but, still harboring bitterness and distrust against the New York establishment for slighting Geto Boys in their early days, declined to participate. He suspected the event would end up mocking the South.

"You know how they make us look on TV? Like we live on the front porch with flies and shit flying around us, with our stomachs all big eating watermelon rinds? That ain't us, man," he wrote, in a statement to *Ozone* magazine before the show. "We're smart, man. Our life is slowed down so we don't miss nothing. When shit gets moving too fast you miss everything."

# 3

# TRAE AND DJ SCREW

■ ■ ■

## Rap Gets Screwed


TRAE'S REAL NAME is Frazier Thompson III, and his nickname is pronounced "Tray," as in "the third." But he's not some Connecticut blue blood, he's a tough Houston rapper with a mean car.

His ocean-water-blue Dodge Challenger has tinted windows, ostrich seats with his name monogrammed on them, and ferocious-looking rims. These tire covers are called "swangers," and their chrome spokes jut out dramatically, as if to slice up another vehicle's wheels. Trae says the swangers cost about $4,000, although he didn't have to pay since he's endorsed by the company who makes them.

Corpulent, with droopy, bearlike eyes, Trae has a voice so deep that it's often hard to understand him. Also like a bear, he is both nurturing—he works hard caring for his son D'Neeko, who was born with a chromosome aberration that made him mentally and physically handicapped—and occasionally dangerous. His temper swelled at the *Ozone* magazine awards show in Houston in 2008, and he punched local rapper Mike Jones in the face. "He got it for running his mouth too much," Trae explained, apparently upset that Jones had declared himself the "president of H-Town." Presumably Trae felt he deserved that title.

He can make a good case for this. Having been mentored by the primary architect of the Houston sound, DJ Screw, Trae released a pair of well-regarded albums on Rap-A-Lot Records, *Restless* and *Life Goes On*, before signing with Universal. He's not a profound lyricist, but his low, spine-chilling flow can induce shivers. He's the guy with whom other rappers, like Rick Ross or Three 6 Mafia, collaborate when they want to solidify their hard-core street credentials.

Repping both Screw's Screwed Up Click and a posse called Assholes By Nature (ABN), he considers himself a man of the people and prides himself on being seen out and about in Houston. When I interviewed him over the phone for *Urban Ink*, he offered to show me around town, so when I arrive I take him up on the offer. Accompanied by my friend Shea, a *Houston Press* writer who's hosting me, I drive my rented Hyundai Accent to an eighteen-and-over hip-hop spot called Club Next. Trae sends someone to grab us at the front door, and we're quickly whisked past bouncers without paying the entrance fee.

Trae is wearing platinum grills, bracelets, and a diamond-encrusted, three-dimensional ABN pendant, which can be twisted like a Rubik's Cube. We don't talk much because it's loud, but I'm introduced to his posse, which includes a stand-up comedian, a photographer, a videographer, and James Prince Jr., the son of Rap-A-Lot Records founder J. Prince and an aspiring label mogul himself.

The group also includes other members of ABN, who belong to rival street gangs and seem to function at least partly as his security. Trae says he assembled the group in an attempt to quell Houston gang rivalries. They have fed the homeless and hosted immunization sessions, while Trae himself has put on Johnny Cash–style prison concerts.

In fact, in 2008 his good works inspired Houston mayor Bill White to get the city to declare the rapper's birthday, July 22, "Trae Day." (It helped that White's son was a fan.) Unfortunately, eight people were shot shortly after the following year's anniversary party, which put something of a damper on the festivities.

Trae says he has no idea what inspired the gunshots and notes that he has never belonged to a gang. Nonetheless, not crossing Trae seems like a good general strategy, and his brothers are tough cookies as well. His younger brother Jay'Ton returned from prison not too long ago, and his older brother Dinkie is doing three consecutive life sentences on a murder conviction.

After we leave Club Next we visit a downtown club, where Trae leads our group up the back stairs. Unfortunately, I'm at the end of the line, and a lurking security guard tries to shake me down for twenty bucks. Nobody else had to pay; perhaps I'm singled out for my wrinkled sweatshirt and Asics tennis shoes. In any case, after a few heated moments I meet up with Trae in the booth above the dance floor, where the DJ is giving him shout-outs on the mic.

At 2 A.M. the club prepares to close. Trae plants himself by the door, shaking hands with fans as they file out, as if on a wedding receiving line. In the periphery is a particularly comely girl, whom Trae's associates are hitting on. She ignores them, however, instead inquiring with Trae himself about his plans for the evening. He says we are headed for a strip club across town, should she care to come along.

We make for our cars and hit the road. Cursed with the Hyundai's inferior pickup, however, Shea and I have trouble keeping pace. Not to mention that driving in Houston can be terrifying, what with its never-ending grid of highways, entrance ramps, hairpin turns, and turnarounds. Two-lane roads become seven-lane interstates without warning, and if you slow down to try to make sense of your GPS the good old boys in their giant trucks will shoot you angry looks.

Texas car subcultures are numerous and diverse. White kids often raise their cabs and outfit their vehicles with monster wheels, while black and Latin folks aim to impress with the opposite approach, altering their suspension systems so their coupes hug the ground. These slabs—slow, loud, and bangin'—are often painted in bright, candy colors and filled with TVs in every possible nook and cranny, although I have no idea why someone would need a television in their rearview mirror.

Trae beats us to the strip club, but even after we deposit the Accent in a crowded lot a block away and walk over, he still hasn't parked. The attendants are rearranging the VIP parking area in order to put his Challenger right next to the door. (Presumably the club owner wants some of its cool to rub off on his establishment.) This takes a good twenty minutes.

Once inside, it's clear that "strip club" was something of a misnomer. Due to local ordinances, women gyrate with their clothes *on*. Clad in a variety of skimpy and sparkling outfits, they dance, collect tips, and occasionally disappear with a client into the backroom. Layers of dudes surround a central, oval-shaped stage, watching the ladies put their hands on the floor and stick their derrieres in the air. They shake double-time, borrowing from the Miami bass style.

The "strippers" who are not dancing huddle around tables of food and liquor in roped-off private areas like the one our group has been shepherded into. They're hoping to entice a high roller into a private dance and appear to have the right idea. Myself excluded, the guys here have money to blow.

Armed with thick stacks of cash wrapped in plastic, presumably fresh from the bank, the men toss handfuls of bills in the air, which flutter down over the dancers. This is called "making it rain," something I'd heard discussed in hundreds of rap songs but until now considered as mythical as Sasquatch. The economic downturn obviously hasn't affected this crowd, although many are only altering the weather with ones.

Eventually the money has piled up in small mounds on the stage. The ladies bring out large red dishpans and scoop the bills in. There's so much stray cash floating around, in fact, that I find some underfoot. I consider putting it in my pocket, but think better of the idea.

TRAE IS NOT a major star outside of his hometown, but he's a household name among rap fans here. This is fairly common in Houston, which is the fourth biggest city in the country and something of a hip-hop island. More than other metropolises, H-Town clubs and radio stations tend to play local artists; when Trae became embroiled in a dispute with a DJ from local radio station 97.9 The Box (KBXX), his music was stricken from their playlist. This threatened to choke of his career, and he took action to sue for reinstatement (he eventually dropped the suit).

The situation demonstrated Houston's insularity. Perhaps owing to its geographic isolation from other cultural enclaves, the scene has developed its own slang and sound, which don't always translate in other regions. DJs here like to augment typical rap tracks by slowing them way down and repeating lines a few times over, slurring rappers' speech and infusing their music with an extraterrestrial quality. You can buy much of Trae's music that has been altered in this style, called "screwed and chopped."

The technique was pioneered by DJ Screw, a self-taught producer born Robert Earl Davis Jr. in Smithville, Texas, a tiny town two hours west of Houston. He later came to the south side of Houston to live with his dad, and earned his nickname by defacing vinyl records he didn't like with a screw—so no one else could play them. A DJ since age thirteen, Screw met a local record store

owner named Daryl Scott, who impressed him by slowing down
fast-paced dance records to mix them with R&B songs. But Screw
took it even further. "The first time I popped a tape of his in the
deck, I tried to push stop because I thought it was being chewed
up," Scott told Britain's the *Guardian*.

Screw arrived upon his innovation by accident one day in 1990
while playing music at his apartment for friends who had come
over to throw dice and hang out. Stoned, he mistakenly altered a
record's pitch, braking it to a snail's pace. One of his friends offered
him ten dollars on the spot if he'd record a tape featuring the effect,
he said, and as early as the next day folks were knocking on his
door for their own copies.

To him, the style's appeal was clear. "When you smoke weed
you be laid back and it slows you down," he told *The Source*. "You
don't react fast, so the music sounded better slowed down." Many
thought the effect was even better when you took prescription
cough syrup.

There was another advantage too: you could understand every
word from a quick-spitting MC's mouth. "I may run it back two or
three times to let you hear what he is saying," Screw added to *Rap
Pages*, "so you can wake up and listen, because they are telling you
something."

He began taking 45s and playing them at 33⅓ revolutions
per minute. Using popular rap records of the day, he scratched
on them, edited them digitally, talked over them, and copied the
resulting versions onto tapes. He relocated to a house in southeast Houston, setting up a studio inside as well as the store where
he dispensed his tapes—plain old gray Maxell cassettes, which he
labeled by hand on white stickers. (Some had his phone number.)

He also recorded original compositions in this style, inviting
up-and-coming south-side MCs to rhyme over them, including, later on, Trae. These sessions were sometimes more like parties. The guys would goof around, memorialize associates who

had died, or give shout-outs to friends in prison. Whatever they rapped about, it was almost always a freestyle. "In Screw house, ain't no such thing as a pen, you just had to go in," Z-Ro told writer Jesse Serwer in an interview for Serwer's blog. "When you hit play until the motherfucker stopped, it was just people coming off the top of the dome." Z-Ro added that the tapes were also a good way for their posse to taunt their rivals from the other side of the city. "Back in them times in Houston, it was north versus south. If you was from anywhere north of the Astrodome, you couldn't come on the south side and vice versa. It was really a heated, tension-filled time, man. You could get your best lick at a motherfucker through music."

Most of the big record labels didn't want much to do with Screw, obviously, as he was treading dubious legal waters by using other artists' copywritten material, and he didn't want much to do with them either. But he did a brisk independent business. Tired of folks knocking on his door at all hours of the day and night, he set up regular hours each day for sales, from eight to ten at night. "At 7:30, I'd look outside my window, and there'd be a line of cars down the whole street, around the corner," he said in a documentary called *DJ Screw—The Story*. "Motherfuckers used to trip, like the neighbors, like 'Man, what the fuck going on in this house?'" At least once the police kicked down his door, convinced he was selling drugs, but they didn't find anything, and before long he went downtown to get his tax license.

It's impossible to gauge exactly how many of these tapes he sold, but in 1995 he said he was moving 120 per day, and according to Screwed Up Click (S.U.C.) member E.S.G., he eventually invested in his own tape-pressing machines.

"You could get a tape for like ten dollars," UGK's Bun B told MTV. "Then, for fifteen dollars, you could give him a list [of songs] you wanted and he'd shout you out on the tape. For a little more, you could actually come to Screw's house and shout out people yourself." As word spread, celebrities like Milwaukee Bucks small forward Glenn Robinson commissioned their own versions.

Screw would work through the night, running his recording sessions with increasing vision and authority. After MCs and singers realized they could make names for themselves on these tapes, they lined up to be part of his S.U.C. posse. "Screw was like a radio station," said Z-Ro. "I wanted to get my music on a Screw tape, because that was the best way to promote your music back then." But he wouldn't take just anybody. You had to earn his respect, and, to some extent, his love. Continued Z-Ro, "The statement Screw used was, 'I might know your name, I might know you personally, but if I really don't know your heart, I really don't know you.'" Trae honed his sinister flow under Screw's direction and believes their collaborations helped Trae achieve recognition. When we got together he showed off his tattoo of his mentor on his forearm; in it, Screw wears a propped-up crown atop his head. "He got to know our music, and showed us how to focus," Trae says. "He taught me to stay dedicated and to stay humble. He was one of the most humble people I ever met."

LIKE CALI WEED or Kentucky bourbon, prescription cough syrup is synonymous with Houston. Containing the sedative drug promethazine and the opiate codeine, it's substantially more potent than your over-the-counter Nyquil. Though prescribed to treat bronchitis and other respiratory illnesses, its street value is hundreds of dollars per dose.

Houston rappers say it was popular as far back as the sixties, but it seems to have come back with a vengeance in the early nineties, coinciding with DJ Screw's rise. Syrup use reached epidemic proportions here in the mid-aughts, and a group of pharmacists were convicted of illegally selling more than two thousand gallons of it.

"There's a corner in 3rd Ward folks call the Million Dollar Corner, you go get anything you want over there," S.U.C. rapper and singer Big Moe told *Murder Dog*. "And they all know each other so somebody pull up wants some drank, there's probably drank over there."

As Big Moe notes, syrup is sometimes called drank, and it's also called sizzurp and lean. Its intake is highly ritualized. Here's how you do it, though you shouldn't do it.

(1) Mix a few ounces of the cough syrup into a two-liter plastic bottle of soda.

(2) Add a Jolly Rancher if you'd like, though it will be plenty sweet already.

(3) Put the cap back on and shake the viscous solution.

(4) Remove the cap, and inhale the expunged gas.

(5) Pour the mixture into a Styrofoam cup over ice.

(6) Sip, don't gulp.

Syrup makes you feel warm and slows things down. Connoisseurs of the addictive elixir imbibe while they drive, while they're writing rhymes, or while they're smoking pot. Screw insisted that one needn't be high to enjoy his music, but many consider syrup essential to the Screw experience.

Some would likely tell you the drug is as harmless as weed, but they are delusional. Screw himself died at age twenty-nine in 2000 in his studio's bathroom. The autopsy found syrup, PCP, and Valium in his system.

Big Moe also lived an unhealthy lifestyle and met a similar fate. Seven years after his 2000 album, *City of Syrup*, whose cover features him pouring the purple stuff over the Houston skyline, the portly MC passed at age thirty-three from a heart attack. "Moe was like a big kid," DJ Crisco Kidd told the *Houston Chronicle*. "And with his drank he was like a kid with a lollipop."

Some Houston rappers think it's time to give syrup a rest. "I think about the people we lose daily," Chamillionaire tells me. "I've got friends and people that I know that fell asleep behind the wheel and died, or went to jail over syrup, stuff like that. I don't see the benefit."

He was speaking shortly after the second anniversary of the death of Pimp C, one half of Texas duo UGK. Pimp C, who revered Screw, was also thirty-three, and died just four months after UGK hit #1 for the first time. "People were like, 'Rest in peace, Pimp C.' 'I'm gonna pour up a cup for Pimp C,'" Chamillionaire goes on, dumbfounded by the irony.

SCREW WORE a goatee, had a soft, gentle face, and spoke in a quiet voice. His friends and family remember him as generous to a fault, giving auditions to unproven rappers and lending out money with abandon. In his later years he took poor care of himself, putting on weight, living on ice cream, fried chicken, and junk food, all the while smoking, drinking, and popping pills. He'd reportedly had two strokes before he passed.

Forever absorbed in his music, he wasn't much of a business-man. He dealt strictly in cash, did little to stop massive bootleg-ging of his product, and never gave much thought to the Internet. Yet somehow more than a decade after his death, Screw music remains commercially viable. His posthumous sales could prob-ably keep any self-respecting rapper in swangers and grills, and a store called Screwed Up Records & Tapes continues to do a steady business.

Opened by Screw in 1998 and run by his cousin after his death, the south-side shop is located on a busy stretch of Cullen Boule-vard, operating out of what looks like a former car garage. One story and flat, with bars on the windows and a handmade sign, its lack of corporate pretentions makes it feel inviting, although the swarm of video cameras above the door might give you pause. In the words of writer Kelefa Sanneh, it has "all the charm and elegance of a check-cashing joint."

The store consists of a single, small room, with a foam-padded door leading to a studio that's off-limits to the public. There is no actual merchandise on the floor, just CD covers. If you want to buy something, you tell the guy behind the counter and slide your cash under bulletproof glass. For sale are hundreds of DJ Screw albums and practically nothing else. It's fairly amazing when you think about it; an operation dedicated entirely to the largely illegal products of a single, deceased artist.

For fifteen dollars I buy a CD from his "Diary of the Origina-tor" series, entitled, *Chapter 12—June 27th*. Released in 1996, its title references the date it was recorded, in honor of the birthday of an S.U.C. associate named Big D-Moe. It's easily the most famous Screw album, and Drake's song "November 18th" is the platinum Canadian rapper's homage. The cover features a snazzy cutout in the shape of Texas, and inside are two discs, the first featuring chopped and screwed versions of popular songs from the era by acts like Bone Thugs-n-Harmony and Tupac Shakur. The second has original compositions, led off by an S.U.C. freestyle. Not long ago that track was chosen as the best Houston rap song in history by KBXX. Pretty impressive, considering its thirty-seven-minute length. Its most well-known stanza comes from S.U.C. member Big Pokey, whose line, "Sittin' sideways/ Paused in a daze/ On a Sunday night I might play me some Maze," served as the hook for Paul Wall's hit "Sittin' Sidewayz."

Chopped and screwed music is not for everyone—Z-Ro said the first time he heard it, he thought Screw's equipment needed some new batteries—but it will make you consider hip-hop in a new light. Bordering on psychedelia, it strips songs of their radio-friendly gloss, deconstructing their percussion and distorting their hooks. Menacing songs sound even more menacing, as the lyrics are shoved right into your face, bringing tales of hood mayhem and female conquest into blunt focus.

These are not tunes for dance clubs, but for cars. Guys who bump Screw tapes hope to convey a dark mystique as they amble by. "[Screw] slowed it down so the bang would be a little harder and deeper," Devin the Dude told MTV. "When the music was like that, you could just creep and ride around all night."

Screw's movement didn't truly catch on until an imitator from Houston's north side called Michael Watts brought it to the nation. His artists like Paul Wall, Chamillionaire, and Mike Jones took over the airwaves in 2005; by then nearly every southern rap album was receiving the "screwed and chopped" treatment.

But Screw was the first, which is why UGK's Pimp C called him the Kool Herc of Texas hip-hop. Yet in many ways Screw's music was the antithesis of the New York style, which celebrated the MCs who rapped *fast*, in the style of Rakim, hopping along with the beat. Screw, however, understood that there was nothing fast about southern living, with its hot temperatures and languid pace and its residents' fondness for extra syllables.

Screw took one of rap's signature stylistic elements, its pacing, and completely altered it. In doing so he left an indelible regional stamp, one that has slowly spread throughout the nation. As noted recently on the tenth anniversary of Screw's death, by *New York Times* writer Jon Caramanica, Screw's influence continues to grow, through slowed versions of far-flung genres like cumbia and reggaeton, and something called witch house. But while Screw had to manually manipulate the speeds of his turntables and cassette recorders, these new artists can achieve their desired effect through simple computer programs.

Screw's Houston disciples are quick to note, however, that his tunes were not just an artistic statement, but a cultural one.

"He made people in Houston proud that they had their own sound, showed them that you didn't have to emulate anyone else," says Bun B. "Not only that, but that other people would want to be like you, if you just had faith in yourself."

# 4

# U GK

■ ■ ■

## From Country to Trill

HAILING FROM Port Arthur, Texas, Pimp C and Bun B made "country rap" and were quite proud of it. Ninety minutes east of Houston, Port Arthur is a predominantly African American Gulf Coast town of sixty thousand; it's the birthplace of Janis Joplin and Robert Rauschenberg but not the kind of place rappers came from. Pimp and Bun's music was so full of slang and twang that they never suspected it would appeal to outsiders. Hence their name: Underground Kingz.

Both men were mammoth and wore a chain or two around their necks. They were more articulate than they let on; had they been born in a different time and place, they might have rapped about politics and literature instead of hos and kilos.

They were charming when they smiled, but they usually tried to look tough. Bun was the good cop, an intimidating-yet-fair presence willing to talk some sense into you. On the mic, his speeding train delivery conveys a sense of order, and his rhymes feel sanded-down and coated by heavy lacquer. "Take a look at the bigger nigga/ Malt liquor swigger playa hater ditch digger/ Figure my hair trigger/ Give a hot one to your liver."

Born Bernard Freeman, his hip-hop handle came from his family's nickname for him, "Bunny." He's disarmingly sincere and modest. "I always thought I was OK [as a rapper], but even after we got signed I really didn't think I was good," he tells me.

Pimp, then, was the bad cop, the high-voiced, unstable provocateur, as likely to slap your face as to sing you a love song. Compelling because you never knew what would come out of his mouth—"Bet it feel funny when ya doin' 69/ Knowing that ya sippin' on all my jimmy wine"—he nonetheless contended that only Bun was a true lyricist. For his part, Bun felt Pimp did all the heavy lifting. In addition to rapping, after all, he sang many of their hooks and produced many of their tracks.

Pimp wasn't born a furs-draped, pinkie-blinging lady's man but rather invented his own nickname after growing up a bespectacled marching band enthusiast. Born Chad Butler, he was the son of a trumpet player and sang and played everything he could get his hands on. Piano, drums, trumpet, flugelhorn, you name it, he picked them up by ear before learning to read music in school. As he explained to Andrew Noz, in his typical gutter eloquence, "I come from a classical background, I came up singing Italian sonnets, Negro spirituals, and shit of that nature."

After his parents got divorced each Christmas was essentially two, and he received drum machines, four tracks, and keyboards. He rapped over his own beats, attempting to emulate Run-DMC. But his sound displeased his stepfather, who happened to be the school's band teacher. "That rap shit is noise," he told him. "You put some music in that shit and you might be able to get paid."

Pimp took the advice to heart, and UGK became known for deep bluesy textures, triumphant church organs, thick funk, and meaty soul. He put some music in that shit, straying from the kick-snare template of Run-DMC in favor of hand claps, 808s, and his signature hi-hats.

Along the way he became perhaps the best producer the South has seen. That point is debatable. That he was the genre's most tragic loose cannon is not.

BUN TOO was the child of divorce. His father lived in southwest Houston, and Bun and Pimp would drive to that city to hit trading fairs. They'd joined forces in a high school group called 4BM, Four Black Ministers, but when the other members dropped out they became UGK. In Houston they searched out nugget rings, bracelets, and chains, and at a spot called King's Flea Market they met a record store proprietor named Russell Washington.

Washington was looking to sign an act to his small record label. He liked the UGK's demo and took them on, and Bun moved to Houston and went to work in Washington's shop. Unfortunately, he didn't have sufficient funds to press up the UGK record, so the guys took to selling crack to finance the project. Not only did they make enough for the album, but their drug-peddling stories would inform much of their music.

Their debut EP was called *The Southern Way*, and "Tell Me Something Good" (which sampled Rufus and Chaka Khan's hippie-era song by the same name) earned radio play in Houston. With the help of powerful independent distributor Southwest Wholesale, they moved tens of thousands of copies of the album, drawing the attention of major labels. They signed with Jive, who proceeded to gut their old tracks, add new music, and release them along with some fresh cuts on their 1992 major label debut *Too Hard to Swallow*.

The highlight track "Pocket Full of Stones" features a mournful horn that sounds straight out of a noir film but is actually recycled from LL Cool J's "Going Back to Cali." Bun describes his orderly march to the top of the dope game, developing a solid business plan and staying focused. "Business boomin' daily, the product sellin' fast," he raps. "Me and my nigga C is makin' money out the ass."

Pimp, meanwhile, becomes unhinged by demanding fiends. "They used to run up sayin', 'Pimp C what ya know?'/ I tell 'em get this crack and get the fuck away from me, hoe!" Still, he allows that the work has its benefits, like oral pleasure from addicts, free of charge. The song was chosen for the *Menace II Society* soundtrack, and along with their placements in Wayans Brothers flicks *A Lowdown Dirty Shame* and *Don't Be a Menace*, UGK began to gain traction.

For my money it's hard to beat their 1994 follow-up, *Super Tight*, which turns shit-talking into a religion via Pimp's revival-style compositions. Many, however consider the 1996 follow-up *Ridin' Dirty* to be their most essential work.

Playing down the grandstanding somewhat in favor of gritty realism, it combines scraps of conversation from actual prisoners with Pimp and Bun's tales of how one might land himself behind bars. On the slow, elegiac opener "One Day," which is something of a down south update of Nas's "Life's a Bitch," Bun raps:

> My brother been in the pen for damn near ten
> But now it looks like when he come out, man I'm
>     goin' in
> So shit, I walk around with my mind blown in my
>     own fuckin' zone
> 'Cause one day you here, the next day you gone

*RIDIN' DIRTY* cracked *Billboard*'s top fifteen, the group's first album to do so. It went a ways toward popularizing Gulf Coast Texas's extended vowel sounds ("ball" becomes "bawwwwwl") and slang, particularly UGK's signature adjective "trill," a combination of "true" and "real." It exuded Texas pride in a way that would become commonplace for Lone Star rappers.

"When most people think of Geto Boys, they don't necessarily think of Texas or Houston," says Paul Wall. "But it seemed like UGK were a lot more reppin' for Texas."

It also helped introduce local car and drug culture and DJ Screw's music to the mainstream. Their song "3 in the Mornin'" incorporates Screw's hazy melodies and speaks of the fallout from a dizzying drug trip. The protagonist is "comin' down real shiny like candy paint," and tries to collect himself but he can't, as he's "leanin' off the dank." In fact, just before *Ridin' Dirty* came out, Pimp and Bun went over to Screw's house and recorded a tape together with him and members of the S.U.C., over beats both from their upcoming album and from favorite songs like Notorious B.I.G.'s "Juicy." "It was really just one of those wild nights," Bun B told writer Maurice Garland in an interview for his blog, noting that folks were drinking from four ounce Gerber baby food bottles full of drank they pulled from Screw's fridge. "There was a mic, so we just started passing it around. There was a no forethought about making the tape. . . . It was just about having fun."

To some critics, *Ridin' Dirty* remains the southern hip-hop album for people who hate southern hip-hop. "Long before the great evil of commercial lowest common denominator rap hijacked southern rap (and eventually hip-hop itself) and turned into the worst music ever in the history of mankind," wrote Brooklyn blogger B.J. "The Good Doctor Zeus" Steiner in 2007, only half kidding, "[UGK] were carving a warm, organic sound that was dripping with soul and funk and didn't really sound like anything else. . . . It was fresh. It was funky. It was the South."

Not that they gave a damn what outsiders thought. Pimp didn't feel northerners cared about him, so why should he care about them? "I was listening to KRS-One all the way up to the point where the man said, 'That shit y'all doing down there is not real hip-hop. If you ain't from New York it's not real hip-hop,'" he told writer Matt Sonzala. "I don't know if it was said in them exact words, but that's the feeling I got after a certain point."

Bun felt more of a kinship with west coasters like E-40, DJ Quik, and Cypress Hill, while Pimp admired Oakland's Too $hort and Compton's Dr. Dre, gangstas who employed musically rich compositions. Like many southern MCs, they took their sensibilities not from the East Coast but from the West, which they believed was full of uncompromising innovators. (Indeed, southern and West Coast rap have always felt a special kinship, likely owing to the fact that many black Californians are only a generation or two removed from Dixie themselves.)

Too $hort's brand of regional marketing was inspiring as well. He and other Oakland artists made music for their hometown, sold it straight to the people, and thus maintained a solid, loyal fan base. "We were kind of taking our cue from what the Oakland music community was doing," Pimp told *Murder Dog*. "Instead of just trying to make rap like we were from New York, why don't we just make Texas music for Texas motherfuckers?'"

JAY-Z INVITED UGK to appear on his song "Big Pimpin'," for which heavyweight Virginia producer Timbaland sampled an Egyptian flute, and director Hype Williams filmed a million-dollar-budget video set during Trinidad's Carnival celebration.

The duo initially felt funny about appearing on the song, as it was kind of soft, but it hit the top twenty and became the biggest hit of their career. That same year UGK were featured on another popular track, Memphis group Three 6 Mafia's "Sippin' on Some Syrup." Both Three 6 Mafia and Jay-Z had wisely grabbed onto UGK's coattails to earn new fans and gain a bit of that Texas market share.

But UGK's next album, *Dirty Money*, stalled for five years, effectively sapping their momentum. Bun says the delay was the result of beef with Jive about the direction of the album. "They wanted us to go in a commercialized direction, toward 'Big Pimpin'" and that sort of thing," he says. "They wanted us to get beats from Timbaland, but there was no need for us to go out and get producers. We already had a producer in the group who was making great music."

In the end, *Dirty Money* was relatively poorly received, and other problems had consumed the group. In 2000, Pimp caused a ruckus at a mall. While looking for shoes, he was approached by a group of brash young shoppers, one of whom loudly expressed her distaste for his songs. The two began ribbing each other and, by Pimp's account, she became aggressive, causing him to lift up his jacket and show off his gun. He was charged with aggravated assault—despite the lack of a literal assault—sentenced to community service, and given probation.

Special prosecutors took the opportunity to interrogate him about his relationship with J. Prince and Rap-A-Lot Records, he said. Though at the time he had no formal relationship with the label, it would later release collections of his previously recorded solo tracks, and Pimp said he considered Prince a "family member."

"I felt like I was in the position where I had to take the probation because what they was talking was some way out shit," Pimp said. Two years later, after failing to complete the community service requirements of what he felt were unfair probation terms, he was sent to prison on an eight-year sentence.

Bun went into a tailspin, convinced that Pimp's blunder threatened everything they'd built. He took to drinking heavily and attacking whatever was in his path, inanimate or not. "Nobody wanted to get in my way at that time," he says. "I take my frustrations out in all the wrong ways."

Striking out on his own had approximately zero appeal to him. Pimp, after all, had been the group's driving force, while Bun felt he had never accomplished anything on his own.

But after coming to grips with the situation, he got his head together. As a solo artist he signed to Rap-A-Lot, who released his highly regarded 2005 work *Trill*. He became a southern rap goodwill ambassador, appearing on songs with anyone who would have him and shouting out Pimp's name nearly every time he opened his mouth.

He popularized the slogan, "Free Pimp C," reflecting his and others' belief that his partner's sentence was capricious and excessive. He focused on expanding the duo's marketing and merchandising possibilities, and he opened himself up to the press in a way that few rappers ever have.

Widely acknowledged as the best interview in hip-hop, he remains more open and forthright than just about anyone. We actually spoke for the first time while he was in the midst of the intercontinental road rally Gumball 3000, driving his Porsche Cayenne at speeds up to 120 miles an hour. This was just days after he'd fallen off of a stage in Stockholm and split open his knee and tore up his arm, which somehow hadn't prevented him from racing, doing press, and performing again, in a sling.

PIMP SPENT much of his four years inside working out rhymes and beats, despite not having much access to equipment, and he compiled thousands of songs and sketches. Upon his release there was a pent-up demand for the group's music, and their triumphant 2007 double disc *Underground Kingz* hit the top of the charts.

A stirring rap all-star exhibition, it features a who's who of the group's contemporaries, including Jazze Pha, Scarface, and Lil Jon, as well as their primary influences, like Too $hort and Big Daddy Kane. Gospel-fueled affirmation "International Player's Anthem

(I Choose You)" brought OutKast's Andre 3000 out of hibernation and was nominated for a Grammy.

But it wasn't all love. "Quit Hatin' the South" gives UGK and the Geto Boys' Willie D an opportunity to air out some grievances. Bun calmly explains that he's "Gotta lot of respect, for the ones before me/ But when my time came they act like they ain't know me." Pimp, however, isn't so diplomatic.

> Y'all niggas on y'all period up there, bitch! . . .
> They'll put all y'all records on one side of the store
> And put all the country rap music on the other side
>      of the store
> And see who sell out first, bitch ass nigga!

Though many folks in his position might have been celebrating their freedom and their success, Pimp appeared increasingly unsettled, not just on "Quit Hatin' the South" but in radio interviews and a now-famous editorial penned for *Ozone* magazine.

In the screed, he unleashed a vicious, paranoid diatribe against just about everyone he could think of. He called Houston rapper Lil' Troy a snitch and castigated Mike Jones and Lil' Flip for their gaudy jewelry, which he called "monkey shit." Sharp dressers didn't escape his ire, either, as he intimated that Russell Simmons and singer Ne-Yo were gay—"dick-in-the-booty" types, he called them.

This was in contrast to his own appeal. "My skin is pretty. My toes are pretty. I'm a young funky wild boy and I'm a sexy young motherfucker," he wrote. Equally perplexing was his insistence that Atlanta was not actually the South, because it's on eastern time rather than central.

Perhaps he just skated along the edges of insanity like other geniuses, or maybe his hedonistic lifestyle and years of drug use had caught up with him. In any case, just two years after his release from prison, in December 2007, he was found dead in Los Angeles' Mondrian Hotel. Also in his room were a half-empty bottle of drank and two prescription medications, one intended to control anxiety and another usually used to treat herpes.

Though his death was initially suspected to be suicide, an autopsy chalked it up to an accidental overdose of the syrup combined with his preexisting sleep apnea condition. The drank likely restricted his breathing, piggybacking on his condition and killing him while he slept. The 260 pounds he carried around didn't help either.

Some troubled musicians, like Elliott Smith, descend into a public cycle of substance abuse and depression, and their deaths are somewhat anticipated. But, bizarre outbursts aside, nobody seemed to see Pimp's coming.

Bun certainly didn't. He asserts his friend was never particularly wild or unsafe: "He definitely enjoyed his life, but I wouldn't say he was any crazier than anybody else." Yet Bun implies that the pair started acting more like uninhibited rock stars after they finally found national fame. "For many years people kept us locked out of a lot of things. Once they couldn't keep us locked out any more, we wanted to make sure we could do everything everyone else did."

*Houston Chronicle* shot footage of the crowd coming out of Pimp's funeral, including a bedazzled Flavor Flav look-alike—dressed in a gold crown and cape, holding a pimp cup—and the bulk of the town's rap celebrities. J. Prince quoted a line from the pastor's eulogy: "It's hard out here for a pimp, but there's hope in Christ."

For consolation Bun turned to Joan Didion's Pulitzer Prize–winning loss memoir *The Year of Magical Thinking*. "It helps you understand that grief is something that everyone goes through," he says, "and you're not expected to handle it as gracefully as we would all like to." He also signed on to teach a class in religion and hip-hop at Rice University in Houston, which seems oddly appropriate.

Pimp's death brought him greater fame than he'd had in life, inspiring eulogies galore and breathless TMZ updates on his autopsy report and funeral. It didn't seem right; one suspects that most of the gossip site's readers were latecomer Pimp fans at best. In the end, one wonders if he wouldn't have been better off living out his days as a still-underground king.

# 5

# EIGHTBALL & MJG AND THREE 6 MAFIA

■ ■ ■

## Memphis Goes Hollywood

INTERVIEWING RAPPERS usually requires permeating layers of handlers, childhood friends, and occasionally lawyers, but Eightball, one-half of celebrated Memphis duo Eightball & MJG, answers his cell phone immediately when I arrive in his hometown. His publicist has given me his number, and a half hour later he pulls up in front of my hotel in his own black Hummer. Not one of those smaller, eco-friendlier Hummers, either—the full-on, 2005, "let's exhume some dinosaurs" model.

Eightball is the fat one; we're on our way to meet the skinny one, MJG, his rhyming partner of two decades. En route to their studio we pass through Orange Mound, the largely black neighborhood, built on a plantation, where the pair grew up. There, before the turn of the century, African Americans were able to purchase homes for one hundred dollars or so. Now, a giant neon Kellogg's sign presides over the local plant.

"On the weekends, you could smell the cereal," Eightball remembers in his generous baritone, noting that the odor was preferable to that of the nearby dog-food factory. "That smelled like somebody was cooking a horse."

Memphis once served as a destination for aspiring musicians from all over the country. But it has long suffered talent drain and, not too long ago, was considered a hip-hop backwater. Eightball & MJG didn't expect to get famous in a city without much of a scene, and so they hopped in their cars and attempted to sell their mixtapes in big cities around the South, finally landing in Houston, where they got a record deal.

UGK made it cool to be country, and Eightball & MJG—born Premro Smith and Marlon Jermaine Goodwin—eventually returned home and repped Memphis harder than ever. The town's other famous rap group, Three 6 Mafia, followed their lead, and in fact delights in playing up country bumpkin stereotypes, specifically on their MTV reality show, where their assistant peed on Jennifer Love Hewitt's lawn.

As we approach the studio we pull up behind MJG's 1986 flat-bed Chevy pickup, which sits on enormous rims and spews filthy exhaust. He's got a thing for old cars, and this is his latest reclamation project. We park in front of their studio—the only cars on a sleepy street—and MJG emerges wearing a black knit cap with holes cut out for his thick braids.

He doesn't say much at first, but after the guys spend a few minutes inside sucking on a thin joint, they get into a discussion of why pimping is such a dominant theme in Memphis culture. Indeed, musician and actor Isaac Hayes, a driving force behind Stax Records, is responsible for tracks like "Pursuit of the Pimpmobile" from the *American Pimp* soundtrack. Craig Brewer's 2005 Memphis-set film *Hustle & Flow*, meanwhile, focuses on the struggles of a pimp turned rapper.

"This is a pimpin' city. Everything is pimpin'," says MJG. "The lingo, the motto, the swag, everything is pimpin' here, even if you're not an official pimp. Everybody here wanna be a pimp, used to be a pimp, tried to be a pimp, is a pimp, dreamed about being a pimp—"

"—know a pimp," puts in Eightball, "was raised by a pimp—"

"—stay next door to a pimp—"

"—in jail with a pimp, worked with a pimp, had a job with a pimp—"

"—his mechanic was a pimp. That's how it is here, really. Even the women. Instead of saying, 'What's up, man?' we be saying, 'What's up, pimpin'?'"

Similarly, their use of the "pimpin'" in song usually isn't about prostituting women but rather excelling at one's craft, whatever it is. But they nonetheless cavorted with some sketchy characters at their local pool hall when they were younger, including, yes, some actual pimps.

Still, having found their hip-hop calling while still young, Eightball says they didn't spend much time on the wrong side of the law. In Houston they joined a label called Suave House, founded by relocated Memphis impresario Tony Draper. The first product was 1993's *Comin' Out Hard*; even harder was their album the following year, *On the Outside Looking In*, which featured the crunk-precursor "Lay It Down."

> Lay it down, lay it down
> You hos lay it down!

"When 'Lay It Down' came on, everybody in the club would be crunk as a motherfucker, wilin', letting loose whatever kind of energy was inside," says Lil Jon, who before he blew up as a performer was a popular club DJ. He notes that the song helped inspire his brand of rowdy club anthems.

But there was more to the Memphis duo's catalog than mindless chants. Their next works showcased Eightball's increasingly confident laid-back delivery and MJG's fierce, antsy pleading. Helming much of their own production, they developed a penchant for lush, Memphis-derived instrumentals, which recall everything from the vibrant Stax legacy to the grim reality of bombed-out storefronts.

"We gravitate toward incorporating that southern delta blues sound in our music," says Eightball. Many of their contemporaries relied on sampled tracks, but they found the live sound more satisfying. "We don't try to overthink it too hard," says MJG. "It's just a natural influence, from being here in the music city. That's just what we've come up around."

*On Top of the World* from 1995 went gold, and they realized for the first time that rap could be a legitimate, long-term career option. "What Can I Do" described the alternative:

> I've got to see the judge on the fifth
> Until then, I'm the cake-cutting, cookie-making,
>    baking soda measurer, illegal money treasurer . . .
> Looking for a way out. Prison ain't the way for me, so
>    I'm trying to stay out . . .
> I want to quit and get legit and pay taxes

"At that time, everybody we knew was doing what they had to do to make money for their families, and they wanted to do something else," says Eightball. "That was a serious conversation at the time."

Both rappers can spit fast, but they tend to excel over slower, funkier, percussive R&B. "Space Age Pimpin'," off *On Top of the World*, for example, features airy synths, porn-flick bass, and a breathy hook. It has seduction, and just a little bit of silliness, on its mind. "Slip on the latex and dive in," raps Eightball. "Swish!"

Plenty of Eightball & MJG tracks objectify women and glorify gunplay, but some express regret for these themes. "Not trying to preach, just trying to reach out," raps Eightball on "Starships and

Rockets." "Killing myself, advertising suicide/ Explaining formulas for black on black genocide/ In other words, I apologize."

They're adamant about not following every trend. You won't hear them using Auto-Tune to make their voices sound like robots, for example, and they take pride in maintaining a grounded image. To illustrate, they play me the video for the slow, gothic title track to their new album, *Ten Toes Down*, whose title refers to their commitment to hip-hop.

Filmed at a fireworks store near Chattanooga, it conspicuously eschews many of rap's typical set pieces. "There ain't no dancing bitches, swimming pools, or jewelry," Eightball notes, proudly. Adds MJG, speaking of the duo in the third person, "There they go again, still sounding the same."

THEY MAY call themselves a mafia, but there's nothing particularly intimidating about Juicy J and his counterpart, DJ Paul. Born with a stunted right arm, Paul is full of wry, sarcastic humor, while Juicy is an impulsive fast-talker who regularly acts the fool, sometimes intentionally, but often not.

There wouldn't seem to be two men less groomed for celebrity, which is what made their 2007 MTV show, *Adventures in Hollyhood*, filmed in the wake of their Oscar victory for the *Hustle & Flow* theme song, so much fun.

That was around the time their fame began to dramatically outstrip that of Eightball & MJG, whose debut came just two years before their own, 1995's *Mystic Stylez*. Juicy calls his predecessors "pioneers" and brags that he used to be their back-up DJ when they performed at the local skating rink. Their success, he adds, convinced him it was possible for a Memphis group to make it big.

Paul and Juicy got started as mixtape DJs and crunk trailblazers who combined slowed Miami bass beats with the dark themes of Geto Boys. Paul specialized in crafting fight chants that would get the crowd worked up. In the early 1990s he made songs at home and test-marketed the bassy, pounding results that night at his club, Paul's Playhouse.

This was Memphis-style buck music, and it often incorporated a variation of a dance called the Gangster Walk, in which folks would form a circle and romp around the dance floor hollering lyrics and sometimes throwing elbows.

Paul's music once sparked a melee in the club's lobby involving dozens of people, and someone whipped out a gun. He later found a man lying under a bathroom sink, shaking. "He had been shot through his side, and then it went into his heart," Paul says. "He died right in front of me."


IT WAS a dark coming-of-age for the man born Paul Beauregard, who grew up in the predominantly black Whitehaven neighborhood. His family situation was stable: his dad owned a pest control business and lots of real estate, and he has pleasant memories of eating his favorite meal—a quarter pounder with mayonnaise—with his mom at the McDonald's on Elvis Presley Boulevard (the same spot where he wrote crunk anthem "Tear Da Club Up").

But as he got older he ran wild, doing drugs and toting firearms. He says his disability helped win the cops' sympathy. "The police used to pull me over when I was young. They'd feel sorry for my ass, even though they'd caught me with two fucking .45s," he says with a laugh. "They'd still be like, 'All right, Paul, you can go. You just better get home.'"

From a young age he was obsessed with heavy metal music, slasher movies, and psychopaths, and he later collected a *Time Life* series on serial killers that he kept in the studio. "I was just in love with murder," he says, oddly nostalgic. "Serial killers were real, real smart. It's like an art; it's like a profession. Especially someone like Ted Bundy. They know he killed thirty people, but they estimate that he probably killed up to one hundred. If you can kill almost one hundred people and never get caught, that's crazy. You've got to really have your head on straight."

The group went by Triple Six Mafia until they changed it to the less–Satanic sounding Three 6 Mafia. Though they had their share of not-for-the-squeamish sex romps like "Slob on My Knob" ("Slob on my knob/ Like corn on the cob"), their tales of conflict and dismemberment, demon shout-outs, and references to the occult got them classified as horrorcore. As then-group member Koopsta Knicca puts it on "Mystic Stylez," "Feel the wrath of the fuckin' devil nation/ Three 6 Mafia, creation of Satan."

Juicy J, whose real name is Jordan Houston and whose father is a preacher, now bristles at the suggestion that they honored Lucifer, however. "We do not worship no devil, man," says J, speaking by phone from his Cadillac truck as he drives from L.A. to Las Vegas. "People ask me that shit every day. There's no way you could have had our success worshipping the devil."

That point is debatable—Robert Johnson did all right—but the group went through many sounds and lineups over the years, at times working with artists including Crunchy Black, Mr. Del, Lord Infamous, Gangsta Boo, and Juicy's older brother Project Pat, who himself went platinum in 2001 thanks largely to his critique of orally inclined ladies called "Chickenhead." (He had trouble maintaining his momentum, however, after subsequently going to prison over a gun charge.)

Juicy and Paul became the act's dominant forces and were extremely shrewd about anticipating trends, such as on their 2000 hit "Sippin' on Some Syrup," which also featured UGK and Pat and appropriated Houston's drink of choice. Their desire for national popularity subsumed their obsession with the dark arts, and Three 6 Mafia would eventually whittle down to a duo.

By the mid-aughts they'd pivoted definitively toward the mainstream, segueing into more commercially acceptable subject matter and friendlier club beats. They hit big with tracks like the deliriously upbeat "Stay Fly" (featuring both Young Buck and Eightball & MJG), a boilerplate Auto-Tuned jam "Lolli Lolli (Pop That Body)," and a collaboration with name-brand Dutch auteur DJ Tiesto called "Feel It," which all but demands a glow stick.


THOUGH ONLY in their late thirties, Eightball & MJG have become rap elder statesmen, whether they like it or not. Sure, they're still making a decent living in the rap game, thanks to regular tours through the Chitlin' Circuit, which take them to places like Hattiesburg, Mississippi, and Dyersburg, Tennessee. And every southern rapper worth his salt shouts them out. But they've had a hard time turning their respect into dollars, never managing a big hit other than their contribution to Three 6 Mafia's "Stay Fly."

It looked like they might break big in the mid-aughts, when longtime admirer Sean "Diddy" Combs released a pair of their albums, 2004's *Living Legends* and 2007's *Ridin High*. Diddy gave them the full Bad Boy Records treatment, putting them in Bentleys and coating their sound in a thick pop sheen, but the albums didn't take off.

And so they changed tack on 2010's *Ten Toes Down*, released in conjunction with Grand Hustle, the label of another of their fanboys, T.I. The work recalls the act's mid-to-late 1990s golden era with its slow, intimidating, 808-driven proclamations and threats, and serves as an attempt to fertilize their southern roots and win back fans they lost during the Bad Boy years.

"Once you cross a line, you can't go back," frets Eightball, citing Diddy as an example of a rapper whose blinged-out, highflying image undercut his street bona fides. "I don't think we're one of the groups that can go so far commercial. [Our fans] won't accept it. We had a single, 'Ridin' High,' that was a fast dance song, but people just don't want to hear that from us."

Which brings him, then, to the subject of Three 6 Mafia. Though both Juicy and Paul still keep houses in Memphis, they moved more or less permanently to L.A. after their Academy Award. While they insist they're still making music for their long-time fans, Eightball isn't so sure.

"It's just my opinion, but after the Oscar, they weren't the same," he says. "Even their hood stuff don't sound like that Three 6 Mafia that took over Memphis after we kicked the door open. I think people's music changes with their surroundings, sometimes."

Juicy naturally isn't thrilled to hear of his predecessor's sell-out charges. "If someone said, 'If you do this song, you can make ten to fifteen to twenty million dollars,' would you be like, 'Nah, I'm gonna just chill with my hardcore fan base and nickel and dime here and there'?"

DJ Paul notes that in recent years they've also acquired a legion of international followers and now have a responsibility to cater to them as well. "We have new fans," he explains, "who will hopefully be around as long as the old fans."

Juicy adds that their recent solo albums, mixtapes, and the street singles from Three 6's upcoming album *Laws of Power* have been marketed to an urban audience. "We got so much stuff coming out that sounds like the old Three 6 Mafia," he contends. "Yeah, we got some pop stuff that our underground fan base wouldn't understand, but it's all good when you see the twenty million dollar check in the mail."


DIRECTOR CRAIG BREWER grew up in Memphis, and after his father passed away Brewer used his inheritance to finance his first film, *The Poor and Hungry*, whose name comes from a Memphis bar. As his stature grew, he continued filming his movies in and around his hometown and incorporated his passion for its music into his plotlines. In 2005 he released his hip-hop film, *Hustle*

& *Flow*, and two years later put out his blues film, *Black Snake Moan*.

*Hustle & Flow* features actor Terrence Howard as a small-time pimp who tries his hand at the independent rap game. The film's road to national distribution was a difficult one, partly because Brewer was intent on shooting it on location and casting southern players. Ludacris plays Skinny Black, a cocky local rapper gone big-time, and DJ Paul and Juicy J have cameos.

"I knew it was going to be something big," Juicy J says. "This was something nobody had ever done, shot a movie in Memphis and put 85 percent of Memphis in the movie. It was a blessing."

Eightball & MJG also contributed to the soundtrack, but it was Three 6 Mafia's "It's Hard Out Here for a Pimp" that became the film's theme song and received the Oscar nomination. Eminem won a 2002 Academy Award for "Lose Yourself," reportedly sleeping through the telecast at home outside Detroit. But in 2006 Three 6 was the first rap act to perform at the show, and it was unlike anything the Kodak Theatre had seen, with a cast of would-be johns and streetwalkers cavorting on a re-created Memphis street corner.

Queen Latifah, who announced the winner, could hardly believe the text on her card, and neither could anyone else. This was a year before Martin Scorsese finally won for *The Departed*, and host Jon Stewart quipped, "For those of you keeping score at home: Martin Scorsese, zero. Three 6 Mafia, one."

"I still don't believe it, because we'd never won anything," says Juicy J. "It shocked us, it shocked the world, it shocked the people on Mars." He adds that he frequently takes his statue out of its safe, holds it, and thanks God.

The award led directly to their MTV reality series *Adventures in Hollyhood*, which lasted for just one season in 2007. Sure, the show has plenty of cringe-worthy moments, such as when Paul and Juicy make their hefty assistants do shirtless jumping jacks and instruct one to dump liquor on himself and run around the house screaming, "I am not an animal!"

And yes, it has the dancing bitches, swimming pools, and jewelry Eightball dreads so much. But often the guys find themselves out of their comfort zones, such as when Juicy goes on a date with Ashton Kutcher's assistant Krissy. She mentions that respect is important to her in a man. "I'm so respectful, it's ridiculous," Juicy insists.

If that's the case, she counters, how does he explain songs like, "Slob on My Knob"?

"Umm . . ." he says, as the camera cuts away. Needless to say, he doesn't get any action that night. Nor does he from his next date, *Laguna Beach* star Kristin Cavallari, whom he calls "Kristin Calamari" and begs in vain to come home with him.

"I wish it could have kept going," Paul says now of the MTV experience. "That show took us to a whole other level."

But as to the charge that their post-Oscar move to California has changed them, he doesn't buy it. "I still do the same shit in L.A. that I did in Memphis. I still barbeque on the weekends, drink Bud Light beer, and piss outside."

# 6

# OUTKAST, GOODIE MOB, AND ORGANIZED NOIZE

■ ■ ■

## The Dirty South Blooms

SHORTLY AFTER the 2010 Haiti earthquake, an international nonprofit based in Atlanta organized a charity event to benefit survivors. By necessity it was thrown together quickly, and when I arrive at the plush restaurant on Piedmont Avenue where it's being held, there aren't many people there.

Big Boi has managed to find time for it in his schedule, however. In fact, I'm outside chatting with the valet when a black Mercedes pulls up onto the sidewalk out front. The valet's brow wrinkles and he hurries over, but upon seeing OutKast's senior member emerge from the sedan, the valet decides to permit the unorthodox parking job.

Antwan "Big Boi" Patton has come alone. I scamper behind him into the restaurant, where he is enveloped by a horde of publicists and photographers. Escorted to a photography-staging area without being offered so much as a tapa, he's willingly held hostage for the next hour or so.

Donors rub up next to him for pictures, while various self-important civic types command his ear. Roaming amid the hoi polloi are models who are dressed like ballerinas but moving like robots. They recall his 2008 show with the Atlanta ballet, *big*, for which he did not pirouette but rather performed music.

Big is short but stands very erect, wearing shades and a long-sleeved T-shirt with silhouettes of revolvers on it. He sports a soul patch and thin mustache, and smiles at everyone he meets. He's almost ridiculously obliging, a PR person's dream, displaying not a trace of artistic snobbery or superstar ennui. He acts less like an icon who has sold twenty-five million albums and more like some dude who has reached the second round of *American Idol*.

For the better part of an hour, he gamely answers the same, banal questions he's been hearing for years. What's up with his long-delayed solo album? When is a new OutKast CD going to drop? Is OutKast broken up?

He's got to be sick of that last one. Despite his constant assertions to the contrary, everyone assumes that he and Andre "3000" Benjamin are finished. Of course, it doesn't help that Andre hasn't always done much to squash the rumors. Over the years he's daydreamed aloud about the group's demise, saying things like, "In a perfect world, this would be the last OutKast record." He's suggested that, if not for Big's insistence upon staying together, their collaboration would have terminated years ago.

Andre's not here with his partner tonight, but that's no surprise. No one even seems to know exactly where the peacock-coiffed, Renaissance man of the duo even lives anymore. (His publicist's response when I asked her was, "Hard to answer, Ben. He just goes where his work takes him.") He and Big certainly don't spend a lot of time together. Each has his own studio, for starters, and there are also lifestyle differences to take into account. Big smokes weed constantly, while Andre, who famously became vegan and stopped smoking pot and drinking booze, can't even tolerate secondhand cigarette smoke.

Big would be happy to revel in his celebrity for the rest of his days; so long as he can park his luxury cars wherever he wants, he's happy to answer questions from sycophants like me all night long. Andre, however, long ago got sick of answering these questions, which is why, for the most part, he no longer does.

"Big is a solid and Dre is a fluid," explained Goodie Mob's Cee Lo Green to *Blender* in 2004. "Dre's just eccentric; he has a solitary disposition. They travel on separate buses; on the Smokin' Grooves tour, Dre's bus was him, his cook, and his guitar tutor. Big's a people person—he's got that big heart, and he likes being surrounded by loved ones, so everybody else was on his bus, smoking and drinking."

Andre's the duo's visionary, considered by some the greatest talent hip-hop has ever produced. His studied, self-conscious compositions often succeed via misdirection; he aims to be subversive. Big, however, remains focused on improving his already near-impeccable flow and crafting the perfect gangsta rap track. Andre freely admits his partner is the better rapper; he himself dreams of symphonies.

Their 2003 magnum opus *Speakerboxxx/The Love Below* illustrated the divide. Actually a pair of solo albums, Big's contribution demonstrated his sonic commitment to big bass and thick hooks. Andre's disc was a rock opera.

But their willingness to embrace their influences and passions, no matter how un-hip-hop, has given them gravitas. They're the group your college professor, your drug dealer, and your grandmother can agree on. Crowd-pleasing innovators with an edge, their pop pretensions don't inhibit their artistic ones. They might have gained fame singing about fish, grits, and all that pimp shit, but their fans stayed on board even as they explored heavy metal, jazz, noise pop, and swing.

Even when nobody knew what to make of OutKast, just about everybody loved them. They've shaped the dirty south, hipster, and conscious rap movements, but have also served as tastemakers for the wider culture. How odd was it that in 2004 *Esquire* named Andre, a rapper clad like a polo player, the best-dressed man on Earth?

It's rare for a group to boast near-unanimous critical and commercial appeal, but one could chalk it up to Big and Andre's differences. Their separate musical visions result in a constant push and pull, a series of artistic corrections. Big reels in Andre's more obscure instincts, and Andre reels in Big's more base ones.

But for all their strengths as collaborators, they do poorly as friends. In addition to being wishy-washy, Andre is known to insult his partner in subtle ways. When asked what Big brings to Andre's music, he said, "The common man's ear" before adding that he was sometimes "bored with what the common man likes." Big has put up with other indignities, like missing out on millions in revenue because of Andre's decisions to stop touring and refuse endorsement deals.

Because of either his love for his partner or his pride in being a part of history, Big is forever content to play the part of the abused wife. "They don't really know Dre," he tells me, referring to Out-Kast gossipmongers. "If they knew Dre, half the stuff they say they wouldn't say. It's all day long, OutKast for life. Can't nobody fuck with us."

Tonight, in case no one heard him say it the first few hundred times, Big insists that the group is as strong as ever. They've even done some recording together recently. I ask him if he ever gets tired of answering this question.

"Yeah, it gets a little worrisome," he says, "but until you tell somebody, they'll never know. So you just got to let them know straight up that, 'Yeah, we still doin' it.'" And then, almost reflexively, he repeats the affirmation that has become his mantra: "OutKast for life."

BORN IN 1975, Big Boi came up in the old south river burg of Savannah, on the town's west side, the son of a fifteen-year-old mother and an Air Force and Marines serviceman whose pilot name was Chico Dusty. "He passed away a couple of years ago and he was a real bad man," Big said while promoting his solo album, *Sir Luscious Left Foot: The Son of Chico Dusty*.

A few months later arrived Andre 3000. Born in Atlanta, he and his teenage mother, Sharon Benjamin Hodo, who studied during the day and worked at night, were abandoned immediately. "Single parents, don't tell me what God can't do," she says on a *Love Below* track that pays tribute to her, called "She's Alive." "I made sure you had. I never felt like you should be deprived of anything. If a man didn't want to take care of his child—you move on, and that's what I did."

Big's parents also promptly split, and both young men were shuffled about, each living with their families for a time in Motel 6s. Big was sent to live with his aunt in Atlanta as a young teen, and he met Andre in tenth grade at their mostly white, arts magnet high school, where they were bused from their low-income neighborhoods.

Big got good grades and was, most days, thrilled to be there. "I don't want to say it was cool, [but] the *girls* was cool in school," he says. Andre, meanwhile, didn't want the other kids to know where he lived, so he had the bus drop him off far from home and walked the rest of the way. Big has described the two of them as preps, and says they engaged in some low-level drug peddling and sometimes stole cars.

But their main thrills came from listening to progressive East and West Coast hip-hop and rapping together. When they were sixteen, a girl at their school championed their talents and hooked them up with an amateur beat maker named Rico Wade.

Wade, only nineteen himself, worked at a beauty supply store called LaMonte's at a shopping center in nearby East Point, Georgia. Also employed there was Tionne Watkins, later known as T-Boz in the wildly successful R&B trio TLC.

A performer and dancer who came up in Atlanta's bass scene, Wade fancied himself a producer. He joined forces with a studio whiz called Ray Murray and a synth-specialist named Sleepy Brown, who was also a more-than-serviceable singer. The trio set up a studio at a skating rink called Jellybeans and christened themselves Organized Noize. They began recruiting hip-hop wannabes.

Big and Andre took the bus over to LaMonte's one day and performed an impromptu audition before members of Wade's crew. They freestyled over a tape of an A Tribe Called Quest song, playing off each other with a seemingly endless cache of rhymes. Though not everyone was sure what to make of their long-winded, esoteric freestyling, Wade was impressed and invited them over to his place in Lakewood Heights.

Wade and the guys had been kicked out of their previous apartment for making too much noise. And so, they had set up shop in the small house, crashing on sleeping bags and recording in an unfinished section of the basement. The room, Wade remembers, was notable for its red dirt clay, exposed pipes, and rats. "It kind of gave you a dungeon vibe," he said during Organized Noize's Hip Hop Honors induction. Thus was named their crew the Dungeon Family, which became the first family of southern hip-hop, sprouting OutKast and Goodie Mob.

Andre and Big relished the creative atmosphere away from their parents and lubricated by malt liquor and marijuana. "I thought it was going on over there," Big Boi told Roni Sarig. "Ten, 15 people in the studio downstairs. Niggas just writing on pads everywhere, smoking their herb, 40 ounces. The atmosphere said, 'Damn, this is where we need to be.'"

IN THE first part of the 1990s, producers Jermaine Dupri and Dallas Austin created an early template for the emerging Atlanta urban pop style. Their artists included slick female R&B groups TLC and Xscape, and kiddie rap acts Another Bad Creation and Kris Kross, the latter known for wearing their clothes backward.

Their accents and slang were minimal, and their subject matter was universal. They could have been from anywhere, but the fact that Atlanta was becoming recognized as a place for hip-hop music movers and shakers was news. The city had never been particularly prominent in the music business, though since the late 1970s it had hosted the annual Jack the Rapper convention, which drew black musicians and other industry types for networking events and soirees.

Dupri says his and Austin's presence drew Los Angeles–based executives L.A. Reid and Babyface to Atlanta, where they set up their soon-to-be-powerhouse label LaFace Records. L.A.'s wife Perri "Pebbles" Reid was also TLC's manager, which gave Organized Noize an important contact at LaFace.

But Wade, Brown, and Murray felt it was time to move beyond their predecessors' glossy styles toward something more distinctly Atlanta. "We put our brains together and decided we were going to take it further than Jermaine, who had introduced Kris Kross and brought in a little bit of hip-hop from the South," said Ray Murray.

Reid was interested in signing hip-hop acts, but, unfamiliar with the scene, came to rely on Wade's expertise. He introduced

Reid to OutKast, who performed in front of Reid's staff at his office. "I don't think L.A. got it," Andre said, "but he's a business-man and understood hip-hop was about to go off."

Reid initially passed on the group but later enlisted OutKast to contribute a song to a LaFace Christmas compilation album. This track would become the impetus for the duo's first single, "Player's Ball," which, to this day, represents platonic OutKast perfection to many.

The track commemorates a yuletide celebration complete with Cadillac Sevilles, herb, and some spiked eggnog, and in the video Andre plays pool shirtless and struts his stuff in the woods. Big Boi, meanwhile, looks almost shy, riding along in the passenger seat of a convertible lowrider. Sleepy Brown sings the hook, speak-ing on afros, braids, and gangsta rides.

The song hasn't aged a bit. Both MCs were still teenagers upon the song's 1993 release, but their deliveries already feel polished. Andre commences with a flurry of staccato rhymes.

> You thought I'd break my neck to help y'all deck the
>     halls?
> Oh no, I got other means of celebratin', I'm getting
>     blizzard at HoJos

Big, meanwhile, rides the quick beat easily, cramming in some syllables while letting others breathe.

> I'm a player doing what the players do
> The package store is closed? Okay my day is ruined

The song ushered in OutKast's seminal 1994 debut *Southern-playalisticadillacmuzik*. Composed entirely by Organized Noise, its music is flush with driving southern funk and live instrumentals. The production group strove not for the en vogue intimidating, otherworldly sound of Death Row Records, but rather for an earthy, down-home, celebratory vibe. "We wanted Atlanta brothers to be proud of where they were from," said Sleepy Brown.

The album has activist moments, noting that the Georgia Dome was still flying the Confederate flag, for one thing. But it's far from preachy. Though it hints at the sonic expansion that was to come, southern rap set pieces like pimps, drugs, and classic rides are in abundance, and Big casts himself as a pimp-slappin', lady-baggin' smooth operator. It may not have been as enlightening as the work of Atlanta-based Afrocentric hip-hop collective Arrested Development, but it felt a lot more fun.

*Southernplayalisticadillacmuzik* still resonates with OutKast fans, and "Player's Ball" remains particularly beloved. At its core, it's a nostalgic tale of two best friends embracing shared ideals, which perhaps explains why it stays so close to Big's heart and why Andre would prefer to forget about it.

"I don't want to be forty years old doing 'Player's Ball,'" he said, speculating that Big would love to be doing exactly that. "He'll be like, 'I want to do this shit. Let's run it.'"

*SOUTHERNPLAYALISTICADILLACMUZIK* featured the work of the entire Dungeon Family, and introduced the public to the quartet Goodie Mob, whose name stands for "Good Die Mostly Over Bullshit," among other things. Political but practical, tuneful but tough, Goodie Mob offered a southern take on conscious hip-hop. Though they never moved many units, they continue to serve as a moral compass of sorts to rappers today, and their debut album *Soul Food* set a standard for artistic fearlessness.

"I credit them for being people who were willing to take chances where other artists may have been concerned about commercial viability," Bun B told Andrew Noz. "They probably sacrificed a lot financially to make an album that really resonated with people."

In 1994 TLC released their second CD, *CrazySexyCool*, which sold eleven million copies, largely due to its Organized Noize–produced smash, "Waterfalls." The colossal hit won the beat-making trio some capital with LaFace, who gave them an opportunity to present a new artist. Whereas OutKast were the Dungeon Family's charismatic, overachieving world beaters, Goodie Mob was meant to represent the crew's moral framework and aesthetic ethos.

"To me, music from the heart is better than music from the pocket," Sleepy Brown later explained to the *Atlanta Journal-Constitution*. "Just sampling something and throwing somebody on the track works for some people. Yeah, you get rich. Get paid. Get your cars. Get your crib. But music from the heart always stays with you."

Bearing this mentality, Organized Noize assembled Goodie Mob's lineup of Cee Lo Green, T-Mo, Big Gipp, and Khujo. All four members had attended the same Atlanta high school, Benjamin E. Mays. Before their formation Gipp was a cosmetology student, and T-Mo and Khujo had a group called the Lumberjacks. Cee Lo was introduced to Wade by Andre, a childhood friend. (In fact, Cee Lo had nearly become a third member of OutKast.)

Organized Noize crafted the act's sound from scratch, composing substantive, mid-tempo beats that were never less than deadly serious. "We thought, 'Let's go a little further than we did with OutKast,'" said Ray Murray. "OutKast was a little more playful; Goodie Mob was a lot harder."

Though the youngest in the group, Cee Lo became the group's de facto leader, a short, rotund, Buddha-like figure who speaks in parables. A self-described childhood thug, he was the son of two Christian preachers who both died before he could legally drink, his mother in a horrific car accident that left her quadriplegic for a time.

He says their deaths led to his embrace of the spiritual, and his music has long had Gospel overtones. "I can relive certain situations, because music tends to be a reenactment of an experience or an emotion," he tells me. "So, some of the things I chose to address aren't present-day for me, but they are cathartic. [The music] is very hopeful for me."

Both a rapper and a singer, his vocals aren't technically perfect, but they convey great vulnerability and pathos. On a track off of Goodie Mob's 1995 debut *Soul Food* called "Thought Process," he raps:

> I wanna lie to you sometimes, but I can't
> I wanna tell you that it's all good, but it ain't
> It's niggas hurtin' and uncertain 'bout if they gon'
>     make it or not

To Goodie Mob, Cee Lo brought an emotional honesty and commitment to black empowerment that shaped the group's thematic milieu. "A person like that, it drives you to be the best," Big Gipp told Marsha Gosho Oakes for the website SoulCulture. "It's not about being the new hot thing, and girls screaming 'cause they want you, it's about a person being touched emotionally and spiritually."

Though Andre and Big make appearances, *Soul Food* lacks the playful bent of OutKast's first work. It's a proclamation, not a party, a treatise on unemployment, depression, and low-income survival. The group members introduce themselves as blue collar champions of the downtrodden. "We consider ourselves the working class," T-Mo said. On "Thought Process," he raps:

> Lookin' for a come up, workin' from nine to five
> Just to get some change so T-Mo can stay alive

Using as its central metaphor the rich, communal staple of the southern diet, *Soul Food* confronts lies of American history and the persecution of African Americans, often in a surreal way.

"Dirty South" opens with a bizarre drug transaction involving Bill Clinton and *The Beverly Hillbillies'* Jed Clampett. Dungeon Family member Cool Breeze raps:

> See, life's a bitch then you figure out, why you really
>      got dropped in the Dirty South
> See in the third grade this is what you told, "You was
>      bought, you was sold"
> Now they sayin' juice left some heads cracked
> I betcha Jedd Clampett want his money back

The term "Dirty South" immediately went into widespread usage despite the fact that Cool Breeze, who coined it, remains largely forgotten. Though to many it refers to southern rap in all its raunchy glory, Goodie Mob was referencing the region's corrupt political nature and racial legacy. In the documentary *The Dirty South*, Khujo says the phrase refers to "the old prune-face ass-white folk" in Atlanta who are still running things. (For their parts, Luke Campbell and Scarface take umbrage with the term, with Luke insisting it applies only to Atlanta-area hip-hop, and Scarface unsatisfied with the implication that there's something unclean about their music.)

*Soul Food* was an unequivocal critical success, and remains a, if not *the*, quintessential southern hip-hop document. But though it won Goodie Mob the somewhat dubious title of "your favorite rapper's rappers," commercial success was elusive. The album and its 1998 follow-up *Still Standing* went gold, but this was before fans had begun rampantly stealing music digitally, and so half a million for a major label release wasn't considered much. The group members grew frustrated, particularly as OutKast's star continued to rise, and began to suspect their message was too narrow for mass consumption.

Third disc *World Party* tried a more saleable sound, but it too failed to move great numbers. Cee Lo left to pursue a solo career, while Khujo lost a segment of his right leg in a 2002 car accident. The group nonetheless plowed forward, releasing a new CD, mainly for financial reasons, called *One Monkey Don't Stop No Show*, which they insisted (with straight faces) wasn't a direct reference to their former mate. "It's a period in my career that I try not to even remember," said Big Gipp later.

Cee Lo went on to release well-regarded works on his own and collaborations with a former University of Georgia DJ named Danger Mouse, who specializes in musical mash-ups with songs from disparate genres. The pair called themselves Gnarls Barkley, and they mostly abandoned Cee Lo's politically conscious ideals in favor of universal themes, ironic humor, and *The Big Lebowski* costumes. "Crazy," a song about the intolerability of living inside your own head from their 2006 debut *St. Elsewhere*, became one of the most popular songs of the decade. A year later they posed with a model for the *Sports Illustrated* swimsuit issue.

Goodie Mob subsequently reunited in full, played a series of shows, and began working on new music. "Monkey" comments aside, they seem refocused on their original, values-oriented mission. "We represent a truth that most people would love to deny, wish they could, but can't and better not," Cee Lo told *Hip Hop Weekly* in 2010. "But we want to be equal parts enlightening and entertaining."

The group managed to eschew the self-aggrandizement, thug posturing, and wishful thinking that has long dominated hip-hop. Though southern rap has never been particularly cerebral, before or after them, Goodie Mob made art out of their own hard truths. This, as much as anything, is what the Dirty South is all about.

THE 1995 Source Hip-Hop Music Awards was quite possibly the most dramatic, momentous evening in the genre's history. Hosted by venerable Gotham rap magazine *The Source* at Madison Square

Garden's Paramount Theater, it stoked the fire of rap's famed East Coast/West Coast feud, was a precursor to tragedy, and anticipated the uprising of the South.

Things kicked into high gear when the ever-brazen Suge Knight lumbered onto the stage. The cofounder of Los Angeles–based Death Row Records was dressed down in a brightly colored polo shirt and not looking to make friends. He proceeded to diss hometown hero Sean Combs, mocking him for appearing on his artists' tracks and in their videos.

Rappers tired of this treatment should come to Death Row, he went on, to boos. Many in the crowd got up out of their seats and became even more infuriated when Snoop Dogg took the stage and began taunting them. This wasn't the mild-mannered Snoop Dogg of recent years, mind you, it was the bandana-clad, Crip-affiliated Snoop of old, a look of righteous fury in his eyes. "The East Coast ain't got no love for Dr. Dre and Snoop Dogg, and Death Row?" he asked, cussing the crowd out and seemingly ready to fight everyone at once.

Two years later Combs's and Knight's marquee artists, Notorious B.I.G. and Tupac Shakur, would be dead. Both murders remain unsolved, though members of the opposing camps have been tossed around as suspects for years. Besides making martyrs out of the rappers, the killings would permanently divide rap into two camps, at least in the mind of much of the public. The conventional wisdom has long held that you've got the East Coast, and you've got the West Coast, and they hate each other.

Or course, there was a third coast, as UGK called it, and it was coming of age right before everyone's eyes. The show also included a performance from Jermaine Dupri and his female protégée Da Brat, as well as an award for OutKast, chosen as best new group.

Yet no one in the audience seemed to know what to make of OutKast. Perhaps the evening's tension brought out the worst in the crowd. Whatever the reason, as Big and Andre made their way to the stage, folks began to boo. "We wanna say 'What's up' to New York, 'cause we from down south," said an ever-diplomatic Big Boi in his acceptance speech. "This y'all city. We just want to say 'What's up' to all the original MCs."

"I'm tired of folks, closed-minded folks," put in a shaken Andre, before restarting. "It's like we got a demo tape and don't nobody want to hear it. But the South got something to say, that's all I got to say."

Though it probably didn't seem like much at the time, Dre's offering became a rallying cry for underappreciated MCs from the bottom of the country. "I felt like that was the turning point," says Ludacris. "No one realized how big the South was going to blow up after that. I think [they] made a mark, making people take a second look at Atlanta and the South, period."

Andre and Big were initially upset. They weren't expecting a warm embrace from their northern peers, but they certainly hadn't foreseen outright hostility. "We were surprised at the hate," Big says, adding that it nonetheless spurred them forward. "From that moment it was nothing but motivation."

They buckled down in the studio, channeling their frustration and pride into 1996's *ATLiens* and its watershed follow-up, 1998's *Aquemini*. A track off of the latter album called "Rosa Parks" was specifically inspired by the Source Awards diss, inviting listeners to "move to the back of the bus," which served as a metaphor for hip-hop's new, OutKast-dominated order.

Andre's beat is driven by nonsense chants, down-home guitar riffs, and, during the breakdown, the sounds of a stomping country hootenanny complete with a harmonica solo performed by Andre's stepfather. It's a collage of southern influences from blues to country to folk.

"Rosa Parks" wasn't really about the titular civil rights icon, but that didn't stop an octogenarian Parks from filing suit for using her name without permission. Her niece said she didn't believe a dementia-addled Parks was behind the dispute, however, suggesting her handlers may have sought profit for themselves. OutKast quietly battled the charges, and the suit was settled out of court shortly before Parks's 2005 death.

TAKING OVER some production duties from Organized Noize, Big and Andre experimented with sound. They hauled in a baby grand piano and instructed their bass, guitar, and percussion players to play live in the studio, improvising everything from stoner funk to prog rock. "It was almost like a Motown," engineer Neal H. Pogue told *Creative Loafing* about the *Aquemini* sessions, likely referencing the sessions' collaborative, instrument-focused nature, atypical for rap records. "That's what I loved about it. It brought back that whole feeling of making records. It was organic."

*ATLiens* edged off of the gangsta motif and recast them as George Clinton–style extraterrestrials, and Andre underwent a major image overhaul. While visiting Jamaica and swimming in the ocean with beat maker Mr. DJ, they undid their cornrows and pledged to stop combing their hair. Before long Andre had dreadlocks, which he sometimes wore in a turban.

"I was young and wilder and some of my fashion choices people didn't accept at the time. I started getting flak from some people, so they were like, 'Either he's gay or on drugs,'" Andre said. But the reverse was true; though he'd been high throughout the recording of *Southernplayalisticadillacmuzik*, he'd since stopped smoking and drinking altogether and given up meat. "I was a young man searching, a young black man, so I was looking into Rastafarianism, Islam, whatever," he said. "I started to notice that all the stories were similar; it was more about a mutual respect and exchange of energy."

He was also inspired by his love interest, neo-soul singer Erykah Badu, with whom he became involved and had a son. A breakout star from Dallas who appears on *Aquemini*, Badu is known for her consciousness-expanding verses and eccentric sartorial taste. No one begrudged Andre his relationship with her, but his left-turn rhymes and style-overhaul—in a genre still obsessed with white Ts and sagging jeans—provoked a backlash. He responded on an *Aquemini* track called "Return of the 'G.'"

> The question is, "Big Boi, what's up with Andre?
> Is he in a cult? Is he on drugs? Is he gay?
> When y'all gon' break up? When y'all gon' wake up?"
> Nigga I'm feelin' better than ever. What's wrong with
>      you?

"At the end of the day, you've still got to go through the same neighborhoods so sometimes you have to say stuff to let people know what it is," Andre said. "I'm a man so you can't say some of this stuff to me."

Andre, the Gemini, was changing in ways his partner, the Aquarius, clearly didn't understand. At one point, when Andre began singing and using a pitch-corrector to modify his voice, Big advised him in no uncertain terms that the fellas in the streets weren't fans of his approach.

But they remained committed to each other, for the time being anyway, and in fact *Aquemini* won them a whole new caste of fans. By not attempting to please anybody, the work ended up pleasing everybody.

*The Source* gave it a perfect rating, and fickle northeasterners got on board as well. This was partly due to an assist from Raekwon, the Wu-Tang Clan member whose crew had won Best Group at the Source Awards. Having moved part-time down to Atlanta, he ran into Big one day at the mall. One thing led to another, and Raekwon was invited to the upgraded Dungeon, located in the basement of Rico Wade's new house.

Raekwon collaborated the Organized Noize–produced *Aque-mini* track "Skew It on the Bar-B," a futuristic jam determined sufficiently dope by New York radio. He insists it was the first southern song to go into rotation in his neck of the woods. "Before that, the South just wasn't played in New York," he says. "But that song was hot, the flows was crazy. The cycle changed. It really opened up the door for southern rappers."

NO MATTER how much Andre experimented, he couldn't shake his fans. *Stankonia*, which features mostly his and Big's genre-divergent production work, represented another commercial and critical peak, selling over four million copies and popping up on every critical best-list worth mentioning.

*Pitchfork* named frenetic first single "B.O.B. (Bombs Over Baghdad)" the number one single of the aughts, lauding the metal, electro, and rap-fused track for inspiring a decade's worth of crossover music. Its video begins with Andre sprinting out of a housing project into bright sunlight, pursued by a legion of children across purple grass. He jumps into a car that pulls off into traffic, and Big climbs into a tractor-trailer that doubles as a mobile strip club. Despite its antiwar overtones, the song reportedly became a favorite of American soldiers deployed overseas.

Another hit from the album, "Ms. Jackson" referenced Dre's relationship problems with Badu. (Her mother is the title character.) But around this time OutKast fans had something else to worry about—the increasingly frequent rumors that Andre was done with OutKast. The speculation was understandable, considering that the pair were now recording in separate studios. Yet even Big was shocked when Andre announced his next project would be a solo record.

Already experimenting with singing, he would begin taking guitar, saxophone, and clarinet lessons. He'd grown increasingly out of touch with the Dungeon Family's hip-hop aesthetic, which Big still embraced, and planned a more unconventional new work.

But their record label was not having it, so a tense negotiation ensued, resulting in a compromise: OutKast would release a double CD, *Speakerboxxx/The Love Below*, in 2003, featuring solo projects from each artist. Though it would go on to be the greatest-selling hip-hop album of all time, its creation was fraught with arguments and tears. To his horror, Big was only permitted to appear on one track on Andre's *The Love Below* CD, though Andre appears often on Big's *Speakerboxxx*.

Meanwhile, nearly everyone in Big's royal court makes guest appearances on his disc, from Dungeon Family protégée Killer Mike and Goodie Mob members to Jay-Z. (Even Big's young son Bamboo babbles on a track.) The work is a sonically dense blend of soul and progressive rap that includes a tribute to Screw music and includes the #1 pop hit, "The Way You Move," a love song featuring Sleepy Brown that begins by denying OutKast is finished.

While Big Boi was playing to his strengths, Andre veered almost completely off of the path. *The Love Below* minimizes rap in favor of cinematic jazz, classical interludes, and Prince impersonations. The protagonist is a lady's man named Ice Cold, who thinks he might be ready to settle down. Enlisting none other than God herself in his quest, he pleads his case for eternal love. "I've never cheated on any of my girlfriends. Well, except that one little time in Japan, but that was just head, and head don't count, right?"

God presents him with the perfect woman, but things don't go as planned. "Happy Valentine's Day" builds upon layers of sonic dissonance to reveal its ultimately unromantic intentions. Andre asks, "If you do not know me, then how could you be my friend?" Gargantuan hit "Hey Ya," meanwhile, subversively rallies against the concept of eternal love. "If what they say is, 'Nothing is forever,' then what makes love the exception?" asks the song, which was ubiquitous on easy-listening stations and in grocery stores.

*The Love Below* features almost all of his own beats, shutting out Organized Noize and leaving them embarrassed. The production team had been riding high for years, producing for artists like Ludacris and earning big paydays for gigs like two *Home Alone* soundtracks. But things began to look bleak. Hit with a mammoth bill for back taxes, Rico Wade filed for bankruptcy in 2004 and developed a nasty cocaine habit. Eventually a lien was put on his home and he was forced to move, abandoning the Dungeon.

AVERSE TO relationship commitment, romantic or otherwise, Andre committed himself to personal and artistic growth. Just as Michael Jordan had abandoned basketball for baseball at the height of his career, Andre fixated on expanding his repertoire.

He moved to Los Angeles to foster his nascent acting career, giving hit-or-miss performances in films like *Be Cool* and *Semi-Pro*. Having transitioned from baggy jerseys and  Kangol caps to tailored suits and fedoras, he took up fashion and became a full-on, bow-tie-clad dandy. The late aughts saw the launch of his Benjamin Bixby clothing line, inspired by college football uniforms from the Depression era.

Though he continued asserting that if it was up to him OutKast would be over, as always the duo proved resilient. They worked together on a 2006 film, *Idlewild*, the story of Prohibition-era cabaret performers in a small Georgia town. Andre and Big both give credible performances, and the film features dazzling cinematography, costumes, and dance scenes. Still, writer/director Bryan Barber's flimsy story line and weak stock characters were hard to overcome.

*Idlewild* performed poorly at the box office, and the soundtrack—which featured old and new OutKast creations—didn't stir up much interest. For the first time, an OutKast album performed worse than the one before it.

NOT MUCH OutKast music emerged in the years after *Idlewild*. Andre announced that he and Big would no longer answer questions about their future plans. Rumors of new projects would surface, however, and now and then the two of them would actually appear together on a song. Perhaps the most inspiring was "International Player's Anthem," a 2007 cut featuring UGK.

Ever-so-slightly recalling "Player's Ball," the song's video is set at Andre's (fictitious) wedding, of all places. He wears a kilt, which earns him jeers from an assembled cast of MCs. "The only thing I wanna know is," says Three 6 Mafia's DJ Paul, "why is he dressed like 'Rowdy' [Roddy] Piper?"

"I got Scottish in my family," explains Andre.

Big Boi plays the best man, dutifully flanking his partner at the altar and handing him the ring. Rapping along while Big Boi mouths his words, Andre says, "Keep your heart, Three Stacks, keep your heart."

Hints like this suggested to the faithful that Andre's attitude had shifted, if only slightly. Though he had grown apart from his childhood friend, they still had plenty in common. Perhaps there was a reason they'd stayed together all these years, even at arm's length. Big remained where he'd always been—by Andre's side, waiting for him to come to his senses.

Before I finish speaking with Big at the Haiti benefit, I ask him about any pet peeves he has about Andre. From the outrageous outfits, to the musical experiments, to the subliminal disses, what does he wish Andre would have done differently?

Big pauses, just for a second, to let me know he's given my question as much consideration as it deserves. "Nothing," he says.

# 7

# CASH MONEY, NO LIMIT, AND JUVENILE

■ ■ ■

## Bling and Murder in New Orleans

FOR A TIME Cash Money Records recorded out of a building that had previously housed the Louisiana Center for Retarded Citizens. Their original offices were in a squat building made of cinder blocks, between a body shop and a hot tub dealer. Before they had outgrown these digs, they'd made a deal with Universal Records worth tens of millions of dollars and were on their way to becoming one of the bestselling independent labels in history.

Along with No Limit, another wildly popular imprint started by a New Orleans project boy, Cash Money's greatest influence was its story: that kids from the slums could become rap stars and buy up the biggest mansions and the fanciest cars. Nowadays, you could say that's rap's *only* story.

The products of a dad who fathered some two dozen other children and a mother who died while they were still kids, Bryan "Baby" Williams and his older brother Ronald "Slim" Williams founded Cash Money in the early 1990s. They combined the street savvy they'd acquired in the Magnolia Projects with the entrepreneurial skills their father—who had his own grocery store and tavern—encouraged in them. His cash advance also helped.

Master P was raised in a Second Ward housing project called Calliope, and later followed his mother to Richmond, California, where he opened a record store called No Limit. He quickly learned the business and decided he wanted more of the pie. He wouldn't just sell the music: he'd make it, market it, and use it to sell other products, too.

After popularizing No Limit's label, he signed on with a major distribution company, Priority Records, which had previously paired up with N.W.A. Typically the independent gets an infusion of cash in these types of deals while ceding future profits. P, however, negotiated to keep his master recordings, which meant he would get most of the royalties.

The Williams brothers negotiated a similar arrangement for Cash Money. "Baby got a better deal for Cash Money than any of the suits from Harvard or Howard could have ever gotten," writes Def Jam Records cofounder Russell Simmons in his book, *Do You!* Simmons adds that he'd previously attempted to negotiate with Cash Money for Def Jam, but Baby wouldn't agree to his terms. "The way it went down was so gangster."

Cash Money and No Limit changed hip-hop by employing a new business model. Rather than trusting outsiders, they kept things in the family. If they couldn't hire their own siblings or offspring, they worked with others and made them blood. The only problem was when you're dividing up money among family, you're bound to fight like family.


BEFORE THERE was New Orleans hip-hop, there was bounce music. With the city's each-day-as-your-last mentality, its residents have long thrived on festive rhythms, and for two decades bounce has been New Orleans's party soundtrack.

Known for its bawdy calls and influenced by the cries of Mardi Gras Indians (merrymakers who dress up in Native American–inspired garb and march during Mardi Gras), bounce mimics the exuberance of Miami bass. Yet its rhythmic DNA can be traced to a single 1986 song called "Drag Rap," from a Queens group called the Showboys.

The track borrows the "Dum, de dum dum/ Dum, de dum dum dum" melody from the *Dragnet* theme and is dominated by xylophone and 808 drums. Yes, it's bizarre that an almost-unknown New York City borough act could shape an entire Crescent City subculture, but countless bounce songs sample "Drag Rap," which is also known as "Triggerman," after the tune's protagonist.

The bounce scene served as a proving ground for many rappers who later signed to Master P's and the Williams brothers' labels, including U.N.L.V. (Uptown Niggas Living Violently), Mia X, Soulja Slim, Choppa, and, the biggest of all, Juvenile.

Before he became a bounce celebrity, Juvenile grew up listening to Run-DMC, MC Lyte, and the Beastie Boys, and would buy absolutely any hip-hop tape that came out. "[Rap] was my therapy, my exercise, my football, my basketball; it was everything to me," he says, adding that he started recording raps to test himself. "Was I going to sound like everybody else? Was I going to sound better? Where would I fit in?"

He and his friend from the projects, Magnolia Slim (who later became Soulja Slim), put their own aggressive spin on bounce, which they called "Where They At" music due to its call-and-response chants. Juvenile's 1995 Warlock Records debut *Being Myself* includes tales of drugging, fucking, and beefing—"Snort a powder bag/ Snort a powder bag" is one refrain—that are quite danceable. But he didn't initially have pretensions of emceeing full time. It was the early nineties, after all, and there weren't many break-out southern rap stars for him to emulate.

Besides, he had a family to support and already possessed a good job working for an environmental company. His responsibilities included cleaning out furnaces and installing new catalysts when plants shut down, a job that kept him plenty busy during his city's era of decline.

But by the mid-nineties Cash Money was coming into its own through a number of locally successful bounce releases. Baby and Slim pursued Juvenile partly because they desired a harder sound and partly because their other artists lacked professionalism. "We was trying to teach them the way to do this thing—as far as handling meetings, signing autographs, doing interviews, showing up on time for shows—but they wasn't hungry enough," Slim told *Rolling Stone.* "They'd make a little money and everything would just go to the wind. They were getting into drugs, smoking weed, and it was taking away from them handling their business."

Juve said they needed to pay him $2,000 a week so he could quit his job; they agreed to his terms and promptly dropped just about everyone else on their roster, notes Juvenile. He chuckles, before drawing back his grin and shaking his head. "That made me feel bad, a little bit. I didn't want to be the reason someone got released." (Early label signees Kilo-G, Pimp Daddy, and Yella Boy, in fact, were subsequently murdered, though the circumstances of their deaths are poorly documented.)

A major draw for Juvenile was the label's in-house producer, Mannie Fresh. Fresh had learned his craft on his father's drum machines and joined a local hip-hop group called New York Incorporated in the mid-eighties when he was fifteen or sixteen. The group, which also included future No Limit MC Mia X, has been called New Orleans's first rap act. Though he'd worked with coastal artists, he was adamant about pursuing a regional sound and could seemingly make beats as easily as he drew breath, conceiving songs practically on demand. "I work better fast," Fresh said. "A lot of people are afraid to take a chance on the first thing that pops in their head. They looking for a gimmick. But if you looking for a hit, you less likely to get one than if you just let it come to you."

He felt the market was oversaturated with bounce, so he began developing his trademark brand of apocalyptic electro-funk for which the label would become known. (He made all of their songs from this era, after all.) Though sometimes rooted in "Triggerman" samples, his compositions had dark undertones that appealed to Juvenile. He says he came to Cash Money largely for a Fresh composition called "Bad Ass Yellow Boy," which he eventually appropriated for his 2001 song "Set It Off." "I was like, 'Man, that's a hit. But if I was on it, damn, it would be even more of a hit.'"

Fresh and Juvenile were a transcendent pairing. Scrawny but serious, employing a nearly impenetrable bayou accent and a flow that combined machine-gun raps with off-balance crooning, the MC could ride the producer's bucking bronco beats like no one else. On "Solja Rag," off of his first Cash Money album, 1997's *Solja Rags*, he poses a series of hypothetical questions, chiding a would-be gangsta and daring him to follow through. "Can you hustle like it's legal? Can you avoid da people?/ And hotwire your Regal? You 'bout dat evil?" At the same time, he sketches out his own blueprint for success. "Is you da man? Do you pay all of your bills?/ Did you make a plan? And won't stop till it fulfilled?"

The first single off his follow-up album *400 Degreez*, "Ha," serves as the sequel to "Solja Rag," telling the next bleak chapter of a soldier's ascent, each assessment punctuated by a manic "Ha!"

> That's you with that badass Benz, ha!
> That's you that can't keep yo' old lady 'cause you keep
>     fuckin' her friends, ha!
> You gotta go to court, ha!
> You got served a subpoena for child support, ha!

Its Marc Klasfeld–directed video boasts a journalistic quality, from the pigtailed girl bouncing on a discarded mattress, to the kid feeding his dog lunch meat, to the Rottweiler on guard atop someone's Cutlass. It is set in the now-demolished Magnolia projects, the spot once called "the most likely place to be killed in New Orleans" in a *Times-Picayune* article (and this in a city that regularly has the country's highest murder rates).

By speaking on a moral code in flux, of the struggle between doing what's right and what's necessary, Juvenile became one of his era's fiercest and most compelling MCs. He was the first southern hip-hop artist I ever fell for, and "Ha" still gives me chills.

MOST RAPPERS will say they got their starts selling their CDs "out the trunk." This can be taken both literally and as a euphemism for hustling copies to friends, family, and strangers, as well as putting them on consignment at mom-and-pop record stores, barbershops, and clothing boutiques. The do-it-yourself ethos is especially strong in the South.

"A lot of us put out records on an independent basis before we got signed to a major label deal," says Ludacris. "We promote, market, press up, mix, and master it ourselves, and then we distribute it either through local distributors or by pushing it out the trunk. So that whole process of doing it all on our own, I think that has a lot to do with our success. It's like, we had practice way before we even got on a major scale."

Ludacris signed to the fledgling Def Jam South label around the turn of the millennium. But before the majors started sniffing around down south, a path to the top was less clear. Even selling your album to everyone in your town wasn't going to get you on the radar of the New York types. And so imprints like Luke Records, Rap-A-Lot, and Suave House pressed up CDs themselves and sold them through regional channels like Select-O-Hits and Southwest Wholesale.

Cash Money employed this model, as did Master P. Though he first established No Limit in the Bay Area, after coming back home he created the archetype of the independent rap hustler turned multimillionaire, convincing countless other would-be entrepreneurs they could do the same. Even his name was meant to indicate that the previously disenfranchised had taken control. "We come from slaves, us calling them master," he explained to allhiphop.com. "I look at my grandparents. I said, 'That master thing, I'ma take it to a whole new level. I wanna master what ever I do. Instead of us calling them that, they will call us that.'"

Yet for all his fame, P has always given off an aura of anonymity, with a soft, malleable face capable of exuding fierceness in his rap videos, intensity on the basketball court, and charisma in his comedy films. It's difficult to get inside his head, and none of the profiles on him that I've read do a good job of bringing him to life.

Part of the problem is that he became so successful so fast that he had already made history before anyone really got a chance to write him up. Another is that he manages his image and his story with great gusto but not always with great accuracy. In their 1998 piece about his experience playing professional basketball, for example, *New York Times* journalists found that his currently claimed year of birth (1970) and graduation year from Warren Easton High School in New Orleans (1987) made him two years younger than he'd claimed in college, meaning he either falsified his age then or was doing so now. For such reasons the mythology surrounding him and No Limit Records is difficult to penetrate. But here goes.

Born Percy Miller, P was raised in the also-crime-ridden Calliope projects along with his sister and three brothers. Two of his brothers would become platinum rappers along with him, but the other one, Kevin, was killed while dealing drugs. P sought a better life for himself through basketball, playing briefly at the University of Houston before injuring his knee.

He eventually made it out to Richmond, California, where, after
the death of his grandfather brought a $10,000 windfall, he opened
the No Limit Records shop. As he tells it, the landlord agreed to
wave the rent for six months so long as he fixed up and painted
the building. Before long, P had built a successful business and
began putting together his label. At its center, he decided, would
be himself. Though a largely unpracticed rapper, he believed his
message had appeal.

"I've been through so much in my life," he told Skee.TV. "That's
what music's really about, about a story, about building your culture. . . . It's the way you deliver it and give it to your audience. And
that's what I learned to do, give it to my audience in a unique way."

While many rappers sought to cross over to the presumably
more-lucrative white audience, P's target market was the folks
in the hood, and he focused on them with laser accuracy. He
recruited his two brothers, Corey Miller (C-Murder) and Vyshonn
Miller (Silkk the Shocker)—two guys who shared his story—and
with some other California artists formed a group called TRU, The
Real Untouchables. P even made an album with his wife, Sonya.

The covers of his first works, like 1991's *Get Away Clean* and
1992's *Mama's Bad Boy*, promise a "Booming Album," and the
sound is distinctly West Coast g-funk. The works see him slowly
developing his themes, which can be roughly summed up by the
title of one *Mama's Bad Boy* track, "Dope, Pussy, and Money."
Like every other hard-edged rapper, P contends that he's not so
much glorifying street mayhem as presenting it as it really is,
though Roni Sarig notes the irony of P's celebration of violence
in the wake of his brother Kevin's murder. Another gangsta-rap-
apologist argument is that everyone knows it's fake, just as they
do *The Godfather*. This seems to make some sense, especially considering that gangster movies are common primary source material for rap songs and monikers; as Ned Sublette points out in his
book *The Year Before the Flood*, not only did Cash Money get their

name from the 1991 film *New Jack City*, they co-opted its gang's dollar-sign motto as well. Yet this claim is made more complicated by the fact that Master P and his cohorts claim to make "reality rap" and emphasize its authenticity. (Unless it doesn't suit them, that is. During C-Murder's murder prosecution, his associates claimed his nickname was inspired by his witnessing, rather than committing, bloodshed; that is, that he would frequently "see murder.")

Gangsta MCs' final argument in their own defense is that it's better to be rapping about eliminating foes than actually taking them out, and this logic holds up. Indeed, the number of criminals turned tax-paying ASCAP members is not insignificant, and I have yet to see any evidence that they're making things worse simply by *talking* about crime—any more than *Grand Theft Auto*, at least.

In any case, before long P had built a California following and begun trafficking his music through local distributors Solar Music Group and In-A-Minute. He released a top-selling compilation, *West Coast Bad Boyz: Another Level of the Game*, and attempted to replicate his success with a down south compilation. Touting a return to his roots, he reached out to New Orleans artists like KLC, an Uptown producer who, along with Mo B. Dick, Craig B, and O'Dell, would form No Limit's in-house production team Beats by the Pound. As prolific as their name implies, they would fashion the label's signature brassy, military procession sound.

KLC later brought to P's attention the combustible talent Soulja Slim, who had flirted with Cash Money but eventually signed to No Limit. Since his early teens, Slim had been both a rapper's rapper and a gangsta's gangsta, the kind of guy who might start a jailhouse fight with the purpose of being thrown into solitary confinement—so he could write lyrics in peace. He was an utterly fearless street warrior who would imbibe coke and heroin and then, if he ran out, rob at gunpoint to score more. "I might be out there and jack this nigga this night and be out there at the concert with the gat in my back pocket, rappin' on stage," he told *Murder Dog*.

Though his nihilism made his music a tough sell for the mainstream, his reckless lifestyle and true-crime stories made him a street legend and, by many accounts, the most popular rapper in the city. It didn't matter how many times he was shot up or incarcerated—he spent five years of his short life in the can—he was a soldier to his core. In fact, he claimed to be the originator of the "soldier" trope that would inform the No Limit lingo, its camouflage garb, and its tank logo.

Understandably, Soulja Slim's volatility initially gave P pause, but he would go on to be the spiritual core of the label, the guy who epitomized "reality rap" more than anyone else. It was tragic but not surprising, then, when he was gunned down in front of his mother's house in 2003. There were no serious suspects, and the case went unsolved; Slim had a lot of enemies, after all. Even some of his close musical associates betrayed him after he passed, stealing his Rolex right off of his arm, as well as his clothes, shoes, and laptop out of his mother's house. "I knew God before Slim died, but not like I know Him now," she told writer Nik Cohn.

But Soulja Slim got something in death that he never had in life—a mainstream hit. Less than a year after his murder, his collaboration with Juvenile, "Slow Motion," hit #1 on *Billboard*'s Hot 100. "Slow down for me, you moving too fast," he raps. "My fingers keep slipping, I'm trying to grip that ass/ Keep being hard-headed and I'ma make you get on me/ Got a human-up disguise but my face is a doggy."

THE BODY of Cash Money cofounder Baby is covered in tattooed portraits: of his daughter, his son, his parents, and his brother. On his right pectoral is a giant image of Lil Wayne. Wayne calls Baby his daddy, but they are not related, though Baby has served as something of a surrogate father to Wayne ever since his stepfather was murdered when he was a teenager.

The day of the death, in fact, Baby picked Wayne up at the hospital. "I was in the passenger seat of his car and I was crying and he looked at me and was like, 'Nigga, what you cryin' for? You act like you lost your father,'" Wayne told allhiphop.com. "And from that day on I never lost my father."

"Before I had a child, Wayne and all of [my artists] were my children," Baby told a New Orleans radio station in 2006, by way of explanation for a photo that had emerged of the two of them locking lips, which sent tremors throughout the homophobic hip-hop community. "Wayne to me is my son—my firstborn son."

His second, then, might have been rapper B.G., the honey-voiced "Baby Gangsta," whose father was also murdered and who similarly joined Cash Money before he became a teenager. Juvenile says he too felt like part of the family, though his own parents were alive and well. But the organization also had cultish overtones; Baby and Slim for a time didn't allow their artists to bring friends by the offices, ostensibly so they could stay focused.

"We don't condone outsiders," said Mannie Fresh. "We went through a long time where it was hell trying to get these guys to understand that. Because they young kids, and they think everybody's they friend and everybody's cool with them, but we don't know these people, and you might not really know these people, either."

"I ain't old, but I feel it's too late for me to make new friends, anyway," added Wayne, sixteen at the time.

While the Cash Money artists undoubtedly felt genuine affection for each other, their camaraderie was likely fueled by their success, first and foremost in the form of the lucrative contract they'd just signed with Universal. Having sat on the sidelines while No Limit took off, the major label had been anxious to get into the southern rap scene. And so after seeing Cash Money artists move tens of thousands of albums through regional distributors like Gonzales Music Wholesale, they felt it was time to partner up.

Their 1998 deal entitled Cash Money to ownership of their publishing royalties and masters, a $3 million annual advance, and 80 percent of sales profits. They also got $30 million over three years to use for videos, marketing, touring, and recording. "But the thing just took off, and now they're selling, like, 500,000 records a month, every month, with very little overhead," said Dino Delvaille, the Universal representative who signed Cash Money, in 2000. "That amounts to a lot of money for them and for us. Whatever money we gave them initially, within a year they made it all back. Now we're giving them a check every month that's in the millions."

"I studied Master P, I studied Suge and Diddy, because I didn't wanna make the same mistakes," Baby said, by way of explanation for his extraordinary agreement. "I went into it with that attitude like, 'I ain't giving them shit—if they wanna fuck with us, they'll fuck with us how I want them to fuck with us.'"

The first fruit of their partnership, Juvenile's *400 Degreez*, would also be their most lucrative, selling more than four million copies. To celebrate the windfall brought to the label by this and other platinum works, Baby and Slim purchased a battalion of Bentleys for everybody, souped-up with features like giant chrome rims, televisions, and blue mink carpeting.

"We fucked up everybody by puttin' rims on these Bentleys," Fresh said. "We was up at Justin's"—Puffy's New York restaurant—"and those guys be like, 'Man, what the fuck wrong with y'all? You don't do that to no Bentley.' I was like, 'Fuck that—I bought it, I gonna put some rims on it, some TVs in that bitch.' I had to tear that motherfucker down."

Juvenile's blue Bentley sported a tricked-out sound system and a promotional display; when you opened the trunk a mounted copy of *400 Degreez* spun atop a tiny motor. Of course, after featuring it in a video the car became passé, he decided, so he ditched it for a Rolls-Royce. "I had to get rid of it," says Juvenile, who was twenty-three at the time, "because everybody knew it."

Also taking off was B.G., who was only eighteen when he released the platinum-selling *Chopper City in the Ghetto*. It spawned the hit "Bling Bling," a term which eventually made the dictionary and the vocabularies of old white ladies in Hollywood movies. Oh, and John McLaughlin, whom I was somewhat astonished to hear use it repeatedly on a recent episode of *The McLaughlin Group*.

B.G. was also a member of the Hot Boys—a Cash Money supergroup named for a truly terrifying Uptown New Orleans gang—which also featured Juvenile, Lil Wayne, and another Magnolia rapper, Turk. Everyone except Juvenile was a teen when the act formed, but unlike kiddie group Kris Kross they were genuine spitters with remarkable chemistry.

Per the title of their 1997 debut *Get It How U Live!*, their stories tended to play out in real life. After B.G.'s 2000 follow-up *Checkmate* he cut ties with Cash Money and checked himself into rehab over a heroin addiction, and in 2009 alone he was arrested four times on gun and firearm charges. Lil Wayne was jailed in New York on a gun conviction, while Juvenile had his own scrapes with the law and faced accusations that he beat up a barber who was pirating his music. Even worse, in 2008 his daughter Jelani was slain, along with her mother and half sister. Jelani's half brother was suspected in the murder.

But it was Turk's troubles that most hampered his career. In 2004, acting on information that heroin was being stored on the premises, narcotics officers backed by a SWAT team forced their way into the Memphis home of his girlfriend. A gunfight ensued and Turk, hiding in a closet, allegedly shot an officer in the jaw. (Turk claimed he was unarmed.) Already sought on a probation violation, he was convicted of second-degree attempted murder and sentenced to ten years in prison.

Descriptions of the incident bear similarities to the Hot Boys'
1999 "We on Fire" video. In it, a group of ATF officers surround a
house and attempt a drug bust. Art diverges from life, however, as
the guys escape, jumping through a window and running through
the streets, bags of money tied around their necks.


IN 1998 No Limit's Master P relocated to a gated community outside of Baton Rouge, an hour or so drive away from New Orleans,
near where P's mothers' ancestors had been slaves. His new
hood was called the Country Club. Joining him were his brothers C-Murder and Silkk the Shocker and compellingly aggressive,
oddly lyrical New Orleans barker Mystikal, who would later break
big with the Neptunes' produced track "Shake Ya Ass." Also in tow
was West Coast legend Snoop Dogg, a rapper with family roots
in Mississippi, whom No Limit had snagged from an imploding
Death Row Records. They weren't allowed to join the golf club,
they complained.

But no matter. No Limit was already in the midst of an
unprecedented late nineties run. The roster had expanded to
include artists like Kane & Abel, Young Bleed, Steady Mobb'n, and
Mr. Serv-On, and just about everything they put out became a top
seller. P claims his label moved 75 million copies all told; even if
it's only half that, it's still a staggering number considering that
the bulk of their sales happened in just a few years and that they
lacked much of anything that could count as a crossover hit.

No Limit farmed out many of its covers to Houston design firm
Pen & Pixel, recognizable for their garish props, poor use of Pho-
toshop, lack of perspective, and general awesomeness. But otherwise the label functioned as something of a hip-hop assembly
line, writing and producing their music in-house and putting out
albums as fast as they could be recorded. "My thing was, with No
Limit, when you're hot, you're hot," P told MTV. "When you got

a fan base, feed that fan base. There's no such thing as too much music."

Estimates for No Limit's profits are widely varied, but reports of sales in 1998, one of the label's peak years, are about $160 million, with P said to pocket about $56 million. Before long P was named hip-hop's highest earner by Guinness World Records. Dubbing himself "Ghetto Bill" (as in Gates), he earned spots on lists of the richest entertainers and the wealthiest people under forty. He even made the cover of *Fortune*, which is, believe it or not, the most supreme accomplishment a rapper can hope for.

He could not have been accused of being spendthrift with his money. His vehicles included a Chevy Impala that changed color, a Gucci-customized Ferrari, and a Gucci-customized helicopter, the latter of which can be seen, along with an elephant and various midgets, in the 504 Boyz's video "Get Back." (The group included him and his brothers, and is named for the New Orleans area code, while "Get Back" has a vague safari theme.)

But he wasn't just stuntin'; he aimed to spread the wealth around. "You know me and Silkk started this from nothing and we brothers," P told MTV, explaining the meaning of their tune "You Eat, I Eat." "It's just a song saying whoever got it, it don't matter. If I got a dollar, he got a dollar. If he got a dollar, I got a dollar. Blood is thicker than water."

More than just the brains behind the operation, P continued to be the imprint's marquee star. Despite his lackluster flow, he churned out jams like "Break 'Em Off Somethin'" and "Make 'Em Say Ugh," undeniable sing-alongs despite their unpolished rapping and raw singing. One of his signature songs was "I'm Bout It, Bout It," with TRU, an affirmation of the hard-knock life P and many of his fans were born into. It even birthed a straight-to-video movie, *I'm Bout It*. Filmed in the Calliope projects, it stars P and his label mates and serves as an ostensible biopic about the life and death of his brother Kevin.

Surprisingly, No Limit's film arm proved remarkably resilient. Their poorly written, shoestring-budget first flicks succeeded because they felt real; it seemed obvious that the guys playing the drug dealers had actual drug-dealing experience. As for sheer watchability, the catalog is hit-and-miss. Offsetting low-budget dreck like *MP Da Last Don*—a derivative mafia fantasy in which the undeniably African American P plays the unkillable Cuban mafia heir Nino Corleone—are quite funny Hollywood comedies like *I Got the Hook Up*, where P takes on the role of an urban businessman who tries to get rich quick selling boosted cell phones.

The flicks featured No Limit music, starred No Limit artists, and served as wonderful cross promotion for the label. They also reinforced its brand, catering almost exclusively to an underserved inner-city audience. If Hollywood thought they could have made much money on this demographic, they would have been doing the same thing, and P deserves credit both for his inspired marketing and do-it-yourself spirit, one that a hard-core punk could love.

In other business realms, however, he employed a throw-shit-against-the-wall-and-see-what-sticks approach, which didn't often prove successful. Shortly after their launching, many of his ventures, in rims, shoes, real estate, clothing, toys, telecommunications, gas, phone sex, and sports management, promptly disappeared—if they ever were particularly serious in the first place. Never mind the immodest title of his 2007 motivational self-help book, *Guaranteed Success*.

Indeed, P had overextended himself, and No Limit Records began to fall off around the time he attempted an NBA career. In 1998, when the label was at its peak and he was probably about thirty, he played briefly with the Continental Basketball Association team Fort Wayne Fury, where he famously was paid $1,000 per week, and a $15 per diem during training camp. ("Man, I ain't letting nothing get by me," he explained of his decision to accept the modest meal money.) Yet despite drawing scores of fans to his tryout sessions, he was later cut by the Toronto Raptors and Charlotte Hornets.

The following year Beats by the Pound's lawyer discouraged them from signing a No Limit contract, and they departed. The label itself wouldn't last much longer, as P began focusing on the career of his son Percy Romeo Miller, who went by Lil' Romeo. He released a half dozen or so albums during the aughts and had a successful acting career, highlighted by a Nickelodeon show called *Romeo!* that ran for a few years. Both he and P also appeared on *Dancing with the Stars*.

But, like his father, his story had holes. In 2003—the year No Limit filed for bankruptcy—*48 Hours* reported that the fourteen-year-old had sold twenty million CDs and quoted him saying that he had $50 million in savings. Both figures are preposterous. His acting career had just begun, for one thing, and his record sales were relatively paltry; the Recording Industry Association of America's website reports that only his first album sold as many as five hundred thousand copies.

There is no doubt, however, that Romeo had a hit with his potato chip line, called Rap Snacks; bag covers with his face on them lined gas station shelves in Saint Louis when I was there. "I just wanted to change the chip game," he explained.

But the Miller family faced real problems in 2002, when P's brother C-Murder was charged with second-degree murder in the shooting of a teenager, a fan of his, at a New Orleans–area club. C-Murder served three years before being granted a retrial, but in 2009 he was found guilty again and sentenced to life in prison.

While in jail he began calling himself C-Miller, and he was not able to take part in the 2010 VH1 Hip Hop Honors show, which formally honored his brother P. It was a big moment for the family, and P, in interviews, spent much of the time talking about his brood. He called himself the "Archie Manning of hip-hop," and touted the careers of Romeo and another of his sons, Valentino, who represented the torch-passing New No Limit Records.

But P's plugs served mainly to underscore the speed of the original No Limit Records' descent. As noted by Andrew Noz, by 2008 almost all of the label's Priority catalog had gone out of print, baffling for works that had moved millions of copies only a decade earlier. "I understand that it was more P's carpet bomb marketing plan that sold a lot of this music and not the actual quality of the music," he wrote. "Once the tank was no longer a force, these records were wiped from the national consciousness."

CASH MONEY appeared to be reaching its zenith in 1999, when albums from Juvenile, Lil Wayne, B.G., and the Hot Boys all went platinum, each reaching #1 or #2. The massive success seemed unsustainable, and many expected the label to quickly burn out like No Limit. Indeed, in the coming years Cash Money's most important artists departed, one after another, including each Hot Boy (except Lil Wayne) and producer Mannie Fresh.

Each alleged financial improprieties. Turk contended that he'd signed on without his mother's permission, and B.G. accused the label of double-dipping by supplying his manager. "Your manager is supposed to go to bat for you with the record company," he told HipHopDX in 2005. "When you got both of them working with the same titles, then your business is bound to get fucked up."

Mannie Fresh left Cash Money shortly after Hurricane Katrina and later told *Hip Hop Weekly* that his time on the label was tantamount to "slavery." Though he admitted that his tendency to craft beats all day and night might have hindered his ability to keep his business straight, his financial complaints were echoed by other producers, including Jim Jonsin and Bangladesh. No Limit artists like Soulja Slim complained of underpayment as well.

Fresh and many of the Cash Money and No Limit rappers worked without formal contracts, which was bound to cause friction, and their various troubles with drugs and the law didn't help matters. But Juvenile's relationship with Cash Money seemed especially contentious. He left and rejoined the imprint at least twice and in 2006 went on a tirade against Baby, asserting he was owed money and suggesting they meet somewhere to fight.

"I thought he had a personal vendetta against me," Juvenile says now. "I thought it was personal, and that was why the financial part wasn't happening. It was like, 'Damn, what I do ya but make you rich? Why you don't want to pay me?'"

Yet despite the gutting of their core lineup, Cash Money has not just survived, but prospered. To replace Mannie Fresh, Baby and Slim enlisted a team of slick, largely anonymous, pop-minded producers, and in the late aughts Lil Wayne ascended to the very top of the cultural landscape. He established his own offshoot label called Young Money, and the umbrella company reeled off a series of savvy signings.

These included a rocker named Kevin Rudolf, British R&B singer Jay Sean, and two of the most popular rappers of the early 2010s, the highly theatrical MC Nicki Minaj and Drake, an alum of *Degrassi: The Next Generation* from Toronto. They both became ubiquitous radio presences. All told, in the first week of December 2009 Cash Money artists were featured on eight of *Billboard*'s Hot 100 songs, and another eight were in the R&B/rap top fifty.

Performing as an artist called Birdman, Baby himself has also been a big part of Cash Money's resurgence. Though he's over forty, his flow is stodgy, and his lyrics are dull, he's had a string of hits over the last decade or so, both solo and with Mannie Fresh (as Big Tymers) and Lil Wayne (*Like Father, Like Son*). He speaks the language of youth, possesses a certain gravitas, and understands that materialism never goes out of style. If another artist has one Phantom in his video, Baby has ten. As Sublette puts it, "His image

had great emotional power for children of single mothers: a violently protective, infinitely permissive, surreally wealthy, doting
father, who was into the same thing the kids were"; that is, cars,
jewels, and chicks.

I meet Baby at an entertainment law class on the campus of
Pace Law School, deep in the New York suburbs, where he's speaking before a half-empty room of aspiring attorneys. It's odd that
he's not out somewhere promoting his fourth solo album *Pricele$$*,
which drops today, but apparently he's come at the behest of the
class's linebacker-physiqued instructor, Vernon Brown, who also
serves as Cash Money's lawyer.

To Baby's right on the panel is Jay Sean, whose Cash Money debut
*All or Nothing* is also being released today. Both it and *Pricele$$* will
go on to sell about thirty thousand units in their first week; not
spectacular, but solid. Speaking with an eloquent European diction,
Sean is clearly thrilled to be linked up with Cash Money.

So is Mack Maine, a rapper who serves as the president of
Young Money, who sits at Baby's left. He gets his name from the
New Orleans school he and Lil Wayne attended, Eleanor McMain
Secondary, and his green undershirt can barely contain his biceps.
It's unfortunate to hear him say he isn't too worried about the fine
print in his contract because Cash Money is his "family," but Baby
appreciates this attitude. "Mack is not just an artist," he says, "he's
like my little brother. Other labels aren't trying to look out for him,
but I'm trying to give him a nice deal, nice money."

Baby's brother, the towering Slim, is also in the building. He
arrived in the group's motorcade of four black Cadillac SUVs, but
he hangs out in the back of the hall and doesn't say a word the
whole time. Indeed, it's Baby's show, and he clearly feels comfort-
able before a crowd that is more educated than he. Sporting sunglasses that hide some, but not all, of his facial tattoos, he notes
that, growing up, his family never had TVs. "So now I have forty
or fifty of them," he says.

I later speak with him about his prickly relationship with long-time distributor Universal. "If I was making moves the way corporate wanted us to make moves, I probably wouldn't be in business," he gripes. "I'm still fighting for some of the same shit that they shouldn't be fucking with me about. I understand what an artist goes through because I play both sides of the fence, the artist and the CEO shit. So I understand why a lot of these artists are crippled."

The major labels tend to hamper performers' long-term careers, he goes on, because they don't give them a chance to develop. Unlike Cash Money, they don't put their faith in an MC's vision, and don't take him under their wing. "To corporate, you're just an artist in a box," he says. "But when you fuck with us, you inherit a family."

HURRICANE KATRINA may have decimated what was left of New Orleans hip-hop. The 2005 storm overwhelmed the levees, flooded the city, and caused the deaths of some eighteen hundred people. Many of the survivors relocated elsewhere. The disaster's cultural impact has been similarly devastating, and the rap scene is a skeleton of its glory days.

Much of this was already in the making. Master P, after all, had left the state for Beverly Hills years earlier. Soulja Slim was dead, and, like C-Murder and Turk, Mystikal was in prison, doing six years for sexually assaulting his hair stylist (he ill-advisedly had the crime videotaped). Lil Wayne moved to Miami, and shortly after the hurricane Cash Money relocated there as well.

But Juvenile never considered leaving, even after Katrina destroyed his house in the suburb of Slidell. "Truthfully, I never thought about [not rebuilding]," he says. "I just did it like everyone else in my neighborhood. . . . A hurricane like that happens every fifty years. I don't see another one happening anytime soon."

I spend an afternoon with him in Manhattan, at the CBS building on West Fifty-Seventh Street, where he's filming an episode of BET's video countdown show *106 & Park*. He's popping Halls and drinking Lipton tea to calm his throat—he did a show last night and feels something coming on—and is an hour late for our meeting because his driver initially took him all the way to Harlem, where the show *used* to be filmed.

A slight man, thin and short, Juvenile's still got that deep, gruff voice, and the top row of his teeth are covered in gold grills, so thick that they push his lip out. Now in his mid-thirties, he's been answering reporters' questions for half of a lifetime, so he tries to keep himself entertained while we talk by fooling around with his fancy new Canon. The best part about it, he says, is that it doubles as a high-quality video camera, thus freeing him from needing permits for video shoots.

Juvenile started off as a regional star and, two decades into his career, seems to be regressing back into one. A new Juvenile album isn't the event that it used to be. His 2006 album *Reality Check* didn't sell in great numbers, 2009's *Cocky & Confident* debuted at #49, and 2010's *Beast Mode* barely registered. The track he hoarsely performs today, called "Gotta Get It," is an uninspired ditty that sounds suspiciously like Paul Wall's recent single, "Got to Get It."

It's somewhat painful to experience my idol's fall from grace, and it's jarring to hear him speak coarsely on subjects like the current state of bounce music. "Right now they got homosexuals doing that in New Orleans," he says, "so I don't like my name even being put in a sentence with that." (Indeed, whether he likes it or not, the scene has become famous for its gay and transgender "sissy bounce" performers.)

He's been itching for a Hot Boys reunion for years now, presumably to help relaunch his star. "Hot Boys gon' go down in history with OutKast and N.W.A as one of the best rap groups," he asserts. But they haven't made it happen, in part owing to Wayne,

Turk, and B.G.'s revolving door relationship with the penitentiary system.

Still, it's encouraging to hear him speak of reuniting with the old crew—if only because his music's quality has fallen off in his post–Cash Money era—and he adds that he's got no more hard feelings against Baby. The two of them worked out their differences and he was able to collect his back royalties, he says.

But while he's no longer bitter, there doesn't seem to be much love, either. He says his warm feelings for his old label long ago wore off. "Real family is real family, you can't change it," he says. With Cash Money, however, "you can walk away from that family, and they're not family no more."

# 8

# NELLY

■ ■ ■

## Forty Acres and a Pool

I ARRIVED back in the Midwest in 2003 to start a fellowship at Saint Louis's alternative weekly *Riverfront Times*, which everyone calls the *RFT*. It was the height of the city's notoriously steamy summer, and Nelly fever was in its fourth year and showed no signs of abating.

The man born Cornell Haynes Jr. had seemed like a one-hit wonder in the making with his 2000 debut single, "Country Grammar." The song, after all, is based on a jump-rope rhyme. But *Country Grammar* the album sold nine million copies, and his 2002 follow-up *Nellyville* moved six million more. He was more popular than anyone working, with more platinum CDs to come.

Though known for its Gaslight Square jazz district, Miles Davis, and rock-and-roll early birds like Chuck Berry and Ike and Tina Turner, the Saint Louis area had never spawned a famous rapper. But Nelly was single-handedly putting the town on the map. His group the St. Lunatics had a top-selling album of their own, and Nelly's protégée Murphy Lee had a hit in national rotation called

"What Da Hook Gon Be." A Nelly copycat named Chingy had bro-
ken big with a song called "Right Thurr," a slurring tribute to the
Saint Louis tradition of turning one's "ere"s into "urrr"s. J-Kwon
would become known for a song called "Tipsy," and Jibbs, the
"Zip Coon"-melody-harvesting guy, would have a top ten hit with
"Chain Hang Low."

These artists filmed their videos in front of the Arch, sported
Saint Louis Cardinals' gear, and shouted out the town in every
song. *The New Yorker* wrote that its atmosphere was "now a little
like that of Nashville in the nineteen-thirties, with the Grand Ole
Opry, or of Detroit in the sixties, with Motown Records." One
of my first blurbs at the *RFT* was an interview with a Washington University economics professor about the economic impact
these freshly minted millionaires were having on the city. He suggested that "some of the hangers-on and the wannabes" may have
impacted the local market for bling.

These were the halcyon days, and Nelly's buzz was concen-
trated in the Loop, a strip of inner-ring suburb University City
that housed the *RFT*, used-clothing boutiques, ethnic restaurants,
and a sportswear shop he partly owned. He had grown up just a
stone's throw away and sometimes filmed videos nearby.

Each week, it seemed, we'd get a press release about one of his
new ventures. He already had a men's apparel line called Vokal
(Very Organized Kids Always Learning), which was known for
its oversized denim jeans and velour jogging outfits and received
a synergistic boost when he and the Lunatics wore it in their
videos.

To complement Vokal he cofounded Apple Bottoms jeans,
named for the shape of a voluptuous woman's backside. The company set out on a national search for a model whose natural beauty
best exemplified the name. Ladies from around the country
paraded their stuff before panels of rappers and celebrity judges,
and VH1 aired a special on the tryouts. Though some were thrilled

that the brand was tailored to large black and Latina women's figures—it was marketed to "real women with real curves"—others
felt the enterprise was exploitive. Critics invoked the Hottentot
Venus, a stage name applied to two or more Khoisan women from
southern Africa with prodigious backsides, who were gawked at
like caged animals in European sideshows.

It was hard to accuse Nelly of acting disingenuously, however,
as much of his shtick involved salivating over women, and the
fairer sex constituted the bulk of his fan base. Girls liked the lilt in
his voice, and they found his high cheekbones, chiseled athlete's
frame, and coy smile irresistible; that and his trademark grunted
"uhhh" ad-libs. (Actually, I find those kind of hot myself.)

Then there was his bad-boy-with-heart persona, signified
by the Band-Aid he wore on his cheek as a gesture of solidarity
with his incarcerated crew mate City Spud. Sure, Nelly bragged
about his drug-dealing past and skill with firearms, but getting
you undressed was always at the back of his mind. A 2002 *Onion*
headline read: "Nelly Reiterates Sex-Liking Stance."

And so Nelly Inc. rolled forward. The archetype of the hip-hop
entrepreneur was nothing new, of course, as Puff Daddy, Russell
Simmons, and Master P had established themselves as expert ver-
tical integrationists. But Nelly was the hottest entertainer working,
an ambitious young man who, unlike P, had crossover appeal with
white audiences.

He dipped his hand into countless industries. Besides the oblig-
atory record label (Derrty Entertainment) and charitable founda-
tions, he had a restaurant, energy drink, and sneaker, and in 2004
purchased a minority stake in the Charlotte Bobcats NBA expansion team, owned primarily by BET founder Robert Johnson.

The next year he played a convict cum running back in a big-
budget movie, a remake called *The Longest Yard* costarring Adam
Sandler and Chris Rock. It may be one of the most unfunny films
I've ever seen, but its Saint Louis premiere was exciting, held at

the theater directly below the *RFT* and preceded by a red-carpet ceremony on the Loop.

But being one of the planet's best-known people had its disadvantages. Even while his CDs, jeans, and caffeinated beverages were making him wealthy, a group of gathering adversaries looked to take him down.

He drew scrutiny from folks who didn't otherwise listen to rap and weren't familiar with the genre's customs and codes. At the same time, traditional MCs took umbrage at his unorthodox style and mass popularity. Somewhere along the way he became a symbol for everything that was wrong with pop culture. He was too successful for his own good.


YOU MAY ask why Nelly merits space in a book about southern hip-hop. Saint Louis isn't the South. It's a fair question. Indeed, the Lou' finds itself in that vague expanse of plains, farmland, hills, and lakes known as the Midwest. But Midwestern rap lacks much in the way of defining characteristics, with little seeming to unite artists as diverse as Eminem, Kanye West, and Bone Thugs-n-Harmony.

Regionalism, in fact, breaks down a bit differently in hip-hop. Two of southern rap's main poles are Houston and Miami, for example, cities not considered the traditional South. And though geographically it lies to the north, sonically Saint Louis hip-hop can be classified as southern.

Absorbing bounce, bass, and buck—not to mention Dixie vernacular and styles like candy-painted cars—Saint Louis artists spit it all back out as something even catchier and more radio ready. Southern fads like snap and crunk were quick to take hold here, and Lou' rappers frequently collaborated with their down south brethren. As for Nelly, northerners accused him of familiar crimes: lyrical shallowness, commercial whoredom, and an infantilized sound. For these reasons, Nelly can be considered the godfather of the latest generation of southern rappers.

Born on an Austin, Texas, military base in 1974 as the son of a Vietnam veteran air force pilot, Nelly lived in Spain for three years in his childhood. His parents' breakup caused him to be shuttled among relatives. He says his early school days were full of fights—he was picked on for being short—but his love of sports helped him fit in after arriving in University City as an adolescent. "When he moved to the neighborhood, he came in trying to outrun, outplay everybody, so he automatically ended up being our friend," says Murphy Lee, a St. Lunatic who is the younger brother of another group member, Kyjuan.

University City's thirty-five thousand residents run the gamut from Washington University professors and young professional couples to working-class black families. The St. Lunatics' old neighborhood is a solidly middle-class enclave dotted with utilitarian brown brick houses and well-kept basketball courts and football fields. The area is very safe now, though in the 1980s it was somewhat less so.

Nelly developed his talents as a top-tier amateur baseball player and even attended major league tryout camps. (He's also a good basketball player and tremendous bowler, owning the house record at Saint Louis's Pin-Up Bowl: 257.) He believes he would have gone pro as a ballplayer had he not turned to drug dealing to pay the bills after the birth of his daughter.

But music provided a third way, and he had big expectations almost immediately after joining with the Lunatics in 1993. The group was rounded out by his look-alike City Spud, who worked at McDonalds, and their friend Ali, who cut hair. "We was always the most popular," adds Murph. "Prom kings and homecoming kings—that's what the Lunatics consisted of."

The collective was impressive in its organization. Ali told the *RFT* that members who were late to meetings were forced to do push-ups. They decided early on that they'd rather make feel-good music instead of gangsta rap. "[Ali] said, 'Rap is twenty-plus years old. Ain't nothing being said that ain't been said,'" Nelly told *Rolling Stone*. "Everybody's rapped about politics, the struggle, money, ho's, everything. So it's all how you shoot it now. It's about how you say it, because there ain't nothing new you can say."

Anxious to avoid the tag of a "local group," they kept the details of their enterprise quiet, well aware that Saint Louis rap was something of an oxymoron. But only a week or so after forming they won a local talent show, earning $200 for performing a song called "Ragged and Dirty."

They began recording at a studio housed in a nearby roller rink called Saints and eventually signed a production deal with a pair of identical twins named Darren and David Stith, who hooked them up with a white high school dropout beat maker named Jason "Jay E" Epperson. (Jay E is the still largely unknown, criminally underappreciated producer responsible for many of Nelly and the Lunatics' big songs.) The act's first hit, "Gimme What You Got," featured a loop of a Rakim sample and took off on local radio, leading to a deal with Universal Records.

Universal decided that Nelly was the group's star, and he set to work on his solo debut, released in 2000. That year was an exciting one for Saint Louis—the Rams had just won the Super Bowl, the Cardinals and the Blues were ascendant, and the Catholic faithful were still buzzing from the pope's visit the previous year.

Nelly's success piggybacked on dreams of urban renewal for the blighted town, which had been America's fourth biggest city at the turn of the previous century but was subsequently gutted by industrial pollution and white flight. Nelly painted Saint Louis as a dangerous but warm-hearted place; it had taken him in, and he loved it for that reason. "You may not recognize the landmarks he mentions, but the streets are filled with run-of-the-mill guys chasing expensive cars and cheap dates; Nellyville could be any American city," wrote Kelefa Sanneh in the *New York Times*. "Luck played a big role in Nelly's success, but so did strategy: his style is vaguely exotic and instantly familiar."

The Lunatics also had a deal with Universal and would soon release their own platinum debut. But one of the crew's members couldn't enjoy the spotlight. Not long before Nelly's break, City Spud had decided to try his hand as a small-time drug dealer. As part of a get-rich-quick scheme, he'd agreed to drive the getaway car while an associate robbed one of City's customers. The plan went awry and City's partner shot the customer five times in his back. While the assailant got away, the victim lived and implicated City Spud, who was sentenced to eight and a half years in prison. Hence the title of the St. Lunatics' debut album: *Free City*.

"WE'LL HAVE kids running up and down the block all day, playing ghetto games," Nelly told *Rolling Stone* in 2000. "We can't afford all the high-priced games, so we make up our games and our own chants; 'down, down baby' is just a chant from one of those games."

He was discussing "Country Grammar," which became a top ten hit that fall. Full of sparkly synths, chimes, and gleeful "whoops!" it's a strikingly musical piece of Saint Louis swing, with Nelly abandoning his raps mid-line and breaking into song. Its chorus recalls the children's patty-cake and jump rope rhyme, but instead of the traditional "Down, down, baby, down by the roller-coaster/ Sweet, sweet baby, I'll never let you go/ Shimmy, shimmy cocoa pop, shimmy shimmy pow" (or a similar variation), the lyrics are toughened up:

> I'm going down, down, baby, your street in a Range
>    Rover
> Street sweeper baby, cocked, ready to let it go
> Shimmy, shimmy cocoa what? Listen to it pound
> Light it up and take a puff, pass it to me now

The song's dichotomy—the hardened and the innocent—gives it power and would later be copied by MCs like Gucci Mane and Lil Boosie. Rappers once assumed that if you wanted to talk tough, your music had to *sound* tough, too. But nowadays southern gangsta rap's music is often quite soft, full of sugary riffs, toy pianos, and choruses sung by children's choirs.

"Country Grammar" also smartly big-ups the unsophisticated yokels of fly-over country, from Memphis to Indiana, Kansas City to Alabama, which were then mostly ignored rap demographics. Meanwhile, the St. Lunatics toured well off the Chitlin' Circuit, to burgs like Sioux City and Omaha. "My whole purpose was to make people who speak country grammar not ashamed of how they talk and turn it into the hot slang," Nelly said.

Nelly doesn't get much credit as a rapper, but he rides a beat expertly, incorporating internal rhymes and never sounding rushed. Still, complex wordplay is not his focus; instead, he's all melody and attitude, ad-libbing, grunting, and humming his way into your memory.

"Saint Louis has a lot of blues and jazz history—it's a soulful place, and I incorporate that," Nelly said. "Instead of getting on top of the beat, I get inside it, as if I'm adding another instrument to the groove."

For his second album, *Nellyville*, he teamed up with Virginia Beach–production duo the Neptunes on "Hot in Herre," which incorporates the go-go riff of Chuck Brown's "Bustin' Loose" and implores the ladies to take off all their clothes. It sat atop *Billboard*'s singles chart for seven weeks and hit the top ten in some dozen other countries. With Murphy Lee and Diddy he won a Grammy for another #1, "Shake Ya Tailfeather," from the *Bad Boys II* soundtrack, and he hit the top spot again with Destiny's Child's Kelly Rowland on the ballad "Dilemma."

These were fairly safe collaborations, but Nelly was more than willing to go outside of his sphere. He joined *NSYNC on their

2002 track "Girlfriend," which raised eyebrows at the time, as conventional wisdom held that you couldn't maintain street cred while rapping with a Charmin-soft boy band. This decision proved prescient, however, as street rappers like Game and T.I. were later clamoring to work with *NSYNC's increasingly respected singer Justin Timberlake.

A fan of country music, Nelly went further outside the box on a duet with Nashville star Tim McGraw called "Over and Over." The pair reportedly hooked up after Nelly said of McGraw, the husband of singer Faith Hill, "He's a badass, he's got game, and he's got a fine bitch!" In the video Nelly wears a Saint Louis Rams jacket while McGraw sports a black cowboy hat; the song's teary chorus has both men practically whispering.

Predictably, it was another massive hit, powering Nelly's 2004 album *Suit*, released the same day as a companion work, *Sweat*. A 2005 compilation called *Sweatsuit* contained the chart-topping single "Grillz," which featured Ali, Goodie Mob's Big Gipp, Paul Wall, and production from Jermaine Dupri. Dupri remembers the Saint Louis MC bringing a party atmosphere to his Atlanta studio for the song's construction.

"Nelly was like, 'I need Paul Wall tonight,'" he says. "Paul flew to Atlanta on the spot, and got on the record. We just kept partying and partying. I don't smoke, but they were smoking. I was drinking a little bit of everything: champagne, beer. I tried lean for the first time with Paul Wall."

Those three works moved some five million copies in total but yet are somehow considered Nelly's falling-off point. Even his underrated 2008 work *Brass Knuckles*—said to be the final nail in his coffin—managed to go gold in an era when almost no one was moving many copies.

Indeed, Nelly's ability to sell himself has never been his problem. His issue was respect, which even his hometown didn't always give him, the city whose entertainment culture he helped revitalize and whom he loved dearly.

In 2000, Mayor Clarence Harmon publicly slighted Nelly by declining to honor him at a football game benefitting a scholarship organization. Harmon—a black Democrat—objected to the subtitle of "Country Grammar," which was "Hot Shit," and the *Post-Dispatch* backed him up.

Although the next mayor would embrace him, in 2002 Nelly was callously thrown out of a mall. Arriving at Saint Louis's Union Station shopping center, he was stopped by a rent-a-cop type. He'd come to purchase Cardinals jerseys for a video shoot at Busch Stadium for the remix of Jermaine Dupri's "Welcome to Atlanta," which included a Saint Louis verse performed by Murphy Lee.

Nelly's crime? Wearing one of those stocking-like hairstyle protectors called a do-rag, banned under the mall's dress code as "commonly known gang-related paraphernalia." The incident led to a protest march, although Nelly declined to attend. "He doesn't feel it was a racist thing," said his publicist, Jane Higgins.

But it was his failure to be politically minded that embroiled him in another controversy that year. South Bronx–bred rapper KRS-One took issue with his ethics and his style in a series of attacks.

Also known as "The Teacha," KRS helped shape early hip-hop music and culture through his work with trio Boogie Down Productions and solo albums. Well-respected but past his commercial prime, he accused Nelly of watering down the art form.

"Sales don't make you the authority/ It means you sold out to the white majority," he rapped on his 2002 track "Clear 'Em Out." Though he later insisted these words weren't specifically aimed at Nelly, the Saint Louisan took them that way anyway, assuming they were a response to his song, "#1," in which he expresses frustration with those who are "judging what's real hip-hop." And so he made a diss track aimed at KRS, rapping, "You the first old man should get a rapper's pension/ No hits since the cordless mic invention."

Relishing the chance to rumble, KRS roared back on a track called "Ova Here." "Your whole style sounds like a *NSYNC commercial," he rapped. "Let's give hip-hop a lift, and don't buy Nelly's album on June twenty-fifth/ That'll send a message back to all them sellouts/ House nigga rapper, your bottom done fell out."

What was The Teacha's complaint, exactly? Like much of what he has said these days, it wasn't clear. Recently he made the confusing assertion that Def Jam Records "single-handedly destroyed hip-hop," while also allowing that there would "be no hip-hop as we know it today" if it weren't for Def Jam. His biggest problem with Nelly seemed to be his lack of a black-power-minded message. KRS claimed a lyric off of *Nellyville*'s title track, which went, "forty acres and a mule/ Fuck that! Nellyville: forty acres and a pool," disrespected civil rights leaders. Never mind that "Nellyville" is a well-intentioned track that reimagines hood life as a paradise with no poverty, gunplay, lottery tickets, or hard drugs. KRS didn't understand where Nelly was coming from, and didn't care to understand.

At one point the veteran rapper said he would squash the beef if Nelly agreed to the terms laid out in a document called the "Declaration of Peace," authored by KRS's Temple of Hip-Hop organization.

"The elements of Hiphop Kulture may be traded for money, honor, power, respect, food, shelter, information and other resources"; reads the verbose manifesto, in part. "However, Hiphop and its culture cannot be bought, nor is it for sale."

There was no winner in this battle. A constructive debate over the role hip-hop plays in black culture gave way to self-promotion and name-calling. Yet Nelly likely got the short end of the stick. KRS was able to effectively sing to his choir, who tend to find him a righteous, philosophical gatekeeper.

But Nelly was already short on gravitas, and he didn't do himself any favors by taking on the rap icon. By throwing muck, all he did was make critics and social activists wonder if the cult of Nelly wasn't so harmless after all.


LIKE OTHER rap artists such as Lil Jon, Nelly saw growth potential in the emerging energy-drink market, which was dominated in its infancy by Red Bull. In 2003 he attempted to entice the young and under-caffeinated with a beverage of his own, Pimp Juice, named for a song on *Nellyville*. Stocked with guarana, apple juice, vitamins, and high-fructose corn syrup, the bright green elixir came in a sleek, bullet-colored can.

Before long, the beverage filled refrigerator cases in stores around town, and people in our office were sampling "Pimptinis"—Pimp Juice and vodka. Distributed nationally, it received more than its share of press; it was a good story, after all, considering some of the profits would go to Nelly's nonprofit organization 4Sho4Kids. But wise elders around the country weren't convinced. A nationwide boycott was called by an alliance of black activists who objected partly to the product's reputation as a booze mixer but mostly to its name.

"What's next? Sambo ham sandwiches and Ku Klux Klan juice?" the Reverend Paul Scott said to *USA Today*. He was a leader of the boycott and the head of the Messianic Afrikan Nation in Durham, North Carolina. In a separate statement he added, "The black community is in danger right now. As black men we should be building a nation of strong black leaders, not a nation of super-energized, drunk pimps." A group of California activist groups, meanwhile, asked the Korean Grocers Association—which supplied many convenience stores in South Central Los Angeles—not to stock the drink.

Perhaps a generational clash over the word *pimp* was inevitable, considering it means different things to different age groups. As explained by Eightball & MJG, the word can refer to anyone who excels at something. (Yes, your high school math club president was a "pimp.") Nelly expanded the definition even further, explaining in the "Pimp Juice" song that it referred to mojo. "Your pimp juice is anything [that] attract the opposite sex/ It could be money, fame, or straight intellect." It's worth noting that in the track's video, however, Nelly kicks it with a group of flamboyantly dressed literal pimps.

It would be an exaggeration to say that the boycott killed Pimp Juice, considering that dozens of new energy drink start-ups ceased production in the mid-aughts. The American market simply couldn't bear all the new beverages, each seemingly only distinguished by the extremeness of the name. In 2007 a South African company called Mojalife signed on to distribute the drink, recasting the word *pimp* as an acronym meaning "Positive, Intellectually Motivated Persons," but Pimp Juice is no longer for sale in America.

BEFORE LONG Nelly was in hot water again, drawn into the debate over another complicated social problem, the role of misogyny in hip-hop. Critics took issue with his song "Tip Drill," a remix of his hit "E.I." from a 2003 compilation called *Da Derrty Versions: The Reinvention*.

"Tip Drill" is a crude, straight-faced ode to "butterface" women, ladies with shapely physiques but unattractive faces. It's a dicey proposition for a song, but it wasn't the tune that drew complaints so much as its extra-raunchy video, which includes naked co-eds grinding in a hot tub and a smirking Nelly running a credit card through the butt cheeks of a thong-clad girl.

The video earned slightly edited airplay on BET's late-night program *Uncut* and prompted rebukes like a *USA Today* op-ed piece that compared Nelly's video antics (and his promotion of Pimp Juice) to R. Kelly's indictment on child pornography charges. "The use of women as hypersexualized props for the fantasies of male rappers is endemic in music videos," wrote author Jill Nelson.

The most highly publicized incident surrounding "Tip Drill" occurred in 2004, when Atlanta's Spelman College, a historically black women's college, organized a cancer fundraiser and invited Nelly, whose sister Jackie was fighting leukemia. After viewing "Tip Drill," a number of students threatened to protest the event, and Nelly pulled out.

It's unfortunate that these entirely unrelated medical and social issues were put at odds with each other. But the Spelman women's outrage was understandable, considering that "Tip Drill" is much closer to pornography than art. Unlike typical rap videos, where scantily clad models serve mostly as look-but-don't-touch set pieces, "Tip Drill" is practically an orgy on film.

Nelly claimed it was less risqué than what you see at strip clubs, that the credit card swipe was slyly metaphorical, and that the performers were grown women making their own choices. Indeed, in an era when hip-hop artists like Luke Campbell, Lil Jon, and Snoop Dogg were trying their hands at actual, dyed-in-the-wool pornography, it felt like Nelly was being singled out.

Nelly's family never was able to find a bone marrow match for Jackie, and in 2005 she died. Three years later, Nelly was still angry about the Spelman situation, noting in a satellite radio interview that the event was scheduled to feature a bone marrow drive.

"I [intended] to teach people about leukemia and help benefit and try to help save lives and try to find a donor for my sister," he said, adding that all the attention focused on his "fucking video" would have been better spent educating the community on leukemia. "I don't have my sister today!" he cried. "No, I don't have her today!"

IN THE MIDDLE of my first southern trip I travel up to Saint Louis, where I drop in on some of my old buddies, visit my Big Brothers

Big Sisters "little brother" Jorell, and stop by the *RFT*. For the first time I also visit the Derrty Entertainment offices, home to Nelly's record label. Housed in a squat University City building next to the freeway, it has no sign and abuts something called "American Medical Claims, Inc." There's little doubt I'm in the right place, however, considering the Hummer H2 and Cadillac Escalade parked out front.

Nelly isn't around, but I get a tour from Murphy Lee, Nelly's right hand man these days and the only other St. Lunatic to develop a substantial solo following. The spot contains recording studios, conference rooms, and an office for Nelly's charities—though the latter is oddly empty for a Tuesday afternoon. Derrty Entertainment is a fairly nondescript facility, truth be told, save for the platinum records everywhere and neat touches like the tile mosaic built into the wall that says, "Nelly, Inc."

Sporting dreadlocks and clad in both a Cardinals shirt and scarf, Murphy Lee is repping Saint Louis as hard as ever. He even launches into a passionate defense of the Cardinal's former home run king Mark McGwire, who recently admitted to using steroids. "I don't really give a damn," Murph says. "You still gotta hit that ball. You can have steroids all you want, but if you can't swing that bat on time to hit that ball, then you ain't shit anyways."

As Nelly has receded from the public spotlight, so has Murph. For reasons unknown his record label, Universal, never allowed him to record a follow-up to his successful 2003 debut, *Murphy's Law*, which nearly went platinum. He blames a management shuffle at the company, and he has released a free CD and DVD of his own called *You See Me*. (As in U[niversity] C[ity] Me.) He's been seen around town, in fact, handing them out himself.

Murph doing his own promotion symbolizes Saint Louis hip-hop's ebb in popularity. Though Nelly maintains some level of commercial viability, J-Kwon, Chingy, and Jibbs have all but disappeared. It all feels kind of depressing, especially for Murph, who must rebuild his buzz from the grassroots level despite having logged so many years in the industry and having won a Grammy.

But he doesn't feel that way. He says Saint Louis's national image could use some help from the local sports teams, but his crew is ready to put Saint Louis rap back on the national radar. With City Spud now home from jail a new St. Lunatics album is on the way, fittingly called *City Free*.

His homie Nelly, meanwhile, has "four or five" more albums under his belt, ready to go. "I'm just going to be honest with you," Murphy says. "Nelly is just getting started. That was nothing."

# 9

# TIMBALAND AND THE NEPTUNES

■ ■ ■

## Architects of Sound in Nowhere, Virginia

HIP-HOP'S dirty little secret is that the MCs themselves aren't always essential to their songs' success. Sure, their raps are part of the attraction, but radio popularity depends almost entirely on their backing tracks, the beats that stick in your head and put behinds on the floor.

What directors are to movies, producers are to songs, and the most successful ones are kingmakers. Because they can make rappers famous and record labels successful, they often earn the most money and have the most clout.

No beat makers have been more sought-after in the past decade than three men from southeast Virginia: Timbaland, Pharrell Williams, and Chad Hugo. (The latter two form the Neptunes.) If you heard a spaced-out, stripped-down pop song on the radio in the early aughts, it was probably one of theirs. It had to feel like cheating if you had them on your song—you were virtually assured of a hit. The Neptunes and Timbaland reshaped rap, R&B, and pop by merging and flipping them into something else entirely. They showed that pop fans don't mind a challenge so long as the beat is catchy.

Nurtured in a coastal suburban expanse that was in the South if not necessarily *of* the South, the Virginians recast powerhouses from around the country like Nelly, Britney Spears, and Aaliyah in their own images and propelled Virginia Beach acts Missy "Misdemeanor" Elliott and Clipse to fame.

Pharrell is the Neptunes' more public face. He and Timbaland were childhood friends, playing together as teens in a group called Surrounded By Idiots. They would later epitomize the celebrity producer phenomenon by coming out from behind the boards and releasing their own albums.

Personally, however, the guys could hardly be more different. Pharrell is a svelte, hippie dippy cool kid who speaks without an accent and could be from L.A. Timbaland is a sleepy-looking, body-conscious musical scholar with a deep drawl.

Timbaland obsesses over his songs' chart positions and his listeners' demographics. Pharrell, on the other hand, focuses on the moon and the stars.

NEW YORK'S early beat makers tended to harvest nuggets from soul, funk, or jazz songs. Once the South got involved, producers were big on adding live orchestration. "For a long time hip-hop was just snippets and elements of other stuff," Mannie Fresh told *Scratch*. "You actually got musicianship in southern music."

But the Neptunes don't often use either approach. Instead, they attempt to re-create, from scratch, the sounds they hear in their heads. "Life, love, science, religion, history, that's what I want to pull into my music," Pharrell told the *New York Times*.

Having played in marching bands as kids, he and Chad understand music on a technical level. But they don't limit themselves
to conventional composition methods. Instead, they do things like
empty trash bins from the bathroom and use them for percussion.

Pharrell will often improvise hooks or progressions, and Chad
will fill in spaces and tie the songs together. The pair go back and
forth, creating tracks that sound clean but unnatural, organic
yet otherworldly, often adding video game bleeps and bloops or
instruments reproduced by synths. The Neptunes don't just consider themselves musicians; they're modern artists. So what if they
happen to be richer than God?

Timbaland seems more blue collar. He can't read music and
hasn't had classical training. Baby coos, birdie tweets, or even
ambient noise might serve as melody, and the resulting sounds
are simultaneously disorienting and familiar. His songs are full
of empty spaces; where lesser producers might cram in layers of
effects to fill the silence (and coddle their assumedly ADD listeners), he pulls back.

Rather than simply making a hot beat and trying to match it up
with an artist, as the Neptunes are wont to do, he crafts songs for
a particular performer's voice. His specialty is artist development
rather than one-off hits.

Some have complained about the ubiquity of the Timbaland/
Neptunes sound. But pop music is more interesting because of
them. Previously, singers like Alanis Morissette, Celine Dion, the
Spice Girls, and the Backstreet Boys ruled the charts. Shudder to
think.


TIMOTHY MOSLEY was born in 1972. His dad worked for Amtrak
and his mom for a homeless shelter. They raised him in Norfolk,
home to the world's largest naval base, and he later built a massive recording studio nearby, in a Virginia Beach industrial park.

"Ain't nothing spectacular about it," Timbaland said of the racially mixed suburban area where he grew up. "Ain't nothing going on out there, really."

There certainly wasn't a music industry. But Tim was undeterred, keeping himself busy as a kid by learning drum machines and samplers. He befriended an aspiring rapper named Melvin "Magoo" Barcliff, who became one of his main collaborators, and by his late teens was a popular club DJ. He made beats for an R&B group called Fayze, featuring his high school friend Missy Elliott, whom he'd met through Magoo after Surrounded By Idiots broke up.

"Tim had this little Casio keyboard, and he has big hands," Missy told Roni Sarig. "So it was hilarious to see him play on that Casio. But he had a way of making a record sound like something I hadn't heard before."

Success was still many years away for Timbaland, however, and his high school years were fraught with roadblocks. After work one day at Red Lobster, he was accidentally shot in the lower part of his neck by a coworker, which left him paralyzed for much of a year. "I would work with him, give him the medicine and massage his arm, and he'd still go in the room every single day, messing with that turntable and writing down lyrics," said his mother Leatrice Pierre. Then there was the time in 1991 that Tim crashed his Mazda, killing a friend riding along. "I been through some junk," he told *Entertainment Weekly*. "It ain't all been peaches and cream."

But he received a break through Missy, whose group was invited by Jodeci member Devante Swing to his Warhol-style singer-songwriter compound in New Jersey. Later renamed Sista, Missy's group promptly moved up to the New York suburbs, and later to Rochester, and Timbaland and Magoo joined them.

"Their stay in Rochester was simultaneously a scary and a magical time," studio engineer Jimmy Douglass told journalist Michael A. Gonzales for the website Soul Summer. "DeVante had all of these talented kids living in this house: Timbaland, Ginu-wine, Missy, the group Sista, Magoo, Playa and Tweet. He had all this talent living under one roof and if he had treated them better, DeVante would have owned the world. . . . Although DeVante was supposed to be the mentor, there were times when he just wanted to control everybody."

Though a Sista album saw a quiet release and Missy and Tim contributed to a Jodeci work, the pair felt stifled and decided to break away. They went back to Virginia for a time and, mining their newly developed contacts, came upon more opportunities. Timbaland landed a hit with Ginuwine's "Pony," and in 1996 he and Missy placed tracks on Detroit-bred R&B singer Aaliyah's second album, *One in a Million*.

The teenage superstar had previously worked with R. Kelly and even married the lascivious Chicago singer/producer while still underage (it was quickly annulled). But Tim and Missy's songs came to define her sound, and *Million* went double platinum. The title track, written by Missy and Tim and produced by the latter, is a fairly standard love song ("Your love is a one in a million"), but stands out for its rattlesnake shakes and tranced-out atmosphere.

Even better is their "Are You That Somebody," off the *Dr. Dolittle* soundtrack, another sonic slice-and-dice masquerading as a traditional radio jam. Featuring a choppy beat that shows up when it's good and ready, the song's back-up singers include an infant and Timbaland himself.

Aaliyah's next, eponymous, album had more Missy and Tim productions, and is my personal favorite. But the twenty-two-year-old singer was killed in a plane crash shortly after takeoff in the Bahamas, where she was filming a music video. An autopsy found traces of alcohol and cocaine in the pilot's bloodstream. It was a ghastly end for an extremely likable talent, but Aaliyah's songs would set the standard for a generation of cutting-edge radio pop.

TIM AND MISSY had lost their muse, but they maintained the bond they'd shared since adolescence. "There's a chemistry between us that will never leave," Missy told *Billboard,* calling it "deeper than this music industry thing." As coproducers they introduced Missy as a solo artist with her 1997 debut *Supa Dupa Fly.* It sold a million and a half copies and delighted critics—Allmusic called it a "post-modern masterpiece." Borrowing only slightly from OutKast's earthy sound and anarchist style, she redefined what it meant to be an MC, singing, talking, rapping, or simply making onomato-poeic noises.

Her verses were whimsical or poignant depending on her mood, and full of subjects with universal appeal that nonetheless sidestepped cliché. She often abandoned cerebral concerns entirely, interrupting herself mid-flow to make silly proclamations. "What da dilly, yo? What da drilly yo?" she raps on her 2001 hit "Get Ur Freak On." "If you wanna battle me/ Then nigga let me know."

Her and Timbaland's lackadaisical, spacey beats sought dance floor bliss but didn't seem to have much to do with current trends. "Get Ur Freak On" used a bhangra beat and a plucked sitar to create an unlikely club smash. "Work It," meanwhile, features a chorus line sung in reverse. Despite being painstakingly crafted, her songs often feel improvised. She told *Elle* that she sometimes brought dancers into the studio, played them beats, and took notes on how they moved to them.

But what separated Missy from her rivals wasn't just her music, it was her atypical hip-hop image. She cast herself as a fashion-forward fly chick, moving from neon tracksuits, sneakers, and b-girl attire to jackets and ties. Though she boasts a photoge-nic smile, she put the focus on her clothes and innovative dance moves, not her T and A.

Early in her career she was replaced in a Raven-Symone video by a slimmer woman, but rather than dwell on her weight, she accentuated it, donning what looked like an inflated black garbage bag for her early video "The Rain (Supa Dupa Fly)." Think *Willy Wonka and the Chocolate Factory*'s Violet Beauregarde, after she's been turned into a blueberry.

Though rarely overtly political, she indicated that she didn't care about the prevailing thin, light-skinned model of black beauty. She was proud to be dark and large, and in 2004 after being diagnosed with hypertension and subsequently losing weight, she went so far as to apologize to fans for slimming down. "I still represent for overweight adults and kids," she promised.

She hasn't responded to constant rumors that she's a lesbian, and her numerous sex raps feature male protagonists. "Pussy don't fail me now," she raps on "Pussycat." "I gotta turn this nigga out/ So he don't want nobody else." Unlike other female pop stars, she doesn't spend much time sucking up to dudes, however, instead ridiculing their deficiencies on songs like "One Minute Man." Without being too blatant about it, she's become one of hip-hop's strongest female empowerment advocates, and one can see her musical and aesthetic influence in rap's new queen, Nicki Minaj.

One has always sensed that Missy's music, though thematically complex, has barely tapped into her lurking creativity. "My imagination is so far out there already," she told the *Guardian*, explaining why she didn't take ecstasy pills. "People couldn't imagine what goes on in my brain."

Nonetheless, it's easy to forget how successful she's been, with five platinum albums and one gold one, her own label, and, with Tim, production gigs for A-listers like Janet Jackson and Mariah Carey. With her vast wealth she procured thousands of sneakers, a pearl white Ferrari, a baby blue Lamborghini, and houses in Los Angeles, New Jersey, and Miami.

She also bought a massive pad for her mother in Portsmouth, Virginia, where Missy was born. Her goal, she says, was to ease her mom's suffering through material comforts. Missy's father was a marine who beat her mother daily, and Missy said he once pulled a gun on both of them and forced them both to go outside naked. Her mother leaving him gave Missy a positive role model for a strong woman, she's said, and in 1999 she aided a domestic violence charity through sales of her signature lipstick, Misdemeanor.

Missy remains a complex figure: a devout Baptist who raps about sex, a woman who often seems uncomfortable in the spotlight but makes Gap commercials with Madonna, and a groundbreaking rapper who isn't convinced others see her as "a real hiphop artist," as she says on her album *Under Construction*.

But perhaps her fans' biggest complaint is her stalled productivity. Expressing a preference for production, she all but disappeared as a performer after 2005's *The Cookbook*. Her follow-up, *Block Party*, initially slated for a 2007 release, was pushed back to 2008, 2009, and then 2010, and seems now to have been swallowed up by the abyss.

TIMBALAND BEGAN working alone and with other collaborators besides Missy, creating and jump-starting numerous other careers. Perhaps his greatest challenge was making Justin Timberlake into a credible solo star. No one gave *NSYNC's adorable powder puff much of a shot, considering that the escapist boy band era was thought to be over, what with 9/11 and the resulting economic downturn.

But, along with the Neptunes, Tim made a viable artist out of Timberlake on his 2002 debut *Justified*. Haunting album centerpiece "Cry Me a River"—reportedly about Timberlake's failed romance with Britney Spears—features abrupt starts and stops and eerie snaps and pops. Though Miami producer Scott Storch claimed he deserved credit for the song, it established Timberlake as an artist with actual meat on his bones.

His evolution continued with 2006 follow-up *FutureSex/LoveSounds*, on which he and Timbaland got even more creative. Bare bones hit "SexyBack" is an unusual, almost jarring piece of rave-pop that, along with other techno-influenced tracks like "My Love," vaulted Timberlake to the top of the pops. The ever-modest Kanye West later asserted that only Timberlake could match him for fans and respect.

"Me and Justin is different: it's not work, it's magic," Timbaland told the *Guardian*.

He was nearly as successful with a pair of female artists, Nelly Furtado and Keri Hilson. Under the auspices of his label, Mosley Music Group, he overhauled the image of the Canadian singer Furtado, best known for her earthy inspirational, "I'm Like a Bird." Under his direction she began wearing smaller shirts and veered into hip-hop, with urban turns like "Promiscuous" and "Maneater."

Timbaland's curiously named solo hit "The Way I Are" introduced an Atlanta songwriter turned R&B artist, Keri Hilson. Her 2009 debut *In a Perfect World...* shocked industry watchers with its strong chart performance. Considering it was shepherded by Timbaland, however, they oughtn't have been surprised.

YOU KNOW the song "Rump Shaker." "All I wanna do is zooma zoom zoom zoom and a boom boom. Just shake your rump!" But you may not know that the video for the 1992 Wreckx-n-Effect single featured, in addition to the bikini-clad saxophone player on a beach, a young Pharrell mugging in the background.

He was still in high school when he wrote a verse for the track, in fact, but it was performed by Teddy Riley, the group's in-demand producer. Riley was the king of New Jack Swing, a musically curious hybrid that merged the bravado of gangsta rap with the tempo of smooth jazz.

A member of studly R&B groups Guy and Blackstreet, he also made beats for Bobby Brown and the Jacksons. Indeed, there was hardly a better-decorated early nineties industry player than he, which made his arrival in Virginia Beach so surprising.

He was raised in Harlem, but he'd come to town for a beach party called Greekfest and liked it so much that he set up shop there, not far from Pharrell's high school. Riley sought new acts to work with, and he quickly found some at a local talent show featuring an act called the Neptunes.

Chad and Pharrell met at a music camp for gifted and talented kids when they were twelve. Their original incarnation of the Neptunes was an all-out band, with a lineup that included their friends Shae Haley and Mike Etheridge. Their sound, according to Riley, was roughly "R&B meets techno/new wave/hip-hop."

Impressed, he signed them to a development deal. But, busy with other projects, he didn't have time to put their record out. So he gave them stipends to spur them on. Pharrell and Chad's break came when Riley asked them one day, almost off-handedly, to make some beats.

As a production duo, then, the Neptunes contributed to Blacktreet's 1994 self-titled debut, and came closer to what we now think of as their signature sound on MC Noreaga's "Superthug." That brisk, pulsing track features a hook composed of the rapper repeating "What" over and over. Chad says the group was attempting to create a "new sound" that mixed hip-hop and rock, but, seeing as they couldn't play guitar, employed a clavichord effect instead.

"Superthug" doesn't really rock, but it was a minor hit. Increasingly prominent assignments followed, including tracks for SWV and Kelis and an out-of-nowhere 1999 smash from Wu-Tang Clan member Ol' Dirty Bastard, "Got Your Money."

It wasn't the avant-garde, look-at-me type beat they'd later use on Britney Spears' "I'm a Slave 4 U," but the blaxploitation riff in "Got Your Money" is just about perfect for Dirty's manic musings. "I don't have no trouble with you fucking me," he explains. "But I have a little problem with you not fucking me."

From there the duo shot into the stratosphere, owning the early aughts with hits like Jay-Z's "I Just Wanna Love U (Give It 2 Me)," Mystikal's "Shake Ya Ass" and Nelly's "Hot in Herre." Each was built on immutable bass lines and slight-yet-infectious hooks, stripping away all that was unnecessary. "We do skeleton songs," Williams said.

Their sound worked not just for mainstream artists but for lyric-minded MCs as well. In the early nineties Chad and Pharrell met two Virginia Beach brothers named Gene and Terrence Thornton, whom they later helped secure a record deal. The Thorntons were actually born in the Bronx, and as duo Clipse their music showcases sophisticated rhymes about the dope trade and a distinctly Northeastern flavor. "I was raised here, but Virginia isn't what I know as southern," said Terrence, who goes by Pusha T. "This is the mixing pot of everything; it's dead smack in the middle."

Eventually the Neptunes signed them to their Star Trak Entertainment label and produced their 2002 album *Lord Willin'*, which was both a critical and commercial success. Clipse's 2006 followup *Hell Hath No Fury* featured more stark, atmospheric Neptunes tracks, and while it wasn't a blockbuster, many called it the rap album of the year. My only quibble with that assessment is that *Hell Hath No Fury*'s beats are so hot that it almost doesn't matter who's rapping. As with many Neptunes productions, they manage to eviscerate their MCs' identities.

Timbaland and the Neptunes didn't just dominate radio in the early aughts, they *were* the radio. One August 2003 estimate found that Neptunes' songs comprised more than 40 percent of pop station airplay. I couldn't find such stats for Tim, but he often seemed at least as overplayed as they. Around that same time, Pharrell and Chad's net worth was estimated at $155 million. Timbaland reportedly earned $200,000 per track at his peak, which was not a bad haul, considering he released dozens of songs per year.

The 2004 Grammy Awards served as a Virginia Beach corona-
tion, with the Neptunes, Timbaland, and Missy Elliott nominated
for fourteen awards and winning three. Its mayor offered a proclamation honoring them, and they finally garnered some recognition in their sleepy city, where they'd somehow remained fairly
anonymous.

You know what happens now: artists get too big for their
britches and start doing bizarre things. Timbaland and Pharrell
had already decided they should be known for more than just producing, and began indulging themselves.

HAVE YOU seen the movie *Bruno*? English comedian Sacha Baron
Cohen goes undercover to expose everything vacuous in the fashion industry. Posing as the vain homosexual host of an Austrian
fashion show, he goads self-important, well-to-do people into
demonstrating their detachment from reality. By the mid-aughts,
Pharrell seemed to be auditioning for a role in the film.

He hung with supermodels and designed sunglasses for Louis
Vuitton. He bought a condo in Miami and filled it with mammoth plants, anime-style sculptures, fiberglass monkeys on top
of horses, graffiti artists' renditions of Warhols emblazoned with
spermatozoa, and actual Warhols.

At the suggestion of a Paris art dealer named Emmanuel Per-
rotin, he even designed a piece of furniture called The Perspective
Chair. It stood upon two pairs of human legs, a man's and a woman's. "It's about being in another person's shoes," he told Conde
Naste's *Fashion Rocks* supplement. "It's about being in love, and I
wanted to know what that was like."

He told the *Guardian* that he saw Nigo—the Japanese fashioni-
sta with whom he'd founded two clothing lines—and soccer star
David Beckham as his peers, rather than other musicians. Then
there was his explanation of the connection between music and

fashion: "Fashion and music is like time and space. Without time there is no space and vice versa. Without fashion there is no music. What are you gonna wear in your video? What are you going to listen to going down the runway? It's the same thing."

He stumbled with a 2006 solo album and released four albums with the revitalized Neptunes band, this time called N*E*R*D (No-one Ever Really Dies). The act reunited him and Chad with their old mate Shae Haley and featured dizzying rock, hip-hop, and house fusions with the members' own singing and rapping front and center.

Their first work, *In Search of . . .* , was well reviewed, but the group's music became increasingly unlikable. Whereas their production isolated songs' defining elements and emphasized them, N*E*R*D bludgeoned the listener with as much studio trickery as possible, making for a series of soulless mosh-pit contrivances. Williams sung in falsetto, and their message was an unholy mash of pretentious preachings, stoner musings, and sleazy come-ons. "You ain't gotta tell us," Pharrell raps on the "Everybody Nose" remix. "You spending daddy's cash/ Your girlfriend's jealous/ You got the fattest ass."

"You can really dig into where society is at. Not to get too deep, but look at what's going on in the world right now and then jam to this," Chad said at one point, speaking on an album, *Seeing Sounds*, that has a song dedicated to women standing in a bathroom line to snort coke. "You don't learn much from Pharrell's lyrics except that he's horny," noted *Rolling Stone*.

BY THE EARLY 2000s Timbaland's weight had ballooned to more than three hundred pounds, and he was diagnosed with type 2 diabetes. He began overhauling his body. "I was having problems with simple things like getting up," he told *Men's Fitness*, "and I couldn't maintain energy throughout the day."

Embarrassed about his public image and concerned with his health, he hired a personal trainer who coached him in the weight room and adjusted his diet. Before long Tim had lost one-third of his body weight and began showing off his muscular new look in music videos, where he flirted with leggy costars.

But was his newfound buffness natural? A 2008 report from Albany newspaper the *Times Union* indicated that Timbaland, along with 50 Cent, Wyclef Jean, and Mary J. Blige, may have been shipped steroids or human growth hormone. (The report cited information from cooperating witnesses in an investigation undertaken by the Albany County district attorney.) Timbaland was not reached for comment, and in any case he and the other artists weren't charged—the probe focused on doctors who were illegally prescribing the drugs. But whether his body modifications came from the gym or the lab (or both), it was all part of a conscious effort to recast himself as a smooth-talking solo star.

Like other producers and moguls with lackluster MC talents—Baby and Diddy come to mind—he'd been honing his skills for years. But despite three albums with Magoo (which received mixed reviews) and a 1998 compilation called *Tim's Bio: Life from da Bassment*, it wasn't until 2007 that he put out a fully realized solo record, *Shock Value*.

For the work he enlisted everyone in his Rolodex, from regular collaborators to Elton John and Fall Out Boy. Like N*E*R*D, Timbaland experimented with rock (he even later crafted albums for Chris Cornell and OneRepublic), but his sound was more accessible than N*E*R*D's, and he went platinum.

Yet he never entirely seized solo stardom. His 2009 sequel *Shock Value II* failed to stir up interest among fans or critics. The album was notable for its heavy lineup of female pop stars, including R&B singer Brandy (recast as rapper Bran'Nu), pin-up singer Katy Perry, and teen sensation Miley Cyrus. Lamenting its poor performance, Tim told MTV he was done with hip-hop, explaining that he'd uncovered his true fan base.

"I did this research," he said. "It's the women who watch *Sex and the City, Desperate Housewives*—all the real go-to-the-bar women like Timbaland, and mostly European women." It was an unexpected yet heartfelt admission from a titan realizing his reign over the industry was slipping. The radio was so full of Timbaland impersonators by now that it was time to start over with a fresh sound.

# 10

# LIL JON

**■■■**

## Mosh Pit Hip-Hop

JONATHAN SMITH came up in an upper-middle-class neighborhood of southwest Atlanta. His street, called Flamingo Drive, was home to black lawyers, black doctors, and even the president of Morehouse College. His dad worked for Lockheed Martin, his mom was in the Army Reserves.

Unlike some other future rap stars, Lil Jon didn't rob people, steal cars, or even shoplift. He just partied. He had a massive lair in the basement of his parents' house, an apartment, really, complete with big screen TV, separate living room, and private bathroom. He didn't have to associate with his folks at all if he didn't want to. He would load up his personal fridge with Olde English and Colt 45—maybe even put a keg in there—and invite over everyone he knew. His friend Dwayne "Emperor" Searcy would spin hip-hop and bass records, and they'd get wild by the pool out back.

"We'd have house parties that didn't end," Jon says, in his famous, disorientingly articulate diction. "The party would go all night, until the next day. People would spend the night."

Jon attended Frederick Douglass High School, a technology-focused magnet school flush with a fleet of new Macs. But he wasn't much of a student and would often depart for Benjamin E. Mays, his friends' school, where he'd hang out with a more hardscrabble lot.

Sometimes he'd head out to Piedmont Park to check out the boards, trucks, and wheels at Skate Escape with another set of friends. His multiethnic skate crew introduced him to punk bands like Minor Threat, the Ramones, and Bad Brains, and even New Wave stuff like the Cure and early Ministry.

Jon was a bit nerdy back then. His longtime friend Vincent Phillips has said Jon's mother used to dress him in "fake polo shirts and fake Izods." And, of course, there's that famous high school graduation picture you've probably seen on the Internet, in which he sports a mortarboard, a dull expression, perky ears, and saucer-sized glasses. He confirms its authenticity and notes that before being called Lil Jon he was known as "Little Spike," after Spike Lee, who wore similar spectacles.

But by inviting over his different cliques and getting them drunk, he won a reputation for throwing banging parties. He particularly admired his friend Searcy, who was killing it on the turntables. "I was amazed with how he could control the crowd with records, how he could play a song and make people go fucking crazy," Jon says. His pal showed him the basics and gave him his equipment when he departed for active duty, and Jon began playing house parties. He notes, "By the time he got back from the navy I was the hottest DJ in Atlanta."

Through the skate scene he'd gotten into the British reggae band Steel Pulse, and so at Atlanta club New York Sound Factory he played dancehall and reggae. He became Rastafarian for a time, subsisting on vegetables, attending Rasta church, and cutting off his hair and letting it grow back as long dreadlocks. Eventually, however, he left the club for a hot new disco called Club Phoenix.

The early nineties were an exciting time to be young in Atlanta, which many rappers call a "melting pot" and had become a mecca for middle-class black folk. Fortune 500 companies like Coca-Cola, Home Depot, and UPS drew educated professionals from all over the South. The city's music scene was ascendant as well, and at Club Phoenix Jon mingled with trendsetters like Dallas Austin, TLC, and Arrested Development, not to mention drug dealers and the famed exotic dancers from Magic City. "That's where everybody who was anybody in Atlanta would be," Jon says.

It was there that he started screaming while DJing, which he says he learned from New York turntablist Kid Capri, who talked on the mic over records. Before long he'd developed his signature holler: "Oookaaaay!"

At Phoenix he also ran into aspiring label mogul Jermaine Dupri, who commented that, even when he wasn't DJing, Jon seemed to be *everywhere*. "That's always been my thing, to just be out, to be networking and getting to know everybody," Jon says. The pair developed a rapport, and when Dupri launched his So So Def record label, he invited Jon to come on and do promotions and A&R. "I was like, 'Huh?'" Jon remembers, unsure if he was adequately qualified for such a gig.

But he wisely accepted it, and in 1993 he became one of the first four or five employees of the soon-to-be-big-time imprint, which had a hit with Kris Kross. Jon promoted the label's records by hollering through a megaphone at exiting club goers, and also sought out emerging artists. Then Dupri assigned him to curate the *So So Def Bass Allstars* compilation, and so Jon immersed himself in the high-energy, Miami-style music, which was just a short step away from crunk.

BEFORE OUTKAST and Goodie Mob, Atlanta didn't have a distinctive hip-hop sound. Early nineties rap fans turned to acts like 2 Live

Crew and MC Shy-D, and anyone else who employed maximum bass. Hopefully your car was up to the task.

"You'd take a home stereo speaker from your house and put it in your backseat," Lil Jon remembers. "You'd go to Radio Shack and grab what they called the super tweeter and put it in the back window. When somebody would be driving by in their Cadillac, they'd be playing Keith Sweat's 'Make It Last Forever,' and the license plate would be rattling from the bottom."

Local tastemaker King Edward J helped popularize the bass sound in Atlanta by flooding the streets with his mixtapes. Something akin to a southeastern DJ Screw, he laced radio slow jams with low-frequency beats and sold the tapes out of his Decatur establishment, The J Shop. They had titles like "Solid Gold" and "Super Cuts."

A high school student named DJ Smurf joined J's team of mixmakers and can still remember J's sales pitch to customers who came into the store: "You can get a fifty minute for ten my friend, and a ninety minute for a nifty $13.50." Smurf later became influential on the bass and crunk scenes himself. His first forays into production were on J's tapes; he used four-track players to layer 808 drums over popular R&B and quiet storm tunes.

Born Michael Crooms, Smurf was raised in the inner-ring Atlanta suburb College Park and earned his nickname for his diminutive size. (He also answers to Mr. Collipark.) He went off to college at Alabama A&M, where he studied telecommunications and then business. But academics didn't captivate him. Instead, he saved money from DJ gigs and as a rapper self-released a single called "2 Tha Walls" in 1992. The song's chorus may sound familiar:

> To the windows!
> To the walls!
> Till the sweat drip down my balls!

When that chant landed in Lil Jon's hands a decade later, it would become crunk's siren call. In the nineties it could be commonly heard at black fraternity parties, so Smurf hadn't invented it, but he was the first to get it on wax.

He dropped out of college to team up with Atlanta's first rap star, MC Shy-D, a cousin of Afrika Bambaataa and a veteran of Luke Records. (In fact, it was Shy-D who sued Luke Campbell for unpaid royalties and sent him into bankruptcy.) In 1993 Shy-D released a trunk-rattling work called *The Comeback* on Atlanta imprint Ichiban Records, with Smurf helping out on production.

Smurf proceeded to hook up with Ichiban himself, releasing 1995's *Versastyle* and 1998's *Dead Crunk*. But it was time for him to face facts: his career as an artist had stalled. His flow wasn't very interesting, and, in an era of No Limit soldiers, he lacked a necessary cocksure attitude. But during *Dead Crunk*'s recording he'd stumbled onto a second career as a talent scout. For a track called "One on One" he enlisted a rapper called Kaine and his friend D-Roc, the latter of whom had appeared on hit Atlanta record "Bankhead Bounce" when he was fifteen.

Both men were born with disabilities: Kaine with a type of cerebral palsy, D-Roc with an undeveloped hand with nubs for fingers. Sonically, however, they had little in common, as D-Roc preferred booty-shakers and Kaine gravitated toward the hard sounds of Geto Boys. Still, their pairing on Smurf's track proved to be a memorable one.

"It sent chills, hearing them back and forth," Smurf recalls. "I was sitting in the studio like, 'Oh shit.' I said, 'Y'all might want to stay fuckin' with each other.'" They did, and, despite being unrelated, were christened Ying Yang Twins to emphasize the polarities in their styles.

Smurf signed them to a production deal, and their 2000 debut single "Whistle While You Twurk" roughly splits the difference between bass and crunk. Originally the song had whistling from

*Snow White and the Seven Dwarfs*, but copyright considerations forced them to remove it. (Disney probably couldn't imagine Snow White "moving her body in a way that she is rubbin up against somethin or someone," as Urban Dictionary defines "twurk.")

Two years later Ying Yang brought the "2 Tha Walls" chorus to Lil Jon, and that's when things started to get interesting.

"I don't know who invented crunk," says Smurf, "but Jon branded it."

THE 1996 compilation Jon executive-produced, *So So Def Bass All-stars*, features Edward J and Smurf, as well as a local speed-demon rapper called Playa Poncho, responsible for the delirious track, "Whatz Up, Whatz Up," which consists almost entirely of Poncho wondering aloud, "What's up? What's up?/ What's up? What's up? What's up?"

The album was a hit, and by this time Jon had developed a keen ear for what dance floor crowds wanted to hear. He noticed that driving, combative chants like Eightball & MJG's "Lay It Down" got them particularly sweaty. "At the time, we were listening to stuff like that to get us hyped up in the club," he says. "I noticed there was no music made by Atlanta artists to get us crazy like that. So, I was like, 'We need to make a song just to get Atlanta folks crunk.'"

What is crunk? It's raucous party music with coarse drum machine rhythms and repetitive, electro-style synth lines, not particularly concerned with lyrics or flows. It features strong bass, but it's slower paced than Miami bass, less for shaking than for knocking into things.

Jon would regularly hit spots like Club 559 and The Gate with Playa Poncho and his crew, and one night the group began spontaneously shouting, "Who you wit?" Jon notes, "When you go in a club with your boys and the right song comes on, you just start chanting together. . . . You start bouncing around. Even today, you go in an Atlanta club, they're gon' start chanting, 'Ay!' or 'East Side!' People love to chant shit."

The "Who you wit?" line worked everyone into a frenzy, and Jon resolved to make it into a song. For the task he joined forces with a pair of burly guys from Poncho's posse, Big Sam and Lil Bo—the East Side Boyz.

None of them could rap, but it didn't matter. Jon had decided that rhyming couplets, verses, and other fancy-shmancy rap elements were filler, and that what listeners really desired were short catchphrases shouted ad nauseum. And so on "Who U Wit?" they simply repeat the eponymous phrase over rumbling 808s and hissing hi-hats, peppering this nagging question with commands to, "Grab shorty!" or "Just ride!" When all else fails, they simply yell, "Ay! Ay! Ay!"

The song's success led to the trio's 1997 debut *Get Crunk, Who U Wit: Da Album*, but crunk itself wouldn't take off for a few more years. Jon spent the time streamlining his formula and incorporating slightly more ornate production techniques. By 2002, when pretty boys like Nelly and Pharrell had all but taken over rap, audiences were ready for something grittier.

Lil Jon & The East Side Boyz's new work *Kings of Crunk* fit the bill, as it wasn't for the Cristal-sipping bourgeois types, but rather the roughnecks who could only get into the VIP by force. As Jon notes on "I Don't Give a Fuck":

> You gotta pocket fulla money, nigga, I don't give a
>     fuck!
> You drinkin' off with them hos, bitch, I don't give a
>     fuck!
> In the club wit yo' pussy clique, I don't give a fuck!
> Security on my dick, bitch, I don't give a fuck!

Jon crashed parties in real life, too. He says that though by the early aughts his act was big in the South and Midwest, BET wouldn't play their music or invite them to their annual Florida bacchanal, Spring Bling. But they somehow snaked their way onto stage one year—either 2001 or 2002, Jon says—and tore it up. "People were going nuts, and the BET people were looking like, 'Who the fuck are these motherfuckers?'"

Sure, it's ironic that an articulate, polite, upper-middle-class kid was leading a movement centered around unbridled aggression. But the beauty of crunk is that it offers a platform for constructive acting out, a nonviolent way to unleash your angst. It's dance music for *guys*, so they can mosh, slam dance, or simply stomp around spilling their glasses of Hpnotiq.

Jon was now officially the king of crunk, but he didn't pretend to have invented the word, which had been commonly used in the South for years. "Crunk is whatever cranked the club up," says DJ Paul of Three 6 Mafia, the group Pimp C and others credited with founding crunk. "Back in the day in Memphis that's how the word came up—like when you crank up a car, it's jumping off the starter and it's rolling. So, when everybody was going crazy, that's what crunk meant to us."

The subgenre's tipping point was 2003's "Get Low," an ode to strippers for which Jon used Ying Yang's "till the sweat drop down my balls" chorus and added whistles, 808s, and a high-pitched, cracked-out synth line. Before long hip-hop and crunk were nearly synonymous, and the word was latched onto by the mainstream, like "bling bling." Crunk sprung up entirely outside of white culture, but it was simple enough for anyone to dance to and silly enough to be nonthreatening.

Jon had turned himself into a walking, talking caricature, sporting shiny grills, sunglasses, and jewel-emblazoned pimp chalices, the first of which he says was given to him by Milwaukee pimp-turned-radio-host Pimpin' Ken. There were scattered grumblings about Jon's crazy black man shtick; the *Village Voice*'s Greg Tate called him a "minstrel-poseur genius," and hip-hop purists complained about crunk's coarse, inelegant nature.

Others however, waxed philosophical about the music, calling it a key to the past capable of unlocking long-dormant ancestral pain and unleashing a primal fury passed down since the time of slavery. There's no denying that though it may have stripped away rap's poetry, it also excised its artifice, bloat, and pseudo-intellectualism, not unlike another hard-charging subgenre Jon had dug in his youth. "What punk was to rock," Andre 3000 famously said, "crunk is to rap."

"The difference is between sitting around listening to music and partying to music," elaborates Atlanta's Lil Scrappy, a formerly lyrical rapper who found success when he switched to crunk. He believes that loquacious hip-hop can be boring, especially in a live setting. "You can't just be walking back and forth on stage, otherwise it could just be a seminar."

Crunk presented an opening for raw, unrefined talents whose work might not have been previously considered nuanced enough for the mainstream, like Bone Crusher, Pastor Troy, Petey Pablo, YoungBloodZ, and Trillville, a group responsible for my all-time favorite crunk song, "Neva Eva." That tune is really nothing more than a repeated, angry invective aimed at an unspecified foe:

> Bitch, nigga you could neva eva/
> Eva eva/ Eva eva/ Eva eva/ Eva eva
> Get on my level, ho!

In the video, a group of crunked-up school kids kidnap their teacher and dismantle their classroom.

Along with Lil Scrappy, Jon is featured on the track, and indeed he seemed to be everywhere at once, just like he'd been on the Atlanta club scene. His biggest production hit of the era was Usher's electro-inspired, "Yeah!" in which Jon barks, "Let's go!," "What?," and "OK!" This might not sound impressive, but he leaves an indelible mark on the song; without him, it's just another R&B seduction story.

*Billboard* determined "Yeah!" to be the second most popular song of the aughts, behind Mariah Carey's Jermaine Dupri–produced hit "We Belong Together." But Jon counts among his greatest accolades being parodied by comedian Dave Chappelle on his Comedy Central sketch show. In one bit Chappelle plays Jon arriving at the airport.

**Counter Clerk:** Are you checking any luggage today?
**Chappelle:** Ye-yeah!
**Counter Clerk:** Did you pack your bags yourself?
**Chappelle:** Ye-yeah!
**Counter Clerk:** Your bags have been in your possession the whole time?
**Chappelle:** What?
**Counter Clerk:** Have these bags been in your possession the whole time?
**Chappelle:** What?
**Counter Clerk:** Have these bags been in your possession the whole time?
**Chappelle:** Ye-yeah!
**Counter Clerk:** Mr. Jon, you're all set.
**Chappelle:** OK!

At this point, Jon's character momentarily drops the façade and speaks prissily and with impeccable diction.

**Chappelle:** Pardon me, madam. Will this be reflected upon my frequent flyer miles?
**Counter Clerk:** Did you book your flight online?

**Chappelle:** Ye-yeah!
**Counter Clerk:** Then they will be.
**Chappelle:** OK!

CRUNK WAS now so big that its downfall was inevitable. Ironically, DJ Smurf, who'd helped usher it in, also helped usher it out. After watching Jon get all the credit for crunk, he sought to brand his own sub-subgenre, an even further stripped style called intimate club music, known for its understated delivery and hushed tones.

Mississippi rapper David Banner employed the approach on the biggest hit of his career, "Play," as did Georgia white rapper Bubba Sparxxx on "Ms. New Booty" and Ying Yang Twins on their smash, "Wait (The Whisper Song)." Smurf produced all three of the tracks, but intimate club music's run was nonetheless short; maybe because of its unfortunate name or simply because "intimacy" in dance music is more attractive to the less-lucrative grown and sexy crowd than to the kids.

A similar Atlanta musical fad called snap quickly stepped in to take its place. As on "Wait (The Whisper Song)," it used finger snaps for percussion, and practitioners included Atlanta groups like Dem Franchize Boys, and D4L.

The latter act took over radio in late 2005 with their ode to cellulite, "Laffy Taffy," a song simple enough for a toddler to sing. (But much too dirty.) Wu-Tang Clan's Ghostface Killah promptly began predicting rap's apocalypse, calling "Laffy Taffy" "bullshit" and mocking it in concert. But it wasn't until the arrival of Smurf's next star, Soulja Boy, that the shit really hit the fan.

As for Jon, he gradually descended from his cultural plateau. After 2004's *Crunk Juice* he saw the implosion of his label, TVT Records, and didn't manage another album until 2010's *Crunk Rock*, which sold poorly. He remains an in-demand club DJ, however, and says he doesn't plan to distance himself from the movement he popularized. He proudly notes that artists like lily-white pop star Ke$ha continue to employ "crunk" in their vernaculars.

"I'm never going to stop using the term, because that's a term I grew up with, and it still applies to everything," Jon says. "Crunk music is a great release of tension. It lets you lose your mind."

# 11

# DJ DRAMA AND T.I.

■ ■ ■

## Mixtapes and Turf Wars in Atlanta

DJ DRAMA'S office and studio can be found in a gentrifying section of Atlanta's Castleberry Hill neighborhood. Housed in an unmarked, squat building with bars over the windows, the facilities look abandoned from the outside. The inside maintains a sort of Goodwill chic, with dirty carpet, furniture seemingly procured from a garage sale, and, in the studio, floor-to-ceiling purple soundproofing foam.

It's understandable that Drama doesn't keep the place too tidy, considering the music industry police have been known to tear it to shreds. In early 2007 a SWAT team working in conjunction with local cops and the Record Industry Association of America (RIAA) came crashing in, armed with guns and dogs. The spot had been under surveillance for weeks, and Drama received a call shortly beforehand warning him of the raid. "I thought it was a mistake," he says. "So when they came in and threw me on the ground and handcuffed me and asked for my ID and said, 'We got one of the perps,' then I said, 'This is real.'"

Drama and his DJ partner Don Cannon were arrested and charged with making bootleg recordings and violating Georgia's RICO (Racketeer Influenced and Corrupt Organizations) statute, a law usually associated with the mob. "When I was face down on the floor," Drama remembers, "I just didn't want to move and get my head blown off."

They also confiscated some twenty-five thousand CDs, not to mention recording equipment, computer gear, and four vehicles, two of which (a van and a BMW 645) Drama says he never got back. After he was taken to Fulton County Jail, the police interrogated his studio's employees, he says, demanding to know the location of the guns and drugs. They made a mess of the place and ripped up the purple foam, but didn't find anything.

The story made national news. It was clear that the RIAA had gotten their point across. As the trade group representing major record labels, their task is enforcing intellectual property laws, an increasingly important challenge during the music industry's rapid decline. The RIAA were the ones who sued the pants off college kids illegally downloading music from file-sharing sites, and now they'd decided that Drama and his ilk were the bad guys.

Drama specializes in mixtapes, which can be loosely defined as works that aren't official studio albums. Though they were once actual tapes, now they're usually released in CD or MP3 format and are usually free, although DJs and even Amazon and iTunes sell some. (Drama claims not to make money off of mixtapes, although collaborator Young Jeezy has accused him of doing exactly that. To make things even more complicated, major labels have even begun repackaging mixtapes and selling them through traditional channels.)

Mixtapes are sometimes perfectly legal, but they're often full of copywritten music, which was the case with many of the CDs

Cross-dressing Shreveport, Louisiana, rapper Ms. Peachez is played by Nelson Boyd.

Hospitalized after shooting himself in the eye, Bushwick Bill posed along with Geto Boys group mates Willie D (left) and Scarface (right) for the cover of their seminal album, *We Can't Be Stopped*.

Houston MC Trae,
left, poses with
Rap-A-Lot Records
founder J. Prince.
MATT SONZALA

Houston rapper Scarface is universally considered the South's
best rapper. VINCENT SOYEZ, COURTESY OF UNIVERSAL MUSIC GROUP

Pimp C, left, and Bun B, formed Port Arthur, Texas, duo UGK.

Eightball, left, and MJG
hail from Memphis.
CHRIS STANFORD,
COURTESY OF E1 MUSIC

Houston's Screwed Up Records & Tapes sells DJ Screw's music, and...that's
about it. BEN WESTHOFF

Memphis's other famous rap group has been whittled down to two members: DJ Paul, left, and Juicy J. DAVE HILL, COURTESY OF SONY MUSIC

Virginia Beach producer Timbaland tore down the boundaries between pop, rap, and R&B. ALBERT WATSON, COURTESY OF UNIVERSAL MUSIC GROUP

New Orleans's former bounce star Juvenile sold more than four million copies of his 1998 album, *400 Degreez.*

CISE HD, COURTESY OF E1 MUSIC

With his patty-cake hit "Country Grammar," Nelly inspired a generation of southern hit-makers.

JONATHAN MANNION, COURTESY OF UNIVERSAL MUSIC GROUP

DJ Drama helps rappers build their buzz by crafting semi-legal mixtapes.

ZACH WOLFE, COURTESY OF WARNER MUSIC GROUP

The most successful rap duo ever, Atlanta's OutKast features Big Boi, left, and Andre 3000. COURTESY OF SONY MUSIC

Cash Money Records cofounder Baby is also one of the label's best-known artists.

RAY TAMARRA, COURTESY OF UNIVERSAL MUSIC GROUP

Former child star Lil Wayne went on to dominate the pop culture landscape in his twenties. COURTESY OF UNIVERSAL MUSIC GROUP

A scene from Lil Wayne's Hollygrove neighborhood in New Orleans.
BEN WESTHOFF

Atlanta beat maker and hype man Lil Jon didn't invent crunk,
but he branded it. TYLER CLINTON, COURTESY OF UNIVERSAL MUSIC GROUP

T.I. has been called
the southern Jay-Z.

A scene from T.I.'s Atlanta neighborhood, Bankhead. BEN WESTHOFF

T.I.'s Club Crucial. BEN WESTHOFF

Houston rapper Paul Wall is known for his grills and his love for Texas.

MIKE FROST, COURTESY OF WARNER MUSIC GROUP

Chamillionaire has the biggest hit in Houston rap history, "Ridin."

JONATHAN MANNION, COURTESY OF UNIVERSAL MUSIC GROUP

Tallahassee, Florida, artist and producer T-Pain is best known for his use of Auto-Tune.

The Neptunes, one of the most successful production groups of all time, tried their hands as artists with N*E*R*D. LESLIE KEE, COURTESY OF UNIVERSAL MUSIC GROUP

Atlanta's DJ Smurf broke Soulja Boy, Ying Yang Twins, and other derided southern acts. KEVIN TERRELL, COURTESY OF UNIVERSAL MUSIC GROUP

Besides inspiring a dance craze, Soulja Boy changed the way rappers market themselves over the Internet. MEENO, COURTESY OF UNIVERSAL MUSIC GROUP

Oft-incarcerated Atlanta rapper Gucci Mane has been called both a genius and a doofus. JONATHAN MANNION, COURTESY OF WARNER MUSIC GROUP

seized from Drama. But that doesn't make him the moral equivalent of those dodgy Times Square guys selling burned Alicia Keys albums for two bucks. In fact, his mixtapes are made in collaboration with the artists themselves, like T.I., Lil Wayne, or Gucci Mane, and sometimes with their record companies, too.

The tapes often serve to promote an upcoming studio album. An MC might rap over a beat from a popular radio song, which gives him the chance to show off his stuff over someone else's work, to gain some quick buzz. Since the majority of rappers do this, and they all use each other's songs, none of them complain. Mixtapes are a low-pressure, informal opportunity for MCs to be off-the-cuff and showcase the lighter sides of their personalities.

In fact, by the middle of the aughts, record company executives saw mixtapes as great advertising and began funding them out of their budgets, just like promotional posters or magazine ads. Ironically, then, this meant that the labels had not only helped pay for Drama's mixtapes but, through the RIAA, for his arrest too.

"There's a disconnection," Drama says, distinguishing between label employees who understand his style of underground street promotion and those who don't. "During the raid, there were people [at the labels] that were like, 'Why is this happening?'"

Drama was released from jail the next day and eventually worked out a deal with the RIAA to escape serving more time. He was required to film a public service announcement condemning DJs who leak music without permission, something he wasn't in the habit of doing in the first place.

But, save for the lost van and BMW, the raid actually ended up the best thing that could have happened to him. "The upside is, that situation brought me a lot of fame and exposure and publicity," he says. "So in the long run it benefited my career."

As illegal downloading gained speed in the late nineties and CD sales began to dip—hip-hop sales, particularly—executives panicked and began some truly awful experiments. Remember

Sony BMG's "rootkit" copy protection software? Placed onto some of their 2005 CDs, it automatically installed itself onto your hard drive, making your computer vulnerable to hackers.

There's no doubt that the industry needed a shake-up, and Drama and his colleagues have sent it in uncharted directions, either increasing its popularity and improving its creativity or nearly destroying it, depending on whom you ask. Indeed, taking a commodity (rap albums) that people once used to pay for and making them (largely) free doesn't sound like the best business model.

"I've done nothing but help the music industry, I can say with 100 percent confidence," he counters. "I look at mixtapes like hip-hop's bloodline. It's about feeding the fans."


DJ DRAMA is bulky, wears a beard, and looks like he's seen it all before. The son of a white mother and a black father, he has skin with a Mediterranean hue. He wears a ball cap spun ninety degrees to the side and enormous jeans. Though winter, it's brutally hot in his spartan studio today, causing him to pull off his oversize sweatshirt. Like his offices he's not especially stylish—he's rugged.

During our conversation he holds his BlackBerry impatiently, attempting to fire off messages during the five or ten seconds it takes me to ask my questions. He's also prone to absentminded boasting. "I put together an OutKast [song recently]," he says, "when not many people could do that."

Drama has become synonymous with the mixtape scene, but his contributions are largely intangible. He doesn't produce, rap, or sing. Instead, he conceives his tapes' themes, sequences them, and adds various interludes, shout-outs, and turntable effects. It might not sound like much, but few folks have the connections, bombast, and diplomatic skills necessary for this line of work. He's released traditional albums as well that have sold hundreds of thousands of copies; many listeners believe his stamp of approval ensures quality.

"I'm like a chef," he explains. "Most of the music is pretty much [the artist's], but they still bring it to me to put it out. It's like having a frozen chicken. You can cook it anywhere, but you may bring it to a specific chef because he has a nice oven, and when he puts all his spices on that chicken and cooks it, it just comes out better than if you did it yourself."

The mixtape phenomenon began in hip-hop's first days, when fans and promoters passed around live recordings of DJ sets. The name was later given to homemade compilations, the kind you might make for a girl you had a crush on.

More recently they've often served as a musical curriculum vitae, used by little-known rappers in search of record deals. 50 Cent excelled at this. His early, unofficially released mixtapes took shots at his rival Ja Rule and others, building his fame and bringing him to the attention of Eminem. Nowadays established rappers use mixtapes for promotion, a technique that started in the Northeast and was deployed down south by Drama and others. "I didn't reinvent the wheel," Drama says. "I took southern music and applied the formula to it." Born Tyree Simmons, he came up in a politically conscious Philadelphia household and attended labor rallies as a kid. He acquired his first mixtape on a trip to New York City with his sister, and he later brought his love of East Coast rap to Clark Atlanta University, where he sold mixtapes to his fellow students. Early versions featured underground New York artists and R&B singers, but as his customers began to demand the rowdier southern stuff, he changed course.

His career didn't really take off until he linked up with Atlanta rapper T.I., who would become one of the three or four most famous rap artists working. In 2000 the rapper's Brooklyn-born business partner, Jason Geter, acquired one of Drama's mixtapes at a barbershop and set up a meeting between the DJ and T.I.

"He was fresh out the trap, quiet, didn't know me, so that's probably why he seemed so reserved," Drama remembers of the MC, who was not yet twenty. "He picked a beat, and at the end of [his verse] he said, 'King of the South.'" Drama was stunned by T.I.'s bombast, considering he was mostly unknown in Atlanta, to say nothing of the entire region. "I said, 'That little nigga just said he's king of the South! He's trippin'.'"


BUT T.I. has always taken himself seriously, even when no one else does. In elementary school he rhymed about going to juvenile lockup and getting suspended from school, and even today his words are usually delivered with a scowl. Though he's good-looking and possesses the charisma necessary for his line of work, he seems to only smile when necessary, as if taking the time to do so will slow him, however briefly, from expanding his rap empire.

Equal parts gangsta, hood ambassador, craft-conscious artist, and bottom-line-focused executive, he believes there are always more fans to be won, more wealth to be amassed. Most rappers want to be filthy rich, but only T.I., it seems, will invest each moment toward this goal. "He's a workhorse," says DJ Drama. "Even when he really doesn't want to do something he does the work."

First, about his moniker: His childhood nickname was Tip. But because of his thick accent people frequently asked him to spell it out, and so as a rapper he became T.I.P. After becoming label mates with Q-Tip, however, he morphed into simply T.I.

Born Clifford Harris Jr. in 1980, he coveted the fly life early. With his father away in New York, he was raised by a consortium of family members, including his cool uncles, who were only in their twenties themselves. They listened to N.W.A and 2 Live Crew, smoked weed, and drove beautiful new cars. If he was going to be like them, he was going to have to do what they did—sell drugs. Even the incarceration of one of them on a ten-year bid didn't deter him.

"That just made me even hungrier because I knew wasn't nobody else representing for the family like that, nobody else going to come through on Mother's Day with side-by-side refrigerators and a brand new car for my grandmother," he told *Murder Dog*. "Nobody that was going to take me shopping, to the arcade or give me hundreds of dollars to throw in my pocket when I was 7, 8 years old. So I knew I had to do it for myself at that point. That's really when I really got buckwild, started doing whatever it takes."

T.I. plied his trade in Bankhead, his swath of west Atlanta whose major artery is officially called Donald Lee Holowell Parkway but still referred to by its former name, Bankhead Highway. The road passes through the now-abandoned Bowen Homes housing project, the childhood residence of former D4L member Shawty Lo. (In 2008, Lo began insisting that T.I. wasn't actually from Bankhead like he claimed but rather from suburban Riverdale, Georgia.)

Bankhead is a poor but colorful place, dotted with mom-and-pop stores, salvage yards, vacated properties, and exquisite graffiti. At 2517 Bankhead Highway, in the heart of the neighborhood, is T.I.'s Club Crucial, a popular, retro-futuristic-styled danceteria.

As a young hustler T.I. would set up shop on South Grand Street, in a vacant lot across from his mother's house. He says he got serious about dealing dope in his teen years and would work all night long. But even after going home to sleep he wasn't really off the clock, as anyone needing a fix was welcome to knock on his bedroom window. "I was a young and stupid man," he told MTV.

After seeing a friend get shot when he was fourteen, T.I. bought a handgun, he said, and three years later was arrested for possession of crack with intent to distribute. He served some time in county and received seven years' probation. When he got out, his future producer DJ Toomp and Jason Geter challenged him to get off the streets and try his hand as a rapper. They took him to a studio, introduced him to some influential people, and not long afterward he secured a deal with LaFace.

His debut album bore an appropriate title, *I'm Serious*, but failed to sell well, perhaps because of its release date, less than a month after 9/11. T.I., however, chalked it up to a lack of promotion. He asked for and received his release from LaFace, founded his own imprint with Geter called Grand Hustle Records, and entered into a joint venture deal with Atlantic Records. This placed more of the promotional duties (and costs) onto his shoulders, but also gave him more control over his destiny. He shot his own videos and put out mixtapes, promoting a song called "24s," which became popular regionally.

Finally, his career had legs. "He and Grand Hustle built their buzz through mixtapes in the streets of Atlanta," says DJ Drama, adding that if he had relied on major label support he never would have gotten anywhere.

BONE CRUSHER featured T.I. on his 2003 crunk-era favorite "Never Scared," and that same year T.I. released his second album, *Trap Muzik*. Its title references drug-dealing hot spots, or "traps," and the work boasts the David Banner–produced hit, "Rubberband Man."

"Who I'm is?/ Rubberband man/ Wild as the Taliban/ Nine in my right/ Forty-five in my other hand," T.I. raps. His nickname came from an old drug-dealing habit; he'd arrive at work each day wearing rubber bands on his wrists signifying how much dope he had on offer. Whenever he made a sale he'd take one off his wrist and use it to bundle his cash; when his arms were bare his day was over.

T.I. deliberately incorporated such vocabulary into his music; in his mind, there was a dearth of local rappers speaking to residents of drug-ridden hoods like Bankhead. While OutKast and Goodie Mob may have been making heartfelt music, they came from southwest Atlanta, the wealthier part of town. "Niggas who are from where I'm from can't really identify with them," he said.

His rap persona, then, comes from his life. This isn't a novel concept, but unlike other, less-compelling trap MCs, he doesn't shy away from the dirty details. Instead of simply rapping about being a hard ass, he'll rap about the crimes of his youth, the details of his prison terms, the way they've affected him mentally, and the financial and familial repercussions. It's all intended to feel as authentic as possible.

At one point, however, it became a bit too real. Just when his career was starting to gain traction, he was pinched for drug- and gun-related probation violations and forced to serve seven months. Indeed, untimely arrests would become his Achilles' heel. Though *Trap Muzik* would go gold that year, he remained unsatisfied.

And so, upon his release and in advance of his next album, he sought out DJ Drama, who had inaugurated a mixtape series called *Gangsta Grillz*, identifiable by their Lil Jon shout-outs. In 2004 Drama compiled *Gangsta Grillz Meets T.I. & P$C in da Streets*, featuring Pimp Squad Click (P$C), a group composed of Grand Hustle artists.

While *In da Streets* has its moments, it's dragged down by too many guest features. But T.I. and Drama excelled on another tape that year, *Down with the King*, which references T.I.'s self-applied "King of the South" moniker and includes only T.I. and his crew. Houston rapper Lil' Flip had taken umbrage with this assertion, and the pair were engaged in a full-fledged rap beef. Neither party had a particularly legitimate claim to the title at this point, but the dispute gave T.I. something to get passionate about.

He always sounds best when he's fired up, and during *Down with the King* his voice often lilts slightly, creating a tiny whine that adds sonic complexity to his threats. Over the beat of Jay-Z's "99

Problems" he offers his own version, called "99 Problemz (But Lil'
Flip Ain't One)."

> Lyrically, I murk you
> Physically, I hurt you
> You ain't never ran the streets
> You had a curfew

T.I. makes it clear that he's down with other Houston rappers,
like Paul Wall, Slim Thug, Mike Jones, and Z-Ro. The tape also features phone conversations between T.I. and Scarface, who asserts
that Lil' Flip isn't actually from the hood he claims, Cloverland—
ironically, the same accusation Shawty Lo later made of T.I.

T.I. and Lil' Flip's quarrel would climax with a brawl between
their entourages at a Houston concert. T.I.'s crew was said to emerge
victorious, and it all served as great promotion for his new album,
*Urban Legend*, which quickly went platinum. Lil' Flip's sales have
suffered since then, and it's become a hip-hop truism that T.I.'s
chutzpah and superior rhymes ended his career. (Although the
leprechaun outfit Flip had taken to wearing to emphasize his Cloverland ties didn't help his cause.)

*Down with the King* established T.I. as a force and also put
Gangsta Grillz on the map. It crowned Drama as the premiere
architect of the "mini-album," as he calls it, a work containing
just a single artist that is as good or better than his studio albums.
He'd use this formula to introduce Young Jeezy and jump-start Lil
Wayne's career, as well.

AFTER PHARRELL declared T.I. to be the "Down South Jay-Z," T.I.
went ahead and proved him right. His classic 2006 fourth album
*King* showcases his breath-control mastery, dazzling internal asso-
nance, and mastery of formal rhyme patterns.

In the eyes of myself and other critics, hip-hop doesn't get more sublime than gothic banger "What You Know," produced by DJ Toomp, which touches on the glories, fears, and paranoia of trap life.

Fresh off the jet to the block
Burnin' rubber with the top popped
My partner bustin' shots
I tell 'em stop, he'll make the block hot

*King* sold a half million copies in its first seven days and landed at #1. That same week saw the premiere of *ATL*, a gentle coming-of-age story with T.I. in the lead. The film made $21 million, and *King* became the top-selling hip-hop album of 2006.

Briefly, then, T.I. actually seemed satisfied with the trajectory of his career, which is perhaps what made 2007 follow-up *T.I. vs. T.I.P.* such a slog. The concept pitted his hot-headed hustler alter ego (T.I.P.) against his smooth-talking businessman persona (T.I.) It was a gimmick Eminem had already employed more effectively, and while *T.I. vs. T.I.P.* went platinum, it sold worse than *King* and isn't particularly memorable. The lack of production from DJ Toomp certainly hurts.

But, just as the battle with Lil' Flip had creatively inspired him, so too would real-life drama jar him from his comfort zone. Following a Cincinnati show in May of 2006, he was involved in a lethal dispute at a nightclub. Some attendees asserted that a group of local patrons grew annoyed when one of T.I.'s crew mates made it rain dollar bills; others said the locals resented not being allowed into the VIP section, commandeered by T.I.'s group.

Whatever the case, a scuffle ensued, and a member of the Cincinnati crew named Hosea Thomas was hit in the head with a bottle of liquor. T.I. and his men hustled out of the club and tried to drive away in their two vans but were ambushed by a pair of sport utility vehicles containing Thomas and others.

T.I. was sitting behind Philant Johnson, a childhood friend who now worked as his assistant. He could do nothing as the assailants pulled up next to them and unleashed fifty to one hundred rounds, by T.I.'s estimation. Johnson lost consciousness. T.I. discovered that his van's tires were flat, and when he attempted to drag his friend to the other van, they were fired upon again.

The police arrived and Johnson was taken to the hospital, but he would not survive. T.I. was left with the unenviable task of informing Johnson's young daughter and mom of the tragedy. He told Johnson's mother that he believed the bullets were intended for him.

THOUGH HOSEA THOMAS would be found guilty of the murder in late 2008, the incident left T.I. a nervous, paranoid wreck. The murders of Biggie Smalls and Tupac Shakur—both at heights of their fame—loomed large in his mind, he said, and he prepared himself for another attack.

Only a few hours before his scheduled performance at the BET Awards in Atlanta on October 13, 2007, he attempted to purchase three high-powered machine guns and silencers, valued at $12,000, from his bodyguard in a Walgreen's parking lot.

Little did he know that the bodyguard had been pinched a few days earlier while trying to buy the firearms from a federal agent. He'd subsequently flipped and turned government witness. And so T.I. was arrested by Bureau of Alcohol, Tobacco, and Firearms agents. Another group of officers, meanwhile, raided his house, breaking windows, lobbing stun grenades inside, and knocking open the front door, turning up more unlawful pistols and rifles.

They also took into custody his fiancée, Tameka "Tiny" Cottle, a former member of R&B group Xscape, who was accused of possessing pot and ecstasy. Tiny had delivered her and T.I.'s stillborn daughter earlier that year and would announce she was pregnant again only days later. She delivered their second son in 2008.

After posting a $3 million bond, T.I. was confined to home arrest and served a year there, before being sentenced to nine months in prison and three months in a halfway house. All told it was a pretty lax sentence considering his crimes; as part of his unique plea agreement he received fifteen hundred hours of community service.

Many rappers go to prison. In fact, during T.I.'s incarceration, three of the four other most famous southern rappers were also there or headed there: Gucci Mane, Lil Boosie, and Lil Wayne. (Young Jeezy, who has the most thugged-out image of the bunch, somehow qualified as its most upstanding citizen.)

But T.I. used the run-up to his incarceration as a PR opportunity, mining the drama of his friend's murder and his impending sentencing, which could have sent him away for as long as ten years. In the month and a half before he was sentenced he partnered with MTV for a reality show called *Road to Redemption* in which he toured the country as an antiviolence motivational speaker for at-risk kids.

He made his tribulations the subject of his sixth album, 2008's *Paper Trail*, which he prepared while locked down in his house. "I ain't dead/ I ain't done/ I ain't scared/ I ain't run," he raps on "No Matter What." "I lost my partner and my daughter in the same year/ Somehow I rise above my problems and remain here."

MCs like Lil Wayne and Jay-Z say they don't write down their lyrics before recording them, preferring instead to organize their songs in their heads shortly ahead of time. I find this practice endlessly annoying, akin to Albert Pujols refusing to take batting practice. T.I. had previously used this approach, but for *Paper Trail* he took a different tack. With all the time in the world on his hands, he composed his verses and edited them until he felt they were perfect.

Though he'd started his career making songs for guys in the trap, this new approach coincided with an all-out blitz on his new target audience, mainstream America. "They want a variety, and they don't want to see so much of the ghetto that it's depressing," he told the *Los Angeles Times* years earlier. "But then, they don't want to see so much of the suburbs to where it's not realistic."

*Paper Trail* is an all-out pop album, almost unimaginably catchy. A duet called "Live Your Life" with Rihanna samples "Dragostea din tei" (the "numa numa" song), and the surprisingly tender "Whatever You Like" features a radiant synth beat from producer Jim Jonsin. Both singles went triple platinum. A collaboration with Justin Timberlake called "Dead and Gone," which deals directly with Johnson's death, sold a mere two million.

Real-life drama often makes for great art, and much of *Paper Trail* concerns T.I.'s attempts to come to grips with his situation. On "Ready for Whatever," he explains why his is not a typical rapper-buys-guns-and-gets-caught story.

> If your life was in jeopardy every day is you tellin'
>     me, you wouldn't need weaponry? . . .
> Either die or go to jail that's a hell of decision . . .
> I'm just trying to let you know that I ain't think I had
>     a choice . . .
> Yes officially I broke the law but not maliciously

It almost felt anticlimactic when he finally went in, serving a year total in a Forest City, Arkansas, prison and an Atlanta halfway house. Naturally, then, his early 2010 return gave birth to a fresh promotional cycle in preparation for a new album. This included a mixtape with DJ Drama, *Fuck a Mix-Tape*, and a Larry King interview, in which T.I. spent much of his time squinting and sucking in his bottom lip. The septuagenarian host castigated him for stockpiling weapons and noted he'd been a straight A student as a child. Why then, had he gotten involved selling drugs in the first place? "I was poor, Larry," T.I. said.

Hoping to end on a positive note, King finished by inquiring whether he was happy. Most in his position would have answered in the affirmative, but most don't have T.I.'s drive.

"Am I a happy man? They say when you're completely happy, you die," he said, allowing, "I'm the happiest I've ever been."

Unfortunately, all of this goodwill was squandered when he and Tiny were arrested in Los Angeles in September of that year, after being pulled over and suspected of drug possession. Though he was not prosecuted for the incident, T.I. was cited for a probation violation, and returned to prison on an eleven-month sentence. His fans were left to ponder how he was going to talk his way out of this one.

# 12

# PAUL WALL AND THE NEW H-TOWN MOVEMENT

■ ■ ■

## Shining Diamonds

PAUL WALL is the most curious of hip-hop specimens, and not just because he's white. He certainly is that, though, a pasty, doughy Democrat who underwent gastric surgery to lose one hundred pounds, and whose identity as a rapper is sometimes questioned. One time before a show in Pensacola, Florida, he saddled up to the bar next to a guy who wondered aloud what time Paul Wall would go on. "I'm starting in about twenty minutes," he told the fella, who gave him a dirty look. "'I'm not talking about you, I'm talking about Paul Wall the rapper,'" Wall recalls the man saying. "I thought me and this dude were about to get in a fight."

But Wall's pale complexion is optimal for admiring his plethora of highly detailed tattoos. His work was mostly performed by famed Los Angeles artist Mister Cartoon, who did a portrait of Wall as a clown, complete with gleaming grill and small gray hairs in his beard. The MC's sleeves are full of tributes to friends who are in jail or deceased, including a Screwed Up Click member named Big Hawk, who was shot to death in 2006. On one hand Wall has the state of Texas and the Houston Astros' logo, a star. On his knuckles he's got "F A S T" on one hand and "L I F E" on the other, to go with the title of his 2009 album, *Fast Life*.

It's a curious motto, considering he doesn't often move in a speedy manner. He raps at a leisurely pace, and in his videos he's partial to classic lowrider cars, which move about as fast as the line at the DMV. Right now he's relaxing on his hotel couch. We're in Baton Rouge, Louisiana, where he's acting in a movie for the Syfy channel about a fifty-foot alligator that has begun terrorizing people.

He plays a swamp boat maintenance officer named Froggy, and today they were shooting at a spot called Alligator Bayou. "We were filming the scene where I die, so I have blood everywhere," he says, apologetically. In addition to the carnage, he also sports a closely shaved head, bushy chin hair, and an oversized T-shirt from his clothing line Expensive Taste, which bears an image of a dollar sign made of chain links wrapped around a diamond-tipped microphone.

Wall isn't a trained actor, but like so many other rappers he's trying his hand, having also played a small part in the film *I Hope They Serve Beer in Hell*, based on Tucker Max's randy memoir. Wall's character in that flick is an MC called Grillionaire, whose name is a play on Wall's famed mouthpieces and his former rhyming partner, Chamillionaire. "They told me they wanted me to be, like, a parody of myself," Wall recalls.

In a song for the movie called "One in a Grillion," Grillionaire brags about his ride: "Mink on the seats, gator in the dash/ Like a luxury turducken/ That's stuffed with cash." He also enthuses over his ice (jewelry), whips (cars), hos, and money. Like Wall's catchphrase, "What it do?" Grillionaire has a signature of his own: "Howdy do?"

One could be forgiven for not realizing it's a parody. Wall represents for the gaudy side of Texas culture, and indeed his entire identity is wrapped up in love for his home state. Lots of its denizens have Lone Star pride, but Wall is particularly obsessed, right down to his vowel-heavy accent, which he seems to embellish slightly. (He pronounces his name "Pau Wau.")

But whatever you make of his style, Houston's scene could not have picked a finer ambassador, and he was a big reason why America fell for it in 2005. Just as they'd been consumed by New Orleans's brash hood millionaires a few years earlier, the country was ready for something exotic, and Houston fit the bill.

While paying respects to originators like Geto Boys, DJ Screw, and UGK, Wall and his contemporaries updated their sounds. On paper, it didn't seem like it would work. This was an era of sweaty crunk chants and muscled warriors like 50 Cent. The H-Towners, however, were a motley crew led by Wall, slick-rapping brainiac Chamillionaire, self-referential misfit Mike Jones, colossal Slim Thug, and overconfident Lil' Flip. But their unorthodox images had always been part of the charm. "We had a big fan base that was real broad," Wall says of his early days rapping with Chamillionaire. "We had the gangstas, the computer nerds, kids that went to school, the nine-to-five, regular people."

Mainstream recognition was slow to come to Houston, because for so long rappers there didn't need it to stay solvent. Most never expected to get major label deals or to go platinum. But Wall, a man of one hundred and one marketing schemes, succeeded by being a great salesman. It came naturally to him. He and Chamillionaire, in fact, had once worked jobs giving customer satisfaction interviews over the phone. "We got paid per survey we did, and if they hang up you don't get credit," he remembers. "So, we learned real quick how to use our mouthpieces to be salespeople."


IF YOU'RE ONLY going to be popular in one state, make it Texas. Back before they'd acquired record deals, but were already well known regionally, Wall and Chamillionaire made good money selling their mix CDs in malls around the region, one for fifteen dollars or two for twenty. In the morning they'd drive out to places like Austin, San Antonio, Lafayette, or Lake Charles, Louisiana, ply their wares all day, and then come back at night. Dallas was particularly lucrative. "People would treat us like we were Michael Jackson, would run up to us and be crying and stuff," Wall remembers.

It was a pretty nice gig. Wall had been studying communications at the University of Houston, but the money was too good hocking CDs so he dropped out. He and Chamillionaire quickly sold one hundred thousand copies of their first independent CD together, *Get Ya Mind Correct*, whose title addresses those who intimated they couldn't make it as rappers.

They were making more money than most artists on majors, they say. But it was a moot point. Interscope and Sony BMG weren't exactly beating down their doors. "When we'd try to get major record deals, they'd say, 'Y'all got local sound,'" Wall remembers. Even some of their so-called supporters didn't think they'd get anywhere rapping about swangers and candy paint.

But they had charm, the cocky white kid with an ear for hooks and the fast-rapping black kid who could sing, best friends who'd grown up together in a middle-class section of northwest Houston called Woodland Trails.

Chamillionaire, whose moniker is a combination of "chameleon" and "millionaire," was born Hakeem Seriki and has Nigerian heritage. His mom worked at a hospital, but he somehow never knew what pops did. "I just knew he used to work hard, and he used to hustle, and he used to always be gone," Cham says.

Wall grew up in a devoutly Christian household, the son of a school teacher mother and a heroin addict father who left the family. Born Paul Manry, he was later adopted by his stepfather and changed his name to Paul Slayton. He was dubbed "Paul Wall" in his early teens by a friend, not for any particular reason other than that it rhymes.

He and Cham would play basketball and video games after school and watch *Yo! MTV Raps* and *Rap City*. They'd read *The Source* from cover to cover, including the ads, and pour over production credits in the liner notes of their CDs. In sixth or seventh grade they started emceeing. "I always used to just be rapping about money," Cham remembers. "Before I was Chamillionaire, I always had names like 'Payroll.' I used to make rhymes like, 'I got rims bigger than your house.'"

Wall was a baller in his own mind as well. He rigged up his first car, a miniscule Kia Sephia, to make it look like it had a fancy "pop" trunk, the kind that can be opened and closed slowly by a mechanical switch. His, however, was fake. "I [rigged] some fishing twine from the trunk all the way to the middle of the seat, and I'd release it and let it go," he remembers. "It was a bootleg setup. My parents thought I was crazy."

He worked his way up to Chevy Impalas and Lincoln Town Cars, his goal to bring a hot ride to the annual Kappa beach party, sponsored by a local fraternity. "The freeways were so packed, it was like Mardi Gras," he remembers. "We'd see the other cars and be like, 'Damn, man.'"

AS TEENAGERS Wall and Chamillionaire bribed their way into rap shows and built up relationships with DJs and promoters. They found work distributing flyers for labels like Def Jam and No Limit, and eventually an impresario named Michael "5000" Watts—as in, five thousand watts of shine—asked them to help promote his Swishahouse label.

"He saw us in club parking lots; he saw we were hustling," Chamillionaire says. Watts was a vastly influential Houston hip-hop player, a north-side DJ who chopped and screwed his music. He hadn't invented the style, of course, and many claimed he was simply ripping off DJ Screw. But he'd undoubtedly broadened the genre's appeal through his syndicated radio show and Swisha-house imprint, cofounded by a DJ named OG Ron C. Like their south-side rivals the Screwed Up Click, Swishahouse had a stable of MCs from their part of the city, and Watts's shrewd deployment of far-reaching independent distribution systems helped make his artists, like Slim Thug, local celebrities.

Eventually Wall and Cham convinced Watts to let them rap an intro for his 97.9 The Box (KBXX) radio show, and Watts put the track on a popular mixtape called *Choppin Em Up Part 2.* "Every-body liked it," Cham remembers. "People started asking, 'Wait a minute. Who are these guys, Chamillionaire and Paul Wall?'"

But after coming this far they began growing annoyed with each other. Even during the creation of *Get Ya Mind Correct* they were bickering, the result of logging so many hours together over the years. A creative rift was emerging; Wall wanted to stay true to Texas while Cham wanted to play down the local tropes in favor of more universal subjects. His songs would later reference political and social issues such as inequities in the tax code, the difficul-ties of getting bank loans, and discrimination faced by educated blacks. Actually, all of that comes up in a single verse of 2007's "The Morning News."

"[Paul] sometimes makes music that's directed at one audi-ence, and I feel that he could be greater than that," Cham says, adding, "The best thing I could do for my city is to do stuff that's not just about my city."

"He's right," Wall responds diplomatically. "I think Chamillion-aire has a more global kind of sound, whereas my style is definitely directed toward Texas. He always felt he can be bigger than that, an artist on Jay-Z's caliber, where it's not just for the city or the state. And I always felt like I could be like Juvenile, where there's no question that he's from Magnolia [Projects], New Orleans."

They became further polarized after Chamillionaire's brother Rasaq, a rapper himself, mentioned Wall's mother in a song. It wasn't clear if Rasaq was trash-talking, but Wall and some associates responded by taking him to task physically. "I wouldn't say he got jumped, but we all definitely had a fight with him," says Wall.

Little did the childhood pals know that, after splitting, they would both land deals with different major labels, Wall with Warner Music Group and Chamillionaire with Universal. Chamillionaire had sworn he'd never go corporate, assuming the big boys wouldn't offer him the kind of money he was earning independently. But his sales track record proved a valuable bargaining chip, and he forced the company to play by his rules. His Universal deal allows him to recoup his advances more quickly than most, he says, and he's also entitled to a healthy share of digital profits.

"A lot of these cats learned to make what they needed to make happen outside of the system," says Bun B in the VBS.tv documentary *Screwed in Houston*. "They just said, 'fuck it,' and it's that 'fuck it' mentality that gets these cats these great deals."

FIRST OUT of the gate, however, was another Swishahouse artist, Mike Jones. Before Jones pissed off a group of radio DJs by breaking commitments, before he inspired a mixtape from Chamillionaire dissing him, before he got punched in the face by Trae, Jones took over Houston's underground with sheer dogmatic determination.

The chubby-cheeked MC sold CDs by hand, dressed in a shirt inviting listeners to call him on his personal cell phone. The number actually worked.

He may be one of the most hated men in Houston, but there's no denying Jones's preternaturally catchy delivery, simultaneously warm and sinister, full of laughs, threats, and call-and-response shouts reminding listeners of his identity. "Who? Mike Jones! Who? Mike Jones!"

He signed with Warner Bros. and in April 2005 released *Who Is Mike Jones?*, led off by a song with Slim Thug and Paul Wall called "Still Tippin'," which came to embody the new Houston movement. A slowed Slim Thug freestyle about rims serves as its hook—"still tippin' on fo-fo's, wrapped in fo' vogues"—and the video follows a procession of pimped-out cars riding down the street in a figure-eight pattern. (Horribly inefficient way to drive, that.) Slim Thug pilots a Cadillac truck while a mound of black hair bobs up and down in his lap, and Wall brags about blowing up on the Internet. "Still Tippin'" took over music video rotations despite not sounding like anything else on them.

Before being taken out by T.I., Lil' Flip had gone platinum the year previous, and in 2005 Jones followed suit. Label execs chomped at the bit for more Houston product, and next up, that July, was Slim Thug. A north-side legend, he had done his best to squash the beef with the south side by recording a 1999 track with Screwed Up Click member E.S.G. called "Braids n' Fades," whose title shouted out their respective sections' preferred hairstyles. "Ain't nothin' but players from Houston, Tex, whether we got braids or fades," Slim Thug raps. "'Cause it don't matter where you from, long as you trying to get paid." Though he too had been staunchly independent, he'd grudgingly signed with a major after underground distributor Southwest Wholesale went under in 2003, and he collaborated with the Neptunes on his glossed-up Geffen/Star Trak 2005 work *Already Platinum*. The title referenced his previous successes working outside of the major label system— "How much you could sell in Texas alone was just so stupid," he tells me—but the album didn't actually go platinum. Nor did he make much cash. He complains about having had to pay Pharrell "like forty grand a beat" and says his longtime fans preferred his original, more-grounded sound. Nowadays he's back on an independent label, E1, and says he's "definitely making more money" than he was on Geffen, despite selling fewer copies overall.

Wall's *The Peoples Champ* was an immediate hit upon its September release. First single "Sittin' Sidewayz," with Big Pokey, employs the screwed sound, references lowriders, and offers immutable proof that Wall is, indeed, the "king of the parking lot." Another automotive-themed single with Kanye West later followed, "Drive Slow," and by October *The Peoples Champ* was a million seller.

Houston rap was still more of a curiosity than a vital movement at this point, however. Like Lil Jon, to whom he supplied grills, Paul Wall was seen as something of a caricature, and his catalog is full of groaners like, "I learn from life's lesson if you keep on pressing/ You'll eventually end up on top like salad dressing."

Chamillionaire's single "Ridin'," however, would firmly ensconce the scene in the national consciousness. Found on his November debut, *The Sound of Revenge*, the track pays homage to UGK's *Ridin' Dirty*. Like the other Houston hits that year, it also centers around an auto, one with a PlayStation inside, at that. But it boasts a more complicated story line. To "ride dirty" is to drive with drugs or guns in the car, and Cham admits he's not a model citizen. But that doesn't mean the police have any business racially profiling him.

Forsaking the screwed sound, Cham and Bone Thugs-n-Harmony MC Krayzie Bone spit blistering verses atop a darkly danceable beat from Dallas producers Play-N-Skillz. "Ridin'" hit #1, went quadruple platinum, and dominated the burgeoning ringtone market. It is easily the bestselling song to ever come out of Houston's rap scene, and won the ultimate compliment via a Weird Al Yankovic parody, "White and Nerdy."

"My rims never spin/ To the contrary," raps Al, wearing a set of braces, rather than grills. "You'll find that they're/ Quite stationary."

"Sometimes I'll be like, 'Did I really go through all that?'" Cham reminisces. "I went to Norway and saw hundreds of thousands of people. I got a Grammy. There was the excitement of stepping on stage at the [Video Music Awards] and seeing Puff and Snoop and Jay looking at you."

It sure beat the old days. "I can remember it like it was yesterday," he goes on, "being in some hood club, with the ceiling air condition dripping on the stage, no wireless mic, passing the mic and stepping over the chord. To go from that to riding on private jets and sitting in front row seats at basketball games, it's pretty amazing."

That year also saw the long-awaited Geto Boys reunion album and Bun B's solo debut, which went gold, and two years later UGK would top the charts. Everything had come together for the long-simmering Houston scene. Perhaps most remarkably, Cham and Wall had each managed to excel, apart from each other, by embracing their own instincts.

In 2010 they would reconcile, having made realities out of their childhood boasts to become filthy rich. Particularly so was Chamillionaire, who in 2008 cracked *Forbes*'s list of the top-earning rap stars, tying The Game and OutKast at number fourteen with an estimated $10 million.

As for Wall, along the way he'd invested in two Houston jewelry stores, specializing in custom grills. By sporting the gleaming retainers in his videos, he'd helped drive their popularity. Wall became interested in them as a kid, admiring the sets donned by Houston rappers like Fat Pat and Lil Keke. Wall and his buddies didn't refer to them as grills back then, but rather "pop-outs," "slugs," or just "gold teeth." At seventeen he brokered a deal with an antisocially named entrepreneur called Crime, agreeing to help drum up customers for his grills business in return for his own set. Diamonds were too pricey, so Wall came up with a style that replicated the look, layering bits of white gold atop yellow gold caps.

Crime loved the design and began producing similar sets. He trained Wall, and they sold grills from a stand inside of a friend's Trinity Gardens store. Crime departed for Florida, but before leaving introduced Wall to a wholesaler named "TV" Johnny Dang, a Vietnamese immigrant and former watch repairman who barely spoke English but had a remarkable knack for his new trade.

"Before Johnny, the gold teeth were real simple," Wall says. "They wouldn't take a lot of chances. But Johnny would set the diamonds by hand. It was trial and error, but he ended up really changing the grill game, across the globe."

They opened their own store and sought out a celebrity clientele. Lil Jon was their first big star, showing off his metal mouth on the cover of his 2002 *Kings of Crunk* album, and before long folks like Hugh Hefner and Paris Hilton were getting fitted. Dang endeared himself to Wall's contemporaries and became an unlikely hip-hop celebrity; as if impersonating the titular *Where's Waldo?* character, he popped up regularly in big budget rap videos from artists like Ice Cube and DJ Khaled. You'll easily recognize the goober with the wide eyes, slicked back hair, and squeaky voice.

While in Houston I visit one of Dang and Wall's shops, called TV Jewelry. It sits among many precious-metal emporiums in the past-its-prime Sharpstown mall, and video cameras are trained on each of its solitary carats. Merchandise includes clock-sized wristwatches and diamond pendants galore; one that catches my eye retails for fifteen grand and contains an image of Barack Obama made of red, white, and blue diamonds. "I-Got Change," it reads.

The store is best known for its grills, however, and offers as many different styles and colors as you can conceive. For his part, Wall prefers something called a hand prong set, which has large, round diamonds positioned in a line.

Though it's possible to get your grills installed permanently, like Lil Wayne, it requires having your teeth filed down, and Wall recommends against it. "You can clean your actual teeth and the grills better if they pop out," he explains. "The diamonds will shine a little better."

# 13

# T-PAIN AND HIS FLORIDA HITMAKERS

■ ■ ■

## Rap Robots

A FEW YEARS ago, I wrote an essay about how southern hip-hop is like Fox News, and it annoyed some people. Running in Village Voice Media weeklies, it asserted that the rap subgenre and the cable news station are similarly maligned. "If there's one thing the self-satisfied, liberal, tofu-munching, cappuccino-sipping, in-vitro-fertilization-utilizing coastal elite hate, it's Fox News," I began, adding that the "B-boyin', Shaolin-representin', G-funkin', Golden Era nostalgintelligentsia" feel the same about southern rap.

Both have strong populist appeal, I went on, corralling folks whose passions weren't previously represented on a national level. Prior to Fox, conservatives lacked a TV news outlet to call their own, while coastal rap had long ago fallen out of touch with Midwestern and southern audiences—particularly those who wanted to dance. Though neither has time for your fancy five-dollar words, that doesn't mean they're dumb. Despite giving airtime to reactionary partisans like Sean Hannity and Bill O'Reilly, Fox News also employs thoughtful hosts like Chris Wallace. And coastal rap fans annoyed with "minstrel rap" sometimes forget that genuine spitters like Scarface, T.I., and Big Boi call the South home as well.

"If you're still not convinced that Southern rap and Fox News are one and the same," I concluded, "consider the countless Southern rap odes to big cars and the wasteful misuse of fossil fuel, an indulgence the global-warming deniers on Fox News certainly endorse."

I mostly intended for the piece to be funny, and some found it so, though others believed the association slandered southern rap—or else slandered Fox News. But I maintain that Murdoch's station and down south hip-hop similarly understand the language of their audiences. To wit: while Fox News continues to dominate CNN and MSNBC in the ratings, starting in the mid-2000s a bombastic, inelegant Florida rap crew began taking control of the rap game. They were widely hated on, but there was no denying their ability to put together hits.

The posse couldn't have succeeded without T-Pain, an underrated young Tallahassee singer, rapper, and producer. You probably know him as the guy with the robot voice. Utilizing a software called Auto-Tune, he dominated urban radio and changed the sound of pop music generally. Naturally, a massive backlash followed. He was accused of homogenizing music, dumbing it down, and destroying its humanity.

These accusations, largely from northeasterners, recalled the outcry against Fox News. It made sense, then, when a video of Sean Hannity with his arm around T-Pain surfaced. In the clip, T-Pain plugs Hannity's show and, when prompted, endorses the cause of "conservative victory 2010."

Obama-allied hip-hop fans proceeded to dub T-Pain an "Uncle Tom" and a "coon azzz nicca," which wasn't fair, considering he had no idea who Hannity was. T-Pain contends the smarmy host had been blocking the door to his bus, pestering him for a shout-out; truth be told, T-Pain isn't registered to vote and doesn't care about politics.

This cleared him of being a Republican, but it made him something just as bad: willfully ignorant. To T-Pain haters, this made sense. Of course a man who had no soul (in the James Brown sense) would have no soul (in the political sense).

But there's another reading on T-Pain, one that I prefer. Blessed with neither good looks nor traditional singing talent, he's succeeded by finding rap's heart. His songs focus on love, his lyrics aren't crude by genre standards, and he emphasizes melody. A veritable hip-hop anachronism, he's also a devoted father and husband who pens love songs about his wife.

Think of him as the anti–Lil Wayne, or the anti–Kanye West. Though T-Pain has collaborated with both, and they all use Auto-Tune, he lacks their avant-garde pretentions and rock star entitlement. West, for example, throws temper tantrums when he doesn't win awards, but T-Pain once actually gave up his *Ozone* tastemaker citation in favor of another nominee, Pimp C, insisting he deserved it more.

T-Pain has dark skin, a wide face, and some extra pounds. His stage outfits include hallucinatory paisley vests, topcoats, and Willie Wonka–style top hats over his nappy brown-and-black dreads. His label is called Nappy Boy. "It came from me not knowing how to dress," T-Pain explains of his sartorial approach. "I would just throw shit on. If I found a hat, then I'd wear a hat that day. I just didn't give a damn about being cool."

His music, much of it hip-hop-informed R&B, has a similarly unanalyzed, whimsical appeal. He crafts hits easily, almost as if by accident. One time in 2008, bored in the studio, he was having a few drinks and decided to entertain himself. Riffing on gospel singer Kirk Franklin's song "Silver and Gold" ("I'd rather have

Jesus than silver and gold"), he added a new beat, Auto-Tune, and secular lyrics about combining silver and gold tequila.

"Somebody's gonna have to carry me home/ I done mixed up silver and gold," he sang. The song wasn't for an album or even a mixtape but it leaked, and within a day hundreds of thousands of people had downloaded it.

Fans assumed it was a single off of an upcoming album. Franklin complained, and T-Pain, apologetic, did what he could to squelch it. But it was hopeless. "Silver and Gold" had gone viral. Eventually his camp had no choice but to push his new album back so no one would get the wrong idea.

T-PAIN'S GRANDPARENTS came from the Bahamas, and his folks lived in Miami before moving to Tallahassee to study at Florida A&M. He was born into a Muslim household and named Faheem Najm, but he has little patience for religion these days. "I just think of it as another form of separation and segregation," he says. This too makes him a hip-hop oddball; not praising God in your songs is like not praising Cadillacs.

His dad was a dispatcher for the city electric company, and his mom was an OB/GYN nurse. The family lived on a nice stretch of Ridge Road, but both parents were so busy working that they barely noticed when their son essentially dropped out of school in eighth grade, T-Pain says. By high school he wasn't attending classes, though he'd sometimes drop by the lunch hour and rhyme with his friends, pounding on tables to keep the beat. "I couldn't get in trouble because I didn't go to the school," he says, "so it's not like they could send me to the principal's office."

His showbiz aspirations developed at a young age. T-Pain, in fact, means Tallahassee-Pain, the *pain* referencing the struggle of trying to succeed in a town off the entertainment industry's radar. The youngest child in a musical family, he also had two brothers, aspiring musicians whom he emulated, and their father groomed them for music careers by conducting interviews on the family couch like they were on *106 & Park*.

With some friends, he and his brothers formed a group called Nappy Headz, performing 280 shows one year by T-Pain's count, as far north as DC and as far west as Texas. In addition to their ferocious work ethic, they also had a ruffian image. You can hear T-Pain rapping tough on their minor hit, "Robbery," which he says was the style in Tallahassee at the time.

The thug stuff didn't feel right, however, and one day he had an epiphany—he would sing tender songs, which came more naturally. This activated his creative energies, he says, and helped him learn to stay true to himself rather than following the crowd. Hence the outfits.

He recorded his first demo CD on his home computer using equipment a friend had boosted from a CompUSA store. Armed with a fake gift card, the guy walked out with thousands of dollars' worth of hardware, software, and speakers, and he shared the bounty. T-Pain's demo *Rappa Ternt Sanga* (Rapper Turned Singer) sprouted "I'm Sprung," about a man so in love he's cooking and washing dishes for his lady.

In 2004 he signed a deal with Konvict Muzik, the label cofounded by rising star Akon, for whom, in fact, T-Pain had originally written "I'm Sprung." "I played it for Akon and he was like, 'Wow, this sounds great, but I don't do songs about [women],'" he remembers. And so T-Pain rewrote the track as an ode to his wife, Amber, and it was a surprise hit, leading to Jive's release of *Rappa Ternt Sanga* in 2005.

He and Amber, a former air force servicewoman, had recently been married, when she was twenty-one and he just eighteen. They now have three children together: Kaydnz, Lyriq, and Muziq. "Kaydnz just started walking a little bit," he says. "It's so dope, so awesome."

Not many rappers are espoused, and even fewer talk about their wives publicly. But T-Pain specifically instructs his security team not to let random ladies get anywhere near him. Amber, despite lacking Beyoncé looks, remains the focus of his life. "I feel like I would never have that closure in my life if I never got married," he says. "When I'm by myself, that shit gets depressing." (It's worth noting that, in a rap-star twist on fidelity, she sometimes permits a second woman in their bed.) As he raps on his track, "More Careful":

> They say my girl look regular
> But having a bad bitch don't make you better, bra' . . .
> And I don't get no attitude I get respect
> 'Cause she was with me three years before I got the
>     check

T-Pain became known for songs that were breezy yet insistent, catchy but gentle, more focused on romance than sex. Even his next big hit, "I'm N Luv (Wit a Stripper)," is based on a *friend's* experience, mind you, and isn't nearly as callous as you'd imagine.

> I see you, girl (Spinnin' wide)
> And she lookin' at me (Right in my eyes)
> She got my attention/ Did I forget to mention
> I need to get her over to my crib and do that night
>     thang?

Both it and "I'm Sprung" employ Auto-Tune, and T-Pain's brand of roboticized pop began to take off. Before long he was in demand for guest verses and hooks, collaborating with artists like Jamie Foxx ("Blame It"), Chris Brown ("Kiss Kiss"), and Ciara ("Go Girl"). R. Kelly's people invited him to appear on his "I'm a Flirt" remix but told him he only had an hour to record his part. T-Pain was in the airport at the time, but he quickly wrote a verse anyway, recorded it in the bathroom on his computer's microphone, and sent it in.

Follow-up albums *Epiphany*, named for his personal revelation, and *Thr33 Ringz*, also hit big. In support of the latter he went on a circus-themed tour, calling himself music's "ringleader." His shows, which he says were inspired by his dreams, featured a fire-eater, contortionist, and a midget Britney Spears look-alike. Also on the bill was Lil Wayne, who T-Pain says instructed him to walk onto stage in a very deliberate manner. Instead, he came out riding a Segway, one of those decidedly un-hip upright scooters. "I just kind of did it as a joke to him," T-Pain says, noting that Wayne didn't retaliate, because "he's too cool for that."

AROUND THE TIME of T-Pain's ascension, Miami's DJ Khaled kicked off his own unlikely run. Khaled is a unique hip-hop phenomenon, a comically loud, strangely endearing radio DJ turned artist. He puts out CDs, but many are confused about what exactly he *does* on his CDs.

Like Lil Jon he doesn't really sing or rap, but unlike Jon he's not a respected producer. His main role is suggesting concepts to other songwriters (like T-Pain), and then screaming out catchphrases like "We the best!" and "We takin' over!" as loud as he can. His goal is to create rap bangers in the mode of rock anthems like "We Will Rock You" or "Welcome to the Jungle."

Some are great, some merely grating. But Khaled nonetheless gets credit for assembling a massive Florida contingency and revitalizing a hip-hop tradition called the posse cut, popularized in the genre's golden era and again by No Limit Records. As many as six or seven members of his crew take turns performing on his tracks, and they also regularly appear on each other's solo albums.

Like T-Pain and Akon, Khaled was raised a Muslim—born to Palestinian parents in New Orleans—before chasing a girlfriend to Miami. He came of age as a radio DJ under Luke Campbell and later smartly leveraged his clout as an influential programmer to make his own CDs. His WEDR show gives him unprecedented recruiting power when it comes to filling out guest spots in his songs. "In Miami, he's the boss," says T-Pain. "That's pretty much how he gets all his artists. 'You want your shit played in Miami? You're going to get on this fucking song.'"

Khaled's first work, 2006's *Listennn . . . the Album*, was a moderate hit, but he and the Florida contingency didn't break out until his 2007 follow-up *We the Best*. This was largely due to the album's second single, called "I'm So Hood." T-Pain sings the hook.

> I'm out the hood
> And if you feel me put your hands up, my hood
>     niggas can you stand up
> If you not from here you can walk it out
> And you're not hood if you don't know what I'm
>     talkin' 'bout

I didn't, but reviewers like myself loved the song. Like so many others, its chorus had come to T-Pain almost instantly. Khaled brought him production duo the Runners' lightning-and-thunderclap beat, asked him to develop something around the concept of "hood," and then proceeded to vanish for a few hours. T-Pain completed his task in a few minutes, and so while he waited for Khaled to return he knocked out three other tracks, he says.

WHEN KHALED wasn't using T-Pain on his singles, he often used Akon. The son of a Senegalese percussionist, Akon was raised in Senegal and New Jersey before moving to Atlanta. Though he and T-Pain are often compared, their styles are divergent. Akon doesn't often employ Auto-Tune, for one thing; his voice is more buttery and has better range.

But he lacks his signee's everyman appeal, instead portraying himself as a smooth criminal and claiming in interviews to have served long jail stints for boosting cars. Some of the wind was taken out of his sails, then, when the website The Smoking Gun reported that he'd dramatically exaggerated his incarceration time. In his defense, he claims much of it happened long ago and that the records are inaccessible. He also complains that The Smoking Gun never contacted him. "I got an attorney to expunge a lot of stuff, so I can travel worldwide," he says. "If the site had asked me the questions, I would have given them the story."

Akon gained fame before T-Pain, but by 2007 they were both everywhere, featured on literally dozens of top forty hits, either as featured artists or guests. (T-Pain alone was on four top ten *Hot 100* songs on the December 8 chart that year.) Bringing a softer vocal element to rap is their legacy, Akon suggests. "Hardcore hip-hop wasn't as popular until it started adding melody and song," he says.

T-Pain adds that they share a philosophy in their craft, which is to create songs that *they* like, rather than what they'd imagine a particular demographic might prefer. "I never come out of the booth, like, 'White people are gonna fall over for this song,' or, 'Black people are going to love riding in their car to this song.' Fuck that. I don't care who else likes the song. If I like it, I'm going to make it a single."

Meanwhile, other Khaled-affiliated artists were helping reestablish Florida as a hip-hop hub, something it hadn't been since the days of 2 Live Crew. In the late 1990s, a Luke Campbell protégée named Trick Daddy cemented a large following in Miami, recording on a local label called Slip-N-Slide and collaborating with a raunchy yet mesmerizing rapper called Trina. Another Luke affiliate, Pitbull, boasted dexterous MC abilities and played up his Cuban roots. (In 2004 he told *Ozone*, "These New York labels are fucked right now. Thank you so much for overlooking [the South] and teaching us how to grind and how to sell our own shit and make our own relationships. . . . I will laugh all the way to the bank.")

Also in the mix were Carol City rapper Flo Rida, self-described "goon affiliated" Fort Myers MC Plies, and producers like Miami's Cool & Dre, Orlando's the Runners, and Tampa's J.U.S.T.I.C.E. League, each known for supremely addictive fist pumpers. Lil Wayne and Fat Joe wanted to be a part of the fun so badly that they bought homes in the Miami area themselves, and Cash Money Records came too. In his collaborative song with Wayne called "Make It Rain," the Bronx-reared Joe—associated as much as anyone with the New York borough sound—raps:

> Now why's everybody so mad at the South for?
> Change your style up
> Switch to southpaw

Probably the most successful of the native south Floridians was a weighty Carol City rapper named Rick Ross, who reeled off a string of #1 albums in the late aughts. As an MC he wasn't particularly nimble, so instead he attempted to derive gravitas from a drug kingpin image. "I know Pablo, Noriega," he rapped. "The real Noriega/ He owe me a hundred favors."

Embarrassingly, then, the drug legend from whom Ross got his name, "Freeway" Ricky Ross, sued the rapper for trademark infringement. (The suit was dismissed.) Another report from The Smoking Gun also punctured the MC's self-mythology, finding that he had worked as a prison guard before he was famous. When I ask him about this, he grows flustered and evasive. "First and foremost, man, I'm the biggest boss in the game," he says. "Niggas better get ready for the ride of they life. Just know what it is. Get in the streets."

The Smoking Gun's tidbit about Ross brought widespread criticism from the hip-hop community—rappers are expected to hate the police, after all, not *be* the police. It also proved irresistible to 50 Cent. The Queens-bred MC had a new album coming out and a history of ridiculing other rappers to publicize himself. In early 2009 he bought Ross's baby mama a fur coat and commissioned a series of animated shorts starring "Officer Ricky," a bumbling figure with a cop's body and Ross's head.

The cartoons also mocked the rest of the Florida crew, including T-Pain, who was portrayed with a robot body, singing the Auto-Tuned lyrics, "Hey Baby? How much does your pussy weigh?" Some of this was quite funny, but 50 took it too far when he had someone stalk Khaled's mother, shooting footage of her at work.

The chiseled, top-selling 50 Cent probably thought he had easy targets in these relative newcomers from Florida, none of whom seemed to spend much time in the gym. But in the end, it was they who won out. *Before I Self-Destruct*, 50's late 2009 release, was the worst-performing work of his career, while Ross went on to have one of the most astonishing hip-hop comebacks on record, hitting #1 with his T-Pain-assisted *Deeper Than Rap* and becoming an improbable critic's darling with it and his follow-up, *Teflon Don*.

As for T-Pain, he had bigger problems that year, courtesy of another New York icon, Jay-Z. Jay also had a new CD to promote, and he decided to do it by smearing T-Pain's beloved Auto-Tune.

WHEN CHER'S 1998 song "Believe" hit the airwaves, it sounded like the future. "Do you believe in life after love?" she sang, her voice seemingly wrenched out of the time-space continuum. Hearing the Auto-Tuned effect for the first time made you wonder if someone had slipped some psilocybin mushrooms into your morning omelet.

Auto-Tune was first imagined while a former Exxon seismic data explorer named Andy Hildebrand mingled at a dinner party, contemplating his next move. Only forty, he was already rich enough to retire—he'd developed technology that used sound waves to detect oil under the earth. One of the guests, likely joking, suggested he invent something capable of helping her sing in tune. Undertaking the challenge, he manipulated his oil technology to apply it to music. His creation could slowly bend notes that were sharp or flat, matching them to music in a way that was unnoticeable.

Pitch correction was the original function of Auto-Tune, which a company called Antares debuted in 1997. Indeed, it is still used this way by top artists across genres who want to sound perfect. Mark Taylor and Brian Rawling, the producers on "Believe," however, discovered another use for the software. They realized manipulating the speed in which the notes were corrected would create a metallic, otherworldly sound.

Cher's label wasn't thrilled with the effect, but she loved it, and "Believe" became the biggest hit of her career. For a time Taylor guarded their secret, insisting that they'd made the sound using a vocoder, a voice synthesizer often used in conjunction with keyboards. But the cat quickly escaped the bag and Auto-Tune had caught on around the globe by the turn of the millennium, particularly in North African Arab music genres like Berber and Rai.

The robotic sound wasn't new to hip-hop. Afrika Bambaataa used a vocal distortion effect on his pioneering track "Planet Rock," and vocoder was popular on eighties rap songs including the Showboys' "Drag Rap," which influenced New Orleans bounce music. Funk singer Roger Troutman famously employed the talk box, a device with a plastic tube that created his martianlike chorus on Tupac Shakur's "California Love."

Most people assume T-Pain was turned on to Auto-Tune by Cher's song, but he actually became fascinated with it after hearing the remix of Jennifer Lopez's 1999 Darkchild-produced track, "If You Had My Love," on which it's used briefly. "It sounded cool," he says. "I thought, somebody should do a whole song like that."

The same guy who'd jacked the CompUSA equipment had also pilfered a disc of music software plug-ins, and T-Pain spent an entire day going through them. Discovering Auto-Tune among the bunch was a revelation. "I was like, 'That's the fucking effect! That's the thing I've been telling everybody about!'"

He's been obsessed with it since, but to this day can't put his finger on why it resonates with so many people. "I don't know, man, it's weird," he says. "I think it might be because it makes your voice an instrument. It's like a jazz song, with a saxophone solo over it the whole time. That shit is so soothing, it just makes you feel better."

Accused of being a talentless hack who owes his success to Hildebrand's creation, T-Pain is actually a talented musician who plays drums, piano, and guitar and makes all of his own beats, as well as many others'. Though he's not a trained singer—"I feel like if I get singing lessons, it will take my edge off"—his vocal chops are plenty serviceable. In fact, most folks don't realize that he's not using Auto-Tune at all on some of his biggest hits, like Flo Rida's "Low."

But it's understandable that most focus on the effect, considering its ubiquity in recent years. Kanye West enlisted T-Pain for songwriting help and Auto-Tune coaching for his venerated fourth album, *808s & Heartbreak*, while Diddy reportedly gave T-Pain extra royalties simply for *permitting* him to use Auto-Tune on one of his albums. Players from other genres got into the act as well, including indie-folk group Bon Iver, country act Rascal Flatts, Philadelphia electronic DJ Diplo, and comedy group Lonely Island.

Rap fans might have noticed that no magazine or website interview in the late aughts was complete without the journalist asking the performer for his or her feelings on the technology. Everyone was expected to take sides, whether they used Auto-Tune or not. Detractors called it a gimmicky fad that would sonically date its era, like eighties hair metal. T-Pain doesn't entirely disagree with this assessment. In fact, he had fun with his image, appearing in a Funny or Die comedy sketch where he goes to war with a vindictive, HAL-like vocoder that forces him to record a track called "Thank You Vocoder, You Are Wonderful and Have Helped Me Tremendously." Never mind that he's never actually used vocoder in his life.

He also collaborated with country sprite Taylor Swift (blinged up for the occasion), and made a song with the Brooklyn musicians behind a current-events parody series called "Auto-Tune the News." In their heavily manipulated YouTube video, T-Pain sings a duet of sorts with Katie Couric. But he was also territorial. He penned a track called "Karaoke," aimed at those rappers he believed were ripping him off. Which was just about everyone; only Kanye West and Lil Wayne got a pass.

By 2009 many artists were calling for Auto-Tune's head. KRS-One got in on the action, pairing with Brooklyn golden-era rapper Buckshot for "Robot," which lamented that nowadays "everybody do their thing like a motherfuckin' robot."

Jay-Z was even more confrontational on the lead single of his 2009 album *The Blueprint 3*, called "D.O.A. (Death of Auto-Tune)." Over a squealing electric guitar riff and an interpolation of the song "Na Na Hey Hey Kiss Him Goodbye," Jay decried everything he deemed soft in hip-hop.

> This is anti–Auto-Tune, death of the ringtone,
> This ain't for iTunes, this ain't for sing-alongs . . .
> You niggas singing too much
> Get back to rap/ You T-Pain-ing too much

Jay-Z, a protégée of Notorious B.I.G. who hailed from Brooklyn's Marcy projects, was casting himself as the defender of hip-hop's core values, its lyrical white knight who would save rap from itself. T-Pain wasn't sure if he should feel offended or not—Jay claimed that he didn't mean any disrespect, after all.

And so, since he liked the song, Pain tentatively endorsed it. Shortly after it debuted Jay-Z performed it live at popular New Jersey concert Summer Jam, and T-Pain surprised him by joining him onstage. It was intended to be a gesture of goodwill, but T-Pain took offense when, at the end of the track, Jay-Z yelled out, "Good riddance!" and left the stage without shaking his hand. Now feeling officially dissed, T-Pain lashed back at Jay-Z during a Las Vegas show, calling him "fifty-nine years old" (he was actually thirty-nine, while T-Pain was twenty-three) and insisting, that, if anything was going to die, it should be him.

Though this remark was mean-spirited, many sympathized with T-Pain and saw "D.O.A." as Jay's calculated ploy to reestablish himself as a hip-hop tastemaker at a time when his relevancy seemed to be fading. Then again, "D.O.A." was an undeniably hot song, and *The Blueprint 3* became his most successful album in years. He certainly didn't kill off Auto-Tune, but he may have hastened its decline, as it soon became less prominent on pop radio.

T-Pain himself may have had something to do with its fall from fashion. In late 2009 he hooked up with a technology company to develop an Auto-Tune application called "I Am T-Pain," which let users roboticize their own voices while singing along with his songs.

T-Pain plugged it hard, even showing it off in the video for DJ Khaled's song, "All I Do Is Win." The app sold well, but Auto-Tune's novelty and mystique were starting to fade. Now that anyone could do it, it no longer sounded like the future.

# 14

# SOULJA BOY AND DJ SMURF

■ ■ ■

## Dance, Dance Revolution

I'M STANDING at the corner of Peachtree and Eighth Street in Atlanta when a long BMW pulls up next to me. Driving is DJ Smurf, the former bass and crunk impresario. We've scheduled an interview at a restaurant here in midtown, but after surveying the situation he isn't having it. "Hop in," he says, turning the wheel and steering us north.

Apparently, I'd picked a bad spot. There's a gay bar nearby, and he doesn't want people to get the wrong idea. You see, a few years back the rapper Ma$e was stopped on a traffic violation around here, and before long gossip websites reported that he'd come to pick up a transsexual prostitute.

Smurf's paranoia feels far-fetched to me, if only because he isn't normally a tabloid target. If he were Jermaine Dupri, the producer known for lavish parties and for dating Janet Jackson, that would be one thing, but Smurf keeps a low profile. Clad in a preppy gray sweater with a collared shirt underneath, he's inconspicuous and not wearing much jewelry. When we arrive at a quiet sushi restaurant about a mile or so north, he orders a Grey Goose and cranberry and notes that he doesn't do many promotional photo shoots. "I only pop bottles, maybe, three times a year," he adds. This helps explain why he's not a household name, despite having launched some of southern rap's most popular (and maligned) artists, including Ying Yang Twins and Soulja Boy.

Smurf is short, with a bald head, and talks and moves quickly. In some press photos he smokes a cigar, but it doesn't make him look like Suge Knight. He has none of the world-weariness, for one thing. Though in his late thirties he appears younger, and his speech is peppered with youthful enthusiasm.

Since his days as an unsuccessful bass artist, Smurf has taken on a new role as a veritable anthropologist of talent. His specialty is finding rappers who are popular in their hometowns—particularly those behind dance crazes—unearthing them, and bringing them to the mainstream. "I want to take that group that's dope as fuck, but can't nobody see it but me," he says.

Faddy and unsophisticated, his brand is everything coastal rap fans detest. It is the epitome of what we talk about when we talk about "lowest common denominator" music, and the kind of thing that inspired Nas to title his 2006 album *Hip Hop Is Dead*.

But Smurf makes no apologies. Kids like what they like, he says, and they are rap's most important constituents. "The youth is what always made hip-hop go."


BEFORE DJ SMURF there was Jermaine Dupri, the man as responsible as anyone for turning Atlanta into urban music's capital. Dupri has constructed beats for most of the city's major acts, including TLC, Usher, Monica, and Ludacris, but is probably best known for making nobodies famous.

Like Boston kingmaker Maurice Starr, who assembled the New Kids on the Block, Dupri signed and crafted the images of rappers

like Kris Kross, Da Brat, and Bow Wow, and also wrote and produced their songs. "I create artists from scratch," he tells me. But
his methods have gone out of vogue in recent years. Despite his
label So So Def's long run of success, major label brass won't even
consider his new MCs anymore, he complains, which is why he
went independent recently.

The slumping music industry now prefers to sign performers who already have big local fan bases and proven sales track
records, sparing the companies from investing time or energy in
artist development. It's a cost-cutting measure that has made the
traditional role of Artist & Repertoire nearly obsolete. "Now, if
you're an A&R in New York, it's like, let's go to Atlanta and listen
to what's hot on the radio," Dupri says.

The king of this new approach is DJ Smurf, who doesn't mold
his artists, dress them, or write their songs. Instead, he simply seeks
out already-established independents with hometown followings.
"I believe in organic," he told the *Dallas Observer*. "It's the records
and the acts that are truly on the tips of people's tongues, and that
are truly hot in that market. . . . What's in their cars when they're
driving down the street? Or what's playing in the store when you're
buying your liquor?"

It's not always so easy, however. In fact, Smurf wasn't initially
impressed in early 2007 when he first caught wind of a skinny, hand-
some, charismatic rapper called Soulja Boy Tell'em. Only sixteen,
he reportedly had a massive MySpace following, but Smurf was
unfamiliar with the finer points of that social networking program.

Upon logging on, he didn't particularly care for Soulja Boy's
song "Crank That (Soulja Boy)," and wasn't convinced that his
supposed legions of fans were real. "I didn't understand how it
worked," Smurf says. "When I saw those millions of hits, I thought
that shit was fake."

And so he set out to determine if this kid had any living,
breathing fans outside of cyberspace. At his sons' T-ball game he

asked random children if they were familiar with Soulja Boy, and almost all of them said yes. Astounded, he consulted with influential Atlanta radio DJ Greg Street.

"He said he'd been getting requests for the song ["Crank That"] but he didn't know what they were talking about," Smurf says. Having bypassed the industry machinery altogether, Soulja Boy had somehow built a massive fan base.

BORN DEANDRE WAY, Soulja Boy grew up both in Atlanta with his mother and Batesville, Mississippi, with his dad. At a young age he began recording songs on his computer using a basic digital editing software called FruityLoops.

These tracks included "Bapes," about fashion designer Nigo's clothing line, though he now admits he didn't actually own any Bapes at the time. Then there was "Crank That," which split the difference between crunk and snap, eschewing 808s in favor of steel drums and shouts of "You!"

Though distinctive, the tune seemed an unlikely candidate for a hit, considering he viciously clips the ends of words—"watch" becomes "wat"—and even the lyrics you can understand are hard to interpret. He has denied that its chorus, "Watch me crank that Soulja Boy/ Then Superman that ho," references a bizarre sex act, for example.

Like thousands of other aspiring MCs, he posted his music on sites like SoundClick and MySpace. But unlike most of them he didn't stop there, adding videos of himself doing the "Crank That" dance, which apes the Man of Steel taking flight. At this point his act went viral, and fans taped their own copycat dances, many of which you can still see on YouTube. There's the Crank Dat Homeless Man, Crank Dat Batman, and even Crank Dat Kosher Boy, whose catchphrase is "Jew!"

If Jermaine Dupri had signed Soulja Boy, he may well have revamped his image and changed his songs, but Smurf did no such thing. "I allowed him to be who he is," he says. "His first album was literally just us going in and rerecording songs he had on MySpace."

Soulja Boy inked a deal through Smurf's Collipark Records, an imprint of Interscope, which was known for established street rappers like Dr. Dre and Eminem but nonetheless put its clout behind him. The official video for "Crank That" is an imaginative piece of self-referential meta-art, cutting between shots of Soulja Boy instant messaging with Smurf, girls watching Soulja Boy videos on their cell phones, and actors dressed as senior citizens doing the Superman dance.

Thanks to a perfect storm of corporate bucks and a viral following, by the time his debut album, *Souljaboytellem.com*, dropped in late 2007, he was a pop culture phenomenon. "Think of him as one part Lonely Girl, one part Bruce Barton and one part Dem Franchise Boyz," wrote *LA Weekly*'s Jeff Weiss, "a product of the sort of blurry meld of art and commerce that has inexorably marched on since the day Andy Warhol made his first silk-screen, or at the very least the moment Run-DMC sewed up their first Adidas."

Still, to call Soulja Boy green would be an understatement. Living out his adolescence before our eyes, he did things like pee off of a hotel balcony (and then post footage of it) and purchase not just a Lamborghini but also a diamond-encrusted, remote-controlled Lamborghini toy car, which he wore around his neck. He also sported humongous white T-shirts and sunglasses with his name painted on the lenses in Wite-Out.

But while his taste and his manners needed work, he quickly became the first megastar rapper of the Internet age, racking up some half billion YouTube views. Yes, with a *B*; the clip in which he explains how to do the "Crank That" dance, which contains no music, generated 44 million by itself. Meanwhile, "Crank That" sold more than four million MP3s and five million ringtones, the latter of which had become an increasingly important sales yardstick. (In fact, Soulja Boy epitomizes the disparaging term, "Ringtone rapper," which refers to those deemed simplistic enough to get their point across in the few moments it takes for a cell phone to chime.)

When he actually showed his face, chaos ensued. "It was like some sixties shit with Elvis, how little girls would react when I was with him," Smurf remembers. He pauses, and then adds, "He should go down in history for marketing."

IN THE SUMMER of 2008, Ice-T did something strange. On a mixtape called *Urban Legend*, the MC turned actor, who had recently turned fifty, lashed out at Soulja Boy, someone he didn't know but intensely disliked.

"Soulja Boy, I know you're young enough to be my kid, but you single-handedly killed hip-hop," he said. "That shit is such garbage. You can't do that. We came all the way from Rakim, we came all the way from Das EFX . . . and you come with that Superman shit."

He paused to insult Hurricane Chris, an eighteen-year-old rapper from Shreveport, Louisiana, and concluded with stern words for both of them. "C'mon, man up, you niggas. Stop bullshitting. You niggas is making me feel real fucking mad about this shit. We took it all the way to khakis and straps, and you niggas looking happy, man. That shit's wack."

Soulja Boy couldn't have asked for a better compliment; that he supposedly had the power to destroy a preeminent American cultural institution said a lot about his influence. Still, he immediately fired back via YouTube. "You were born before the Internet was created," he said. "How the fuck did you even find me?"

Why had the streetwise West Coast rapper taken time out of his day for this diatribe? Drumming up publicity for himself didn't seem a primary concern; rather, he was taking what he felt to be a principled stand out of genuine worry for the discipline he helped establish.

The original original gangsta, Ice-T was one of the very first MCs to gain popularity with hard-edged street rhymes, later battling censors over his hard rock group Body Count's song "Cop Killer," before his music career faded and he recast himself as a detective on *Law & Order: Special Victims Unit.*

He wasn't the only rap elder statesman to get in his licks against Soulja Boy. Aging West Coast icon Snoop Dogg and Wu-Tang Clan's Method Man followed suit, calling his songs "bullshit" and "garbage," respectively. Along with their invective, each made impassioned points about the changing state of their business. "It's turmoil, because all of these kids have finally recognized their power. All the downloading and all that, it's crippling the music industry," said Method Man, adding that he put some of the blame on music industry executives. "Now they treat it like fast food. There's no movements anymore, it's just this rapper this week, that rapper next week. No MCs, all rappers."

He almost seemed to be saying that these next-generation artists were hurting hip-hop with their technology-savvy fans; that an elderly demographic unable to pirate electronic music was preferable. That doesn't ring true, and neither does his assertion that "MCs" benefit the industry more than "rappers." Sure, I prefer the chiseled-in-granite stylings of the Wu-Tang Clan to the clunky rhymes of Soulja Boy, but I came up on Wu-Tang. They're my generation. Different people look for different things in their hip-hop; there's more to the music than lyricism, and I can understand why younger folks find Soulja Boy's hooks, singing, and image inviting.

Besides, it's hard to prove that artful music sells better. Inelegant drivel like the Eagles' greatest hits and *The Bodyguard* and *Dirty Dancing* soundtracks, for example, sit atop the all-time best-selling albums list next to the critically respected work of Michael Jackson and Fleetwood Mac. Sure, OutKast has the top rap seller of all time, but *Speakerboxxx/The Love Below* was a double disc, so each purchase counts as two. If you go by individual unit sales, guess who's #1? MC Hammer.

Two more quick points: 1) The popularity of artists like Method Man, Ice-T, and Snoop are waning, and if they're not replaced by a new crop, hip-hop will fade. 2) Divergent styles undoubtedly strengthen the genre as a whole, rather than weakening it. In the words of Luther Campbell: "You need versatility in the music. . . . It can't be all about just one sound because it'll turn into disco or house."

Smurf calls Soulja Boy's detractors "sore losers," noting that once upon a time New York rappers made gimmicky dance records too, like Joe Ski Love's "Pee Wee Dance" and Salt-n-Peppa's "Push It." "Here's one thing I know about East Coast rap: they stopped giving a fuck about the public," he says. "They were making records for each other."

Some MCs came to Soulja Boy's defense, notably the oft-disrespected Nelly, and Scarface, who said Soulja Boy had "the potential to be the next Russell [Simmons]." But most of them weren't exactly falling over themselves to collaborate with him.

Meanwhile, seemingly every critic decried Soulja Boy's lack of substance and wrote him off as a one-hit wonder. (Guilty.) After his second album, *iSouljaBoyTellem*, debuted in late 2008 to lackluster sales, his career seemed headed for the ditch.

IT'S SPRING 2009, barely a year and a half after his breakout, and Soulja Boy has already overhauled his image. Gone are the Wite-Out sunglasses and giant T's in favor of an aqua green shirt and matching ball cap chosen by a stylist. His Nikes match too; they're propped up on a conference room's table.

Physically he's different, as well. He's grown a couple of inches and filled his frame with enough tattoos to join a motorcycle club; they have begun to creep onto his neck and face. Some vestiges of his old style remain, however, like his enormous pendant chain, which he says contains "$100,000 worth of diamonds."

I meet up with the suddenly revitalized eighteen-year-old at the offices of his Manhattan-based handlers. A next generation multitasker of the first order, he simultaneously answers my questions while working on his laptop, pecking at two handheld devices, and eating from a bag of McDonald's.

He's understandably busy considering that his career has taken on a second life in recent months. After *iSouljaBoyTellem*'s first single, "Bird Walk," flopped, he came back with the surprisingly tender hip-hop power ballad, "Kiss Me Thru the Phone." Its plot concerns a pair of separated young lovers who text each other and send iPhone pics to stay in touch, but the song has a universal message and its video features actual old people.

"Kiss Me Thru the Phone" was followed by "Turn My Swag On," an exercise in self-affirmation that featured his own brand of existential contemplation: "I got a question: Why they hatin' on me? I didn't do nothin' to 'em, but count this money." It was also a monster hit.

Though most MCs wouldn't take his calls a few months back, now they were suddenly lining up to work with him. The "Turn My Swag On" remix featured Young Jeezy and Lil Wayne, not to mention New York MCs Fabolous, Jim Jones, and Maino. Gucci Mane, meanwhile, shocked me by declaring Soulja Boy one of the best producers working. And so, for his third CD, *The DeAndre Way*, he joined forces with big names like Trey Songz and 50 Cent, who, in their collaborative song "Mean Mug," asserts he will "pull that trigger [if] y'all fuck with my little nigga." "After the first album, I'm not going to lie, there was no artists that reached out," he says. "Now I have more hits, more rank and pull. Everything is changing."

Though the new album's sales were unimpressive, other rappers were co-opting his promotional approach. "He kind of

revolutionized one of the ways to get on, because the days of walking into a record label and giving them your demo, those have
been over for about six years now," Washington, DC, rapper Wale
told me in 2008. "Now, it's like, 'Get your own buzz. Get your own
thing rockin', maybe do some YouTubes. Prove yourself like that.'"

My time with Soulja Boy is entertaining and surreal. At one
point I ask him about his video for "Turn My Swag On," in which
he blows his nose with one hundred dollar bills and tosses stacks
of the green stuff around a house. Was that *real cash* in the video?

"Yeah," he says. "It was 1.1 million dollars."

How does one acquire that kind of wad? Do you walk up to
your bank teller and say, "I'd like to withdraw 1.1 million dollars,
please"?

"That's how we roll, man. I've got a million dollars cash on me
right now."

Where?

"In my case. Better be careful. I'm strapped at all times."

Robbing Soulja Boy hadn't been on my list of the day's activi-
ties. But his edginess is perhaps understandable. Following an
Atlanta release party for *iSouljaBoyTellem*, he and his friends were
robbed at gunpoint at his home. "Somebody kicked in the door.
One dude ran in, put the AK to my homeboy's head, put him to
the floor," he explained to Los Angeles radio station Power 106 not
long after the incident. "The other two ran in, and my homeboy
jumped in the other room."

In a terrifying twist, two masked men with their voices dis-
guised released a viral video shortly thereafter in which they
claimed credit for the crime. "That shit's fake as hell," Soulja Boy
says now. "Those were just two random dudes making a video. I
guess they were trying to get some hits on YouTube."

Even criminals, it appears, are employing his marketing
methods.

"I LOVE watching peoples' reaction to my new groups for the first time," DJ Smurf wrote in a Twitter message not long ago. "It's this confusing look that I can't explain but it's priceless!"

When rap elitists were looking to blame someone for the downfall of hip-hop as they knew it, they picked the wrong target. Instead of Soulja Boy, it should have been Smurf.

Shortly after Soulja Boy's arrival came the debut of another Smurf discovery, Shreveport teenager Hurricane Chris. Unlike Soulja Boy, Chris could actually spit, but you wouldn't know it from his hits like "A Bay Bay," a simple sing-along with an irresistible ear worm. ("It's so hot up in da club/ That I ain't got no shoes on," he raps.) Ice-T wasn't a fan of the song, nor of Chris's signature braids. "Take them fucking beads out your fucking hair, kid," he said. (Chris is probably most famous, however, for once rapping his rather graphic ode to the Oscar-winning actress, "Halle Berry," on the floor of the Louisiana House of Representatives.)

Up next for Smurf was Atlanta youngster V.I.C. and his Soulja Boy–coproduced title shot "Get Silly."

> My chain too silly/ My wrist too silly
> The girls throw me dish 'cause my rims big billin'
> My ride too silly/ I ride too silly . . .
> I be wilin' on a island somewhere just like Gilligan

It was an example of the increasingly common "fooling around with the Casio presets" aesthetic but even more grating, and the song was a hit. The Hannah Montana crowd couldn't get enough; a friend of mine noted that schoolmates of her Big Brothers Big Sisters program mentee were recording low-budget knockoffs.

In early 2010 Smurf took on a pair of Dallas newcomers called Treal Lee and Prince Rick, who had a local smash called "Mr. Hit Dat Hoe." It had its own dance, naturally, performed by a furiously gyrating Urkel look-alike. Smurf says he knew immediately, just from the song's *name*, that it might be something for him, and after getting wind from his brother Derrick that the song was a phenomenon in Texas, he flew to Dallas to check it out.

Taken to a "hood sports bar" where the song was in rotation, he witnessed pandemonium. At one point a fight broke out, resulting in a girl's weave being thrown across the dance floor. "That's the kind of thing you've got to see to know something is legit," Smurf says. He released the single on his label, but not before changing its title to the somewhat-less-domestic-violence-y, "Mr. Hit Dat."

To Smurf, finding an underexposed southern music scene is like a baseball card fanatic discovering a box of old Topps packs in his grandmother's attic. As he said of Dallas's emerging "D-Town Boogie" movement: "I like it because they remind me of back when everybody was hungry. When you look at a market that hasn't been developed or exposed, you find a certain kind of hunger that [reminds me of] when hip-hop was fresh. See, I'm in Atlanta so everybody is doing it here. Everybody knows that they can put a record on the radio and they're gonna get a record deal. So the creativity, the work ethic, it's not like it used to be."

Whether Smurf has ushered in hip-hop's apocalypse or simply created an ultraefficient way to give fans what they want is up for debate. What is not, however, is his unparalleled ability to predict what an eleven-year-old girl is going to like and what a member of the Wu-Tang Clan is going to hate.

"Some cats now, they've been rhyming for a year, and they blow up overnight because of a certain beat or a certain hook, or a certain brand that's behind them," laments Raekwon. "The kids who are into it are younger, and it's more being driven by having fun. There's nothing wrong with having fun—hip-hop has always been about having fun—but it used to be about being creative and making great albums."

Smurf is now finishing his second vodka and cranberry, and our talk turns to Ms. Peachez, the Shreveport cross-dressing rapper whose song "Fry That Chicken" incensed critics around the country and helped ignite the "minstrel show rap" debate. I'm surprised to learn he's unfamiliar with her.

"That sounds like some bullshit," he says, after I describe her blue wig, pedantic rhymes, and seeming oblivion to the gnarliest black stereotypes. Nonetheless, he's not willing to write her off until he checks her out for himself. "If I go down to Shreveport and see why people like it, I'll probably come out of there, like, 'Fry That Chicken' is the shit."

# 15

# LIL WAYNE

■■■

## Gangster Weirdo

LIL WAYNE gained fame with the Hot Boys, but by 2007 he had a new persona and had become one of rap's biggest solo acts. Meet Weezy: a muscled, five-and-a-half-foot-tall, dreadlocked overachiever whose pants sagged and whose shirt was rarely on.

He traveled the world playing solo concerts, stopping only to record songs and get new tattoos. Some spoke to love of his craft, like the one that said, "I Am Music" above his right eye. Some, like the Frankenstein cracks on his forehead, were simply designed to make him seem sinister. "I think the tattoos intimidate [people] and show them they'd better not walk up to me," he tells me. "Because I'll knock your fucking head off."

He claimed an allegiance to his "Daddy," Cash Money Records' cofounder Baby, his creator ("Fear God" was tattooed on his eyelids), the Bloods gang, and the city of New Orleans—though he no longer lived there. But that was about it.

He'd turned into the world's most famous rapper, which was odd considering that during their late nineties run he wasn't even the hottest Hot Boy, playing second or third fiddle to Juvenile and B.G. "I'll be honest," says DJ Drama. "In the early Cash Money days, Wayne is probably somebody I didn't pay a lot of attention to lyrically." But his skills developed rapidly; eventually, he dubbed himself the best rapper alive and expected you to treat him as such.

"Talk to me like you talk to Martin Luther King or Malcolm X," he castigated an *XXL* writer. "You're not going to ask him about what he thinks about what somebody said about him. You ask him about his greatness, and his greatness only." This made no sense on many levels, but what could you do? At this point, Wayne was so good it didn't matter that he was also insufferable.

OVER THE YEARS, Wayne became more confident in his distinctive, froglike voice, and began ignoring many genre conventions. These days when he is actually rapping—rather than playing his guitar— he doesn't usually spit fast or have a narrative in mind. Instead, he deals almost solely in images, and he has come up with a million and one ways to describe himself. He's a "monster like the Loch Ness," he's a "prisoner locked up behind Xanax bars," he goes hard like "geese erection."

By 2008, the year he threatened to take over pop music, there were two main Lil Wayne story lines going. The first concerned his scads of free mixtapes preceding his latest studio work, *Tha Carter III*. He'd teamed up with Atlanta mixtape king DJ Drama and taken that man's buzz-building promotional strategy to its logical conclusion: he released a mixtape approximately every five minutes. They were well received, but would they backfire? Would his fans bother paying for an official album after being gifted a career's worth of free music?

The second story line was that he had lost control of himself, and was about to die. Already facing a gun charge in New York as well as drug and gun charges in Arizona, he made no attempts to disguise his rampant substance abuse and wild lifestyle. His success justified it, he insisted. "Everybody try to talk about, 'The boy on too much drugs, and Baby need to take him to rehab,'" he said one time onstage. "[But] a junkie can't do what the fuck I do. I am the ultimate high. I am my drug."

He was photographed exhaling viscous gray clouds, and he refused to go into recording studios or hotel rooms where he couldn't smoke his weed. Rarely spotted without his Styrofoam cup of codeine-promethazine cough syrup and Hawaiian Punch, he hinted that no lady was as special to him as his syrup, to which he even penned a love song, "Me and My Drank." ("Thinkin' about a certain somebody/ That perfect somebody/ Sexy purple body.") Wayne admitted that he suffered from sleep apnea, the condition that, in combination with the lean, killed Pimp C in 2007. He feuded publicly with his manager and longtime friend Cortez Bryant, who believed the substance was ruining Wayne.

Still, when a reporter with *The Fader* magazine asked if he was ever overwhelmed by his pace, he grew incensed. "This is not a pace, this is how I live!" Wayne said. "I wake up, smoke weed, fuck bitches, get my dick sucked—a lot—drink my drink and come here and do this shit. What am I supposed to do, take a vacation? Go to Cancun and relax? This the vacation. You got a job, but this the vacation right here."

In 2007 and 2008 he was on the cover of about every music and rap magazine out there: *Rolling Stone, Blender, Complex, The Source, YRB, Billboard, XXL, Murder Dog.* Almost every article talked about how he was killing himself. *Vibe* featured him on the front of their May 2008 issue. "Hendrix. Marley. 'Pac. B.I.G.," the first line of their story read. "History is littered with legends who burned brightest just before they burned out." But Wayne didn't die. Instead, he spent his days and nights in a creative hallucination.

Raised in New Orleans, he moved to Miami shortly before Katrina, not because he sensed the storm coming but to be with his then-girlfriend, rapper Trina. Cash Money followed him not long afterward. Holed up in a small studio, he worked from sundown to sunup, putting together track after track, sometimes three or four per day. He said he felt invincible in the booth, like Roger Federer at Wimbledon, or Michael Jordan in the play-offs. Every time.

"It feels like [going] into a classroom, you know you didn't study everything, the test gets in front of you, and [you're like], 'Damn, I know all the answers,'" he told *Vibe*. "That's how I feel when I get in the studio, like, 'Damn, I know all the answers.'"

He brought his equipment wherever he traveled and recorded constantly, obsessing over every syllable. What was he trying to do, exactly? Sure he wanted *Tha Carter III* to be a masterpiece, but what that entailed he wasn't entirely sure. At one point he said he wanted to smoke blunts with Oscar de la Hoya, Tom from MySpace, and Bill Gates for inspiration.

"I don't have a vision for [*III*], 'cause that means you have a goal, which means you have a limit," he said another time, entering into the third person. "That question is stupid. Why do he do it? Because he is him. How do he do it? Because he is him. I'm not a psychic, I don't see myself doing anything. I don't expect, I live. I live!"


WAYNE WAS once shot following a Florida concert, he said, after a posse of would-be groupies were denied entry onto his tour bus. They fired through the window and a bullet struck Wayne harmlessly in the chest. "I was like, 'Damn! Them bitches wanted to screw bad!'" he told *Blender*.

Another time he nearly took his own life, accidentally. At age eleven, the year he says he lost his virginity, he was watching a Notorious B.I.G. video and showing off in front of a mirror, fooling around with a Glock belonging to his mother. He was in his bedroom and stoned. The gun accidentally went off and the bullet went right through him, dangerously close to his heart. He was saved when police heard him struggling and rescued him.

What kind of mother lets her preteen son play with guns while doing drugs? The kind that arms him herself. "Nigga play with you, you kill him," she told him. Fact is, he and his mother, Jacita, a chef, adored each other. His scripted *C* tattoo between his eyebrows is an homage to her, for "Cita."

Born Dwayne Carter Jr., Wayne never knew his father, which is why he dropped the *D* and goes by Wayne. He grew up in New Orleans's Hollygrove neighborhood in the Seventeenth Ward, a sprawling barrio of squat, one-story shacks and long shotgun houses. Though it wasn't hit as hard as other parts of the city, Hollygrove still shows Katrina's damage, with gutted houses galore and folks working to rebuild them.

It remains a grim spot. Some of the porches are entirely enclosed by iron gates, making them essentially cages, and it's got some of the biggest potholes I've ever seen, the kind your car can almost fall into. It's not a particularly inviting place for an outsider; everyone assumed I was there for drugs or a prostitute.

I couldn't find Wayne's childhood home, but he lived near the intersection of Apple and Eagle streets, where he would go to consort with the older drug dealers. ("I'm a Apple Street killa, a Eagle Street soldier," he raps on one song, and has the words *Apple* and *Eagle* tattooed on his stomach.) The intersection was pretty quiet when I visited. A boarded-up mom-and-pop establishment called Kim's Supermarket sat on one corner, with the word *Liquor* and its phone number handwritten by the door. A group of adults sat on the front porch of a multifamily home on the adjacent corner. In their yard a pair of tots—they couldn't have been older than two— play fought each other wearing red boxing gloves.

Reportedly a standout student at Lafayette Elementary, Wayne made good grades and rapped in a group called Kids With Attitude

(K.W.A.). Jacita initially balked at letting him hang with the Cash Money crew, as she thought they looked like gangbangers. Still, he got his first taste of street life from his stepfather, Reginald "Rabbit" McDonald, a drug pusher who was abducted and murdered when Wayne was fourteen. A year later Wayne had his first child, a girl named Reginae, with his fourteen-year-old sweetheart Antonia Johnson, whom he would marry, though it wouldn't last.

His interest in rap probably saved him from bigger trouble. He introduced himself to Baby and Slim at an autograph session in 1993 at a music store called Odyssey Records, where future collaborator DJ Khaled happened to be working. Only ten at the time, Wayne freestyled for them, and though they were impressed they wondered who was ghostwriting his rhymes. His brothers? No, Wayne said, I'm an only child. His father? No, Wayne said, I don't have one. After the meeting they gave him their numbers, and he began rapping on their answering machines. Impressed, they took him on.

An early track he recorded for the label was called "Fuck tha World," about Rabbit's murder. He also got a tattoo in tribute to his stepfather, and the Japanese characters meaning *strength* on his bullet wounds.

IN 2004 Wayne released his strongest studio album to date, the gold-selling *Tha Carter*, and labels tried courting him away from Cash Money. Baby, who had already seen the defection of his other marquee stars, promoted him to company president and gave him his own imprint, Young Money. In 2006 he responded by going platinum with an even stronger work, *Tha Carter II*.

Finishing *Tha Carter III*, however, wasn't proving very easy. Each time he thought it was done, the work leaked over the Internet and he was forced to go back to the drawing board. From the time an artist records a song to the time it appears in a store, countless people—from sound engineers, to reviewers, to the guys loading the CDs into boxes for shipping—have access to them. It's almost impossible to trace a breach to an individual or to stop it from happening again.

Wayne would regularly learn that songs he swore were still under lock and key had leaked. This bothered him at first, until he simply decided to go with the flow. "Between the bootleggers, the downloading, and someone leaking my music to both, I had to come to an understanding of the world changing," he told *Murder Dog*. "If I can't beat them, I'll join them."

And so he went on a mixtape tear. The run-up to *Tha Carter III* saw his offerings like *The Leak*, *The Drought Is Over 2 (The Carter 3 Sessions)*, and *The Drought Is Over 3 (Who Is the Predator)*.

His 2006 tape *Dedication 2* showed up on year-end critical best lists, and 2007's *Da Drought 3*, was even better received. Over beats first used by rappers like Young Jeezy and Jibbs, it's a flurry of jokes and boasts so original and well constructed that it changed the way critics thought about mixtapes. From "Live from 504," which he raps in a half-speed, crazed Jamaican accent:

> Kids, drugs kill, I'm acknowledging that
> But when I'm on the drugs, I don't have a problem
>     with that
> And my niggas got guns the size of toddlers,
>     be-yotch!
> And we aiming right at your fucking collar, be-yotch!

His lyrics were a blend of the threatening, the cocky, the non-sensical, the misogynist, and the slightly profound. Much of it concerned outer space and metaphysics. It was drugged-up talk, yes, but it sounded like he was on a really good high. The songs felt intimate, their stoned musings bringing the listener into the room with him.

A year earlier some of my editors had forbid mixtape reviews in their pages, as they considered the medium too banal. But by 2007 they'd changed the policy. That was the same year MTV named Wayne their "hottest rapper in the game," and *Vibe* magazine compiled a list of Wayne's seventy-seven *best* songs of the year.

"The mixtape game, he just dominated it," says Drama. "He lived it and he breathed it. You started seeing his lyrical progression." Adds Baby, "Lil Wayne *is* the Internet."

The marketing plan for *Tha Carter III* was to give away as much music as possible. But what if *Tha Carter III* wasn't as good as his mixtapes, the appetizer more tasty than the main course? At least Radiohead, who distributed their 2007 album *In Rainbows* on the Internet using a "pay what you'd like" model, *allowed* their fans to donate if they wanted to.

But Wayne wasn't as established as Radiohead. He wanted to communicate with his fans directly to build his brand. His mixtapes were his way of getting around the media idiots who didn't appreciate him properly. He even told his parent record company, Universal, that he didn't want them to hire people to pass out promotional T-shirts and hang up posters for him.

And his strategy seemed to be working. In an essay for *Oxford American* called "I Will Forever Remain Faithful: How Lil Wayne helped me survive my first year teaching in New Orleans," author David Ramsey painted Wayne as a beacon of hope for his hurricane-ravaged hometown. Most of Ramsey's students described Wayne as their favorite musician, and one brought Ramsey a stack of his mixtapes. A pair of fifth graders even enlisted his expertise in a debate over some lyrics. "Mr. Ramsey," one of them pleaded, "will you *please* tell him that if you go into space for a year and come back to Earth that all your family will be dead because time moves slower in space?"

Wayne charmed the mainstream as well. As his star rose, everyone began asking him to collaborate, and he never said no.

Enrique Iglesias wants to do a track? Absolutely! Destiny's Child? You bet. Shakira? No problem. Many of the features were forgettable, but some were delightfully whimsical, like his verse on DJ Khaled's "We Takin' Over," complete with *Kindergarten Cop* joke at the end.

> I am the beast, feed me rappers or feed me beats
> I am untamed, I need a leash, I am insane, I need a
> shrink . . .
> I have more jewels than your jeweler
> Touch and I will bust your medulla / That's a bullet
> hole, it is not a tumor

Though some speculated he would dilute his brand, he saw these features as a way to keep himself flush (up to six figures per pop, he said) while he released his free mixtapes. Noting that 50 Cent had called him an industry whore, *XXL* asked if there was anyone he would turn down for a collaboration. "Hell no," Wayne said. "Whores get *paid.*"

I penned a widely read, but fictional, article for *OC Weekly* about an imagined Wayne collaboration with teen actor Zac Efron, star of *High School Musical.* They were putting together a remix album called *High School Musical 2: Non-Stop Dance Party,* the story went.

> On "All for One," Efron sings the chorus: "Everybody all for one, a real summer has just begun! Let's rock and roll and just let go, feel the rhythm of the drums. We're gonna have fun in the sun!" Meanwhile, Wayne raps, "I'm a dog, you're all a bunch of fleas on my dick. Driving a Jag, er, like my name was Mick. I'm so sour like cream with chives, and my sperm will make your face break out in hives."

Widely believed to be true, the piece got picked up by publications including UK's *The Sun* after Perez Hilton ran with it. That anyone believed this silliness indicated just how much Wayne had crossed over.

YOU PROBABLY already know how the story ends. In an era when platinum albums are increasingly uncommon, *Tha Carter III* sold a million copies in its first week. It ended up as 2008's bestselling album, in any genre, by a long shot. (It sold 2.88 million that year; Coldplay's latest was second with 2.15 million.) As a congratulatory gift, Baby bought him a silver Rolls-Royce.

The album deserved its success; it is at turns mischievous, bizarre, rambling, and tragic, everything that is crass and wonderful about rap music. Featuring beats tailor-made for his slow, improv-heavy verses, it contains both radio-friendly melodies and weird, off-kilter ones that stop and start abruptly.

Over a squealing, classic rock beat on "Playin' with Fire," he speaks of battling an abusive mate of his mother's ("I went into the kitchen got the cleaver . . . He could see the devil in my features") and inviting death. "I'm doin' the same shit Martin Luther King did," he yelps, "Checkin' in the same hotel in the same suite, bitch, same balcony/ Like assassinate me, bitch."

The album's first big hit "Lollipop" offers a fairly basic "candy as sex organ" simile, but follow-up "A Milli" boasts a memorable machine gun loop that served as a platform for other rappers to strut their stuff on mixtapes. Just as Wayne had developed his style by jacking other folks' songs, now they were using his toward the same end.

The work transcends the southern rap tag, and Wayne knew it. "I'm the only down south nigga [that] could have been in the Firm, or the Commission or Wu-Tang," he told *YRB*, referencing groups of elite northeastern lyricists. And so, having proven himself the best rapper alive—or, at least, the most saleable—he decided he'd rapped enough for the moment.

Instead, he did a lot of singing (the Auto-Tune helped) and stepped up his guitar lessons. But strapped for time in preparation for the rock album he was putting out, he took to practicing onstage during his concerts. I was unfortunate enough to see one of these performances; it's hard to imagine behavior more self-indulgent.

The resulting 2010 work *Rebirth*, then, is as bad as you'd imagine. Convinced that emulating rockers like Iggy Pop or Perry Farrell required nothing more than lustful wails and come-hither whispers, he lived out his guitar-god fantasies over the course of twelve tracks, but they sounded more like the work of a guy playing a rocker in a movie than an actual rocker.

The customary next step in megacelebrity, then, was jail. Shortly after *Rebirth* he landed on Rikers Island to serve a one-year sentence from his New York gun conviction. As painful as the incarceration may have been, it likely didn't compare to the agony he faced in a dentist's chair beforehand, where he underwent surgery to get his grills removed, had eight root canals performed, and had dental implants put in. Turns out the drank's true damage had been to his teeth.

Indeed, before going in he announced that he'd quit drinking the stuff, finally admitting that his pace was unsustainable. Time, he feared, might catch up with him after all. "Me and that nigga [time] got a serious problem against each other," he told *Complex*. "You already know who's winning, man—that nigga."

# 16

# GUCCI MANE

■ ■ ■

## True Crime Rap

MANY YOUNG RAPPERS emphasize the poverty of their upbringings, the drugs they've sold, and the time they've served. But when they get famous, everything changes. They move to the suburbs, their production budgets go up, and they try to appeal to a wider audience. They may still talk tough, but mostly they're concerned with padding their 401(k)s.

The list of former tough guys turned rich softies is quite long. Crip Snoop Dogg showed off his parental prowess on the E! reality show *Snoop Dogg's Father Hood.* Jay-Z invested in restaurants with fancy wine lists. The much-shot 50 Cent got to work developing cologne lines. N.W.A's Ice Cube cast bratty four-year-olds for his family comedies. As for Wu-Tang Clan's Ghostface Killah? He made an R&B album. "I ain't shoot nobody in like . . . since the early nineties, man," he said.

But even though they've changed, hip-hop hasn't. Authenticity remains in demand, and those rapping about dope, detention, and double-barreled shotguns are expected to live that lifestyle. Someone had to step in and fill the void.

Though the West Coast maintains its reputation as a gangsta's paradise, in recent years the South has emerged as the premiere purveyor street rap with an edge. Its landscape has something of a Wild West flavor, a breeding ground for young, cocky, lawless artists who believe they have nothing to lose.

MCs like Gucci Mane, Young Jeezy, and Lil Boosie owe their popularity, in part, to a backlash against other wannabe miscreants who were found to be fakes. They also had southern ties: The Smoking Gun showed singer Akon to have exaggerated his prison time and discovered self-purported drug kingpin Rick Ross to be a former corrections officer. A HipHopDX report, meanwhile, showed that Fort Myers rapper Plies wasn't as much of a thug as he claimed and had actually studied sociology for a time at the University of South Florida.

The new crop of gangsta rappers (more likely to be called trap rappers), however, maintained quite real ties to the criminal underworld. The most interesting of the bunch was Gucci Mane, whose rhymes were as compelling and unlikely as his story. Though he had a hard time promoting himself behind bars, where he often found himself, his troubles with the cops only enhanced his credibility. "When you hear me, you hear a lot of pain, a lot of hood," he says on his MySpace page's biography, "you hear what's going on in the inner city in Atlanta."

IN MARCH of 2009, Gucci was released from Atlanta's Fulton County Jail. He'd served half a year for violating the terms of his probation, stemming from a 2005 incident in which he beat a promoter with a pool cue. Upon his emergence, the twenty-nine-year-old MC went straight to the studio and began recording songs, determined to take his career to the next level. "I got a lot of ideas together," he told me. "It was a time for me to refocus."

His music, released on mixtapes and unauthorized albums, had been widely distributed while he was away, and his popularity had exploded. Though known regionally since the middle of the decade, when he had a hit with Young Jeezy called "Icy," his name was now one of the hottest hip-hop brands in the country. Pittsburgh-based promoter William Marshall has booked Gucci for numerous shows over the years. He notes that in 2005 the going rate was $6,500, in 2006 it was $8,000, in 2008 it was $15,000, and upon Gucci's 2009 release from prison it had ballooned to $50,000.

Lines of frenzied fans stretched for blocks to see Gucci's homecoming appearances in states beyond the South, including Ohio, New York, and California, and some had to be moved from clubs to arenas. Labels fought to release his music. "This is a pinnacle point in Gucci's career," Melvin Breeden, president of Gucci's former label Big Cat Records, told me at the time. "He's as hot as he ever has been."

Indeed, there were signs that he could finally take his place next to such Atlanta rap immortals as T.I., OutKast, Ludacris, and Gucci's collaborator-turned-rival, Young Jeezy. In the midst of recording his second major-label album with contributions from Lil Wayne, Cam'ron, Usher, Keyshia Cole, and Bun B, he was making his presence felt nationally like never before. By the summer of 2009 he had done a verse on a Mariah Carey song, appeared on XXL's cover, and was the talk of the blogosphere. Affiliates like OJ da Juiceman, Nicki Minaj, and Waka Flocka Flame were riding his coattails to success in their own right.

Known for his awe-inspiring diamond pendants featuring Bart Simpson and Odie (Garfield's nemesis)—as well as a tattoo of an ice cream cone on his face—Gucci raps in a deep twang over thick, syrupy club beats. He's prone to funny asides and brutal honesty as he details his difficult childhood, his struggles to stay solvent, and his various material passions. There's nothing contrived about him, and he built his following through years of underground marketing efforts. Without much help (or interference) from major label record companies, his style evolved naturally.

I've twice talked with Gucci over the phone, and he's hard to understand. Owing to his Alabama upbringing and what he calls a speech impediment, he always sounds like his nose is stuffed. But he's excitable and can be hilarious. In a 2010 interview with satellite radio host Angela Yee, he noted that he'd been on probation since he was seventeen, but was scheduled to be free the next year.

"I want to go to Antarctica!" he cried, proceeding to reel off his crimes throughout the years, both real and imaginary. "Murder charge, pistol charge, assault charge, pimping and pandering . . . aggravated motherfucking ice game!" He also called himself the "Langston Hughes of East Atlanta," and complimented Yee on her shoes, which he called "leave 'em ons."

Born Radric Davis, Gucci spent the first years of his life in the former steel town of Bessemer, Alabama, on the outskirts of Birmingham. He was raised by an elementary school teacher and a "hustler" stepfather, in Gucci's words. Pops was the original Gucci Mane, so-called by people in the neighborhood for his propensity for the finer things in life. ("Mane" comes from the heavily accented pronunciation of "man.") Nonetheless, his early years were difficult, as he spells out in a song called "Neva Had Shit."

> I ain't never had shit, nigga, that's the truth
> Rich kids in the school used to jone my shoes . . .
> Now, my daddy hustle hard but he love some liquor
> And my momma wanna leave him but she love the
>     nigga

Arriving in East Atlanta at age nine, Gucci was ridiculed by other students. "I got [picked on] because of how I spoke and my diction, which was different," he says. "I would talk with a country slang because I was from Alabama." Nonetheless he excelled in his classes, not so much because he studied a lot but because of his natural abilities. "I was always naturally smart," he boasts. "I had a high IQ." Gucci's former manager, Debra Antney, seconds this characterization, calling him "damn near a genius." Adds one of his producers, Drumma Boy, "Gucci is a very intelligent guy. A lot of people don't realize how smart he is."

He graduated from high school and won a scholarship to Georgia Perimeter College, starting computer programming classes there in 1998. But he says he was forced to sell drugs to make ends meet and fell in with a delinquent crowd. "Badass kids took a liking to him," Antney says. "They took him in and loved him unconditionally, when [others] ridiculed and condemned him." School had only been in session for a month when he was caught with dozens of bags of crack. The police nabbed him while selling on a corner, he says, and beat him before taking him in.

Stripped of his scholarship, he began living like an outlaw, trafficking drugs in greater quantities and recklessly robbing and stealing. "A lot of shit niggas be talking about they have done inside them streets I done really did them," he told *Murder Dog* in 2005. "I'm like one of the wildest niggas in Atlanta."

Along the way his rap career began gaining steam. He'd been writing poetry since he was a kid and possessed a uncanny knack for wordplay and rhyme. A combination of sensibilities informed his style; he rapped fast, but his slang and accent showed he wasn't totally slick. "My upbringing, the way I see shit comes from the east side of Atlanta, but my diction and the way I pronounce words, it comes from Birmingham," he said. "When I blend that in with the city shit it's like best of both worlds in a rapper."

Though his images were often ugly, his lyrics, internal rhymes, and delivery dazzled. "Run it back just like I'm a running back/ While my diamonds doing jumping jacks, my pockets getting fat," he raps on "Running Back (Getting Fat)," which was recorded early in his career on Big Cat Records. "I'm getting fat, obese/ I won't stop, man, I just keep eatin'."

He and his associates recorded their music and sold it in their neighborhood, and after gaining a following Gucci founded his own label. He flew to New York to talk with some imprints there, but they were slow to understand his appeal, and so he paired up with the independent Atlanta imprint Big Cat Records.

His regional break out came with the 2005 CD *Trap House*, which included the infectious "Icy," a tribute to his chains and jewelry featuring a beat from his longtime collaborator Zaytoven. In its video he wears a diamond-studded watch designed by New York hip-hop jeweler Jacob Arabo and a gold pendant spelling out the words "So Icy" in, supposedly, $40,000 of diamonds.

The song was a collaboration with Young Jeezy, a soon-to-be multiplatinum rapper born Jay Jenkins, from near Macon, Georgia. It was Gucci's first hit, but the situation turned sour after he rebuffed Jeezy's attempt to include the song on his 2005 debut, *Let's Get It: Thug Motivation 101*.

YOU WERE more likely to hear other rappers on the radio, but no one dominated the South's club scene in the late aughts like Young Jeezy. On my trips to discos from Houston to Athens to New Orleans, I heard his snarl and defensive boasts on one track after another.

He doesn't claim to be much of a lyricist and indeed has the annoying habit of rhyming the same words with themselves. "You niggas out of order like soda machines," he raps on *Trap or Die (Gangsta Grillz Edition)*. "But Jeezy keep the cola like soda machines." I don't know what this means, but I'd imagine it's a coded drug reference, much like his song "24-23 (Kobe, Le-Bron)," which is not, in fact, about basketball. Instead, the players' numbers correspond with prices for cocaine kilos; he used to pay "Kobe," he explains ($24,000), but now he only pays "LeBron" ($23,000).

He and Gucci claim similar backgrounds as small-town kids turned big-time hustlers, and Jeezy's cocaine-referencing nickname is "Snowman." But he takes himself more seriously than Gucci, always rapping like he's a bit angry. His slow beats have a haunting quality, like the part in the movie when the main character's brother, about to escape the ghetto on a football scholarship, gets shot up by the bad guys. Appropriately, he was once in a group called Boyz n da Hood.

Though he's gone platinum, he claims his target audience is the pushers on the corners. There's no moralizing here; instead he offers "thug motivation" (to quote his album titles) not to go straight, per say, but to make a lot of money.

Indeed, the trap rappers portray themselves differently than the old gangsta rappers did. While N.W.A and Geto Boys proudly boasted of their nihilistic, antisocial tendencies, Jeezy and company lay out a moral case for drug dealing. With few options in the hood, Jeezy argues, pushers feed their families the only way they can. "This is America," he told MTV. "This is what y'all made us. At least I'm out here trying to get people to do right. I'm not saying, 'Go kill you a couple of cats.' I'm telling cats it's out here if you want to go get it." Added T.I. in the documentary, *Don Vito Presents: Crunk & Famous*: "What about the dope man that rebuilt the neighborhood, that gave back to the football team, that did for all the old ladies? . . . Those men are pillars to our community."

As Jeezy's career gained speed, he moved to Atlanta. Though he says he stopped dealing when he became an MC, he was closely affiliated with a national drug syndicate called BMF, Black Mafia Family, which had a major hub there. He buddied up with the ring's cofounder Demetrius "Big Meech" Flenory and other members and shouted them out in song: "You don't want me to get the streets involved/ Better yet make a call and get Meech involved (Yeah BMF)."

Meech and his brother Terry "Southwest T" Flenory eventually received thirty years for running the organization, and their underlings remain suspects in unsolved murders. But in their heyday they moved millions of dollars of cocaine and were awash in cash. Big Meech, the ostentatious one, threw a birthday party for himself with live jungle animals and posted billboards in Atlanta reading, "The World Is BMF's." He also started a record label and helped launch Jeezy's career.

Despite a wave of BMF-related arrests and incarcerations, Jeezy was spared. Still, he's not someone on whose bad side I would want to be, but that's where Gucci found himself in 2005 after refusing to let Jeezy use the song they'd made together, "Icy," on his album. Jeezy released a diss track called "Stay Strapped," which begins with some run-of-the-mill digs ("You pussy nigga, everything's coochie about you") before offering a $10,000 bounty for Gucci's "So Icy" pendant. "I want that motherfucking bullshit-ass 'Icy' chain," he says. "So if he come to your town and you happen to snatch that motherfucker off his neck, or knock that motherfucker off his neck, when I come to town, shoot it to me."

This was the rap equivalent of posting a "Wanted: Reward" poster with a picture of Gucci's chain on it in the town square, and not long afterward trouble found him. As reported by Mara Shalhoup in her book *BMF*, Gucci went to a strip club called Blazin' Saddles, hoping to convince some girls to perform to his songs. A dancer named Foxy invited him and one of his friends back to her Decatur home, where they were when a van pulled up outside. Five men emerged, armed with a gun, brass knuckles, and duct tape. The crew included a man named Henry "Pookie Loc" Clark III, a member of a Macon rap group called Loccish Lifestyle, that was on the verge of signing with Jeezy's Corporate Thugz Entertainment label. Clark was apparently an acquaintance of Foxy's, but this was not a social call.

They entered the house without knocking. One man punched Gucci in the head, and another hit his friend with the gun. Gucci, however, was packing himself, and he took aim and shot Clark. All five men ran out of the house, but Clark became separated, making his way into the nearby woods, where he fell to the ground. His body was found by a group including one of Clark's crew mates and Corporate Thugz Entertainment's co-owner, three days later. It was covered in flies.

The next week Gucci turned himself in. He admitted to the shooting but claimed self-defense. "I found myself in a predicament, and even though there was an attack on my life, I truly never intended to hurt anyone," he told SOHH.com. "I was just trying to protect myself."

Gucci's lawyers implied that the "Icy" dispute led up to the attack and even claimed that the assailants were BMF. Jeezy, however, denied any involvement, insisting he'd never even wanted "Icy" for his album in the first place. The charges against Gucci were dropped.


THOUGH TRAGIC, the shooting certainly wasn't bad for business. Released the same week Gucci posted bond from DeKalb County Jail, his debut *Trap House* went on to sell some 175,000 copies according to Big Cat's estimates, impressive for an independent album.

But though Gucci's volatile, fearless nature may have endeared him to fans, his lack of self-control has repeatedly gotten him in trouble. His brutal tendencies are on display on a YouTube video, said to be filmed at a 2005 record release party, in which he performs at a small club next to Atlanta rapper Mac Bre-Z, a former romantic interest. At one point he asks Bre-Z to step off the stage.

When she refuses, he pushes her violently. She appears to hurl a glass at him, causing him to lunge and coldcock her in the face.

In 2005 he began serving a six-month sentence for beating a concert promoter named Troy Bufford with a pool stick. Apparently Bufford used Gucci's name to promote an event without his authorization. "I'm just too rebellious, man. I gonna do what I want, when I want," Gucci explained to Angela Yee. "I only got one of these lives. God didn't give me two of 'em, he gave me one, so I'm going hard every day."

Shortly after beginning that stint, Gucci was badly beaten by another inmate and placed into twenty-three-hour-a-day protective lockdown for most of his remaining sentence. Upon release he was assigned six hundred hours of community service but was later forced to return after completing only twenty-five of them. He and his manager say he'd actually completed his obligation, but it wasn't properly documented.

Gucci's lawyer Dwight L. Thomas argues that the rapper's troubles owe to a lack of counseling after the killing. "He was going through emotional issues that obscured his ability to think straight," Thomas told MTV. "He never got therapy for the killing. When a soldier kills somebody, we give them therapy. When a police officer kills somebody, he gets therapy."

There were more slipups in 2008 and 2009, including arrests for DUI, marijuana and illegal weapons possession, and then rehab. He was pinched on another probation violation and sent back to prison right before the December 2009 release of his anticipated new album, *The State vs. Radric Davis*. This may have been bad timing, as jail prohibited him from promoting the CD properly, though then again his fans expected nothing less. In any case, the work didn't sell as well as expected despite Gucci's having dominated the rap press all year.

It seemed likely that what made him popular in the hood— his thick slang, his lack of polish, his arrest record—made him unpalatable to a mass audience. Similarly, Baton Rouge rapper Lil Boosie has yet to entirely break through to the mainstream. He's a lyrically gifted loose cannon who was indicted on a first degree murder charge in 2010 and potentially faced the death penalty.

As for Gucci's beef with Jeezy, it came to an end in late 2009 during a peacemaking session on DJ Drama's Atlanta radio show. Drama had helped build both rappers' careers, and his own fortunes were intertwined with theirs, so he had a vested interest in making sure they avoided a tragic showdown.

"It's about that time, we're getting older, growing," Gucci said, calling from prison. "So, let's do it for the city."

"What are we doing?" Jeezy asked, understandably skeptical about welcoming back the guy who'd killed one of his affiliates. But before long, Jeezy agreed to reconcile. "We're gonna do this for the city," he concluded.

THOUGH HIS arrests made the headlines, Gucci was writing and recording at a torrid pace behind the scenes. By sheer force of will, he'd developed from a unique-sounding braggart into a sophisticated storyteller.

You wouldn't know it from mainstream outlets like *Rolling Stone* and Pitchfork, who, until he was a rap household name, virtually ignored him. Among blogosphere critics, however, a heated debate raged over Gucci's merits, with scribes arguing their points in the high-minded manner of graduate students. Normally, critics cluster together when it comes to praising or maligning an MC. You won't meet one who doesn't love MF Doom and Scarface, but good luck finding somebody to stick up for Plies or Flo Rida.

But rap writers split down the middle when it came to Gucci. Some found him a wildly innovative outsider with charisma to spare. "Make no mistake, Gucci Mane loves language. He's a classical rap thesaurus addict but not in the . . . 'find the biggest most obscure synonym' sense," wrote Andrew Noz. This camp also found him authentic in ways corporate-backed rappers were not. They admired how he'd shaped his own image and culled his following from the streets rather than relying on major label marketing plans.

To others this was pure nonsense, and Gucci was simply materialistic, chauvinistic, and flat-out untalented. Sure, he made some catchy songs, but even those had little substance or redeeming value. Jeff Weiss opined that, though Gucci was tolerable in small doses, listening to his albums was like eating pizza three meals a day. "At first, it's awesome but by the 22nd time, you feel bloated, indolent and suspect that you might be too old for these sort of harebrained schemes," he wrote. "The defense is that the streets want Gucci. That's fine—the streets also want Coldplay, Kings of Leon, and Nickelback. It just depends what street you're on."

Blogger Brandon Soderberg applauded Gucci's "nontraditional form of lyricism" and maintained that folks tended to pigeonhole him either as an ignorant southern type or a postmodern genius. Neither characterization had much to do with Gucci himself, he said, but rather more to do with their own backgrounds and prejudices.

"It's only a matter of time before the mixed metaphor of bloggers/white writers as colonialists wanders into the debate or accusations of flat-out racism get tossed around when someone like Gucci's given a good critical look-over," he wrote, adding, "Gucci's cultural context switches in a way that's simply not available to white or essentially, nonblack listeners."

Indeed, it was long assumed that for a rapper to be great, he needed to be verbose and fairly intellectual in a streetwise way, while simultaneously maintaining a value system palatable to liberal, white critics. But through the juxtaposition of his gutter morality with his obvious craftsmanship Gucci began to challenge those assumptions and showed that some critics were having a hard time taking their own biases out of the equation.

Still, the fact that Soderberg and most of the other critics weighing in were white themselves threatened to send the debate into the realm of absurdity. Thankfully, then, it culminated with a satirical piece by blogger Gordon Gartrelle. In a post called "Gucci Mane: Lyrical Genius, Outsider Theorist" for the blog We Are Respectable Negroes, he gave the rapper the full dissertation-style treatment.

"How much 'unh' can one girl take/ How many cakes can one man bake?" he wrote, quoting Gucci's song "Booty Shorts," and proceeding to break it down.

> In this context, "unh" refers to penis. For Gucci, this rhetorical question is not a macho sexual boast; it is a nod to radical lesbian feminist awakening. Another way of framing the question is, how much rapacious male sexuality must a woman endure before she rebels against hegemonic patriarchy and becomes a fully realized, liberated human being?
>
> An alternate version of the second line has Gucci asking "how much cake [i.e. money] can one man make?" This alternate question's proximity to the previous one links liberation from patriarchal norms to liberation from the capitalist drive for greed and acquisition. Gucci's choice to stress a man's cake baking instead suggests that he preferred to stay with the theme of subversive gender acts, in this case, a man engaging in domestic labor, a realm traditionally associated with (or thrust upon) women.

This sidesplitting post comments on critics' tendencies to overanalyze hip-hop, to rationalize their love of artists or songs by assigning them cultural importance. (Or else to dismiss them on the grounds that they lack such significance.) In my mind, the best rap artists aren't necessarily intellectual or politically forward thinking, they simply display originality, mastery of the form, or passion. I believe Gucci does all three.

IF RAP has gone through a civil war, then the South has undeniably emerged victorious, at least for now. From sales to influence, it dominates despite efforts from coastal players to hold it back.

But winning is not enough. Before too long, its run on the charts will cease. Its popularity will die down when kids stop buying the music. Responsibility will then fall to adults to keep the discipline from being forgotten. Writers, historians, fans, and collectors will need to fight to establish its place in the pantheon, as partisans have done for blues, jazz, and, to some extent, early Bronx hip-hop.

Why is the subgenre that brought us the "Stanky Legg" and the "Laffy Taffy" worth saving, you ask? Because it is the true populist music of its time. It is "authentic" in the way prized by devotees of the Delta blues, a southern music that is celebrated and preserved with great vigor. When blues fans evaluate a performer, his appeal to poor folk, his humble beginnings, and his aversion to corporate manipulation are taken into consideration. These are attributes that the artists profiled in this book have in spades. Perhaps, then, in the same way that Delta bluesmen like Robert Johnson and Son House didn't become critical darlings until the 1960s, it will take decades for southern hip-hop to win appreciation among hip-hop scribes and tastemakers. I look forward to the day they're teaching college courses about Soulja Boy.

And speaking of so-called lowest common denominator artists, many of today's popular Dixie MCs also share similarities with the purveyors of early century "race records"—music that is

known to offend white folks' taste—who, unlike the Delta bluesmen, were popular in their own time.

Columbus, Georgia-born Ma Rainey, the "mother of the blues,"
specialized in such recordings, and her spirit is alive and well. One
suspects, however, that if her signature twenties-era euphemistic
dance instructional "Ma Rainey's Black Bottom" came out today, it
would be maligned comparably to "Laffy Taffy."

> All the boys in the neighborhood
> They say your black bottom is really good
> Come on and show me your black bottom
> I want to learn that dance

The prevailing notion is that hip-hop should—nay, must—be
about something bigger than self-expression or having fun. But
who came up with this? Overeducated men, mainly, those who
have traded in their baseball cards and Dungeons and Dragons
sets for golden-era music and would rather sit at home with their
vinyl than go out and party in a coeducational fashion.

These cultural reactionaries overlook the qualities that make
southern rap singularly compelling: its giant, overpoweringly
catchy beats, its inventiveness, its humor. Unlike the bulk of
coastal hip-hop being made these days, it doesn't take itself seriously, and it has got character (and characters) to spare. And, yes,
it tends to speak to black folks in a more exclusive way than the
alternative—which is not to say that it doesn't speak to plenty of
other folks as well.

It certainly speaks to me; its vivacity brings me a joy that I don't
get from other styles. Sure, it's sometimes nonsensical, sometimes
preposterous, but it's always unpretentious and always concerned
with hitting your pleasure centers. If music can have a more
important raison d'être than that, I don't know what it is.

# ACKNOWLEDGMENTS

I'D FIRST like to thank everyone who read this book. It means a lot to me. Tell me which chapter you liked best.

I'm in debt to the rap artists who suffered through my horribly invasive questions, often for hours at a time. Particularly accommodating were Luke Campbell, Rico and Dale Lynch, Bushwick Bill, DJ Drama, DJ Smurf, Big Boi, Trae, Murphy Lee, Juvenile, Eightball & MJG, Slim Thug, DJ Paul and Juicy J, Scarface, Lil Jon, T-Pain, Paul Wall, Chamillionaire, Soulja Boy, Big Mike, and Bun B.

Thanks to my editors, Yuval Taylor and Michelle Schoob, and to the editors at the weeklies, magazines, and websites I write for, including Rodney Carmichael, Mara Shalhoup, Rob Harvilla, Chris Gray, Arielle Castillo, Marcus Blassingame, Nancy Staab, Joe Keyes, Stephen Thompson, Andy Van de Voorde, Jonathan Fischer, Spencer Patterson, Paul Gambino, Dan Brown, Jonathan Cunningham, and Pete Freedman. Also thanks for Bob Duffy, Tom Finkel, and everyone at the *RFT* for helping me develop my style.

On my southern trips I crashed with a lot of people and ate a lot of their food. Thanks to Leah Roeber and Jonathan Rovick, John

Wehr, Jamila and Rodney Carmichael, Larami and Shea Serrano, and Doug Garrett and Inna Park. Thanks also to John Lomax, Jorell Cleveland, and Jeremy Blackburn for showing me around.

Special thanks to Shea Serrano not just for hosting me but for his enlightenment on the Houston chapters. Other people who get credit for assists (on their way to triple doubles) are everyone on The What? message board, Elijah Wald, Justin Graham Maginn, Craig Malisow, Jon Milde, Stefan Merrill Block, Dave Cohn, Julia Beverly, and the guys from The Frozen Food Section. RIP Helias and Sean Rowe.

For every unresponsive publicist I encountered there was another outstanding one, including Giovanna Melchiorre, Tamiko Hope, Nancy Byron, Jane Higgins, David Bosch, Ticeman Merriweather, and Roberta Magrini.

I'm especially grateful to my agent, Marissa Walsh, who has made my dreams come true.

Love always to my wife, Anna, who along with my parents Cathy and Norm and siblings Alex and Julia have been more supportive than they know.

# RECOMMENDED LISTENING

*The 2 Live Crew Is What We Are*, The 2 Live Crew

*We Can't Be Stopped*, Geto Boys

*The Fix*, Scarface

*Diary of the Originator: Chapter 12, June 27th*, DJ Screw

*Ridin' Dirty*, UGK

*On Top of the World*, Eightball & MJG

*Most Known Unknown*, Three 6 Mafia

*Aquemini*, OutKast

*Soul Food*, Goodie Mob

*400 Degreez*, Juvenile

*Ghetto D*, Master P

*Country Grammar*, Nelly

*Aaliyah*, Aaliyah

*Under Construction*, Missy Elliott

*Lord Willin'*, Clipse

*Kings of Crunk*, Lil Jon & the East Side Boyz

*Down with the King*, T.I., hosted by DJ Drama

*Get Ya Mind Correct*, Paul Wall and Chamillionaire

*We the Best*, DJ Khaled

*Souljaboytellem.com*, Soulja Boy

*Tha Carter III*, Lil Wayne

*Murder Was the Case*, Gucci Mane

# RECOMMENDED READING

*The Adventures of Grandmaster Flash: My Life, My Beats*, Grandmaster Flash with David Ritz (Crown Archetype, 2008)

*BMF: The Rise and Fall of Big Meech and the Black Mafia Family*, Mara Shalhoup (St. Martin's, 2010)

*Can't Stop Won't Stop: A History of the Hip Hop Generation*, Jeff Chang (St. Martin's, 2005)

*How the Beatles Destroyed Rock 'n' Roll: An Alternative History of American Popular Music*, Elijah Wald (Oxford University Press, 2009)

*In Search of the Blues*, Marybeth Hamilton (Basic Books, 2008)

*Our Band Could Be Your Life: Scenes from the American Indie Underground 1981–1991*, Michael Azerrad (Little, Brown, 2001)

*Third Coast: OutKast, Timbaland, and How Hip-Hop Became a Southern Thing*, Roni Sarig (Da Capo, 2007)

*Triksta: Life and Death and New Orleans Rap*, Nik Cohn (Vintage, 2007)

*Vixen Icon*, Buffie the Body (Triple Crown, 2009)

*The Year Before the Flood: A Story of New Orleans*, Ned Sublette (Lawrence Hill Books, 2009)

# INDEX